TEACHING BASIC GYMNASTICS

A COEDUCATIONAL APPROACH

Third Edition

Phyllis S. Cooper
Trenton State College

Milan Trnka
West Chester State University

Illustrated by A. Bruce Frederick

Macmillan College Publishing Company
New York

Maxwell Macmillan Canada
Toronto

Maxwell Macmillan International
New York   Oxford   Singapore   Sydney

Editor: Ann Castel Davis
Production Editor: Stephen C. Robb
Art Coordinator: Ruth A. Kimpel
Text Designer: Susan E. Frankenberry
Cover Designer: Russ Maselli
Production Buyer: Patricia A. Tonneman

This book was set in Times Roman and Optima by The Clarinda Company and was printed and bound by Custom Printing Company, Inc. The cover was printed by Phoenix Color Corp.

Copyright © 1994 by Macmillan College Publishing Company, Inc.

Printed in the United States of America

All rights reserved. No part of this book may be reproduced or transmitted in any form or by any means, electronic or mechanical, including photocopy, recording, or any information storage and retrieval system, without permission in writing from the Publisher.

Earlier editions copyright © 1989 by Macmillan College Publishing Company and © 1982 by Burgess Publishing Company.

Macmillan College Publishing Company
866 Third Avenue
New York, New York 10022

Macmillan College Publishing Company is part of the
Maxwell Communication Group of Companies.

Maxwell Macmillan Canada, Inc.
1200 Eglinton Avenue East, Suite 200
Don Mills, Ontario M3C 3N1

Library of Congress Cataloging-in-Publication Data
Cooper, Phyllis.
  Teaching basic gymnastics : a coeducational approach / Phyllis S.
Cooper, Milan Trnka.— 3rd ed.
    p.   cm.
  Includes bibliographical references (p.   ) and index.
  ISBN 0-02-324701-0
  1. Gymnastics—Study and teaching.   I. Trnka, Milan.   II. Title.
GV461.C654   1993
796.44—dc20   93-7874
                                                                                       CIP

Printing: 3 4 5 6 7 8 9   Year: 8

Preface

Teaching Basic Gymnastics: A Coeducational Approach provides methods of teaching and spotting for many beginning and some intermediate gymnastic skills. Emphasis is placed on guiding instructors in working with students in typical physical education classes. Instructors are urged to encourage students to seek their own individual levels of success rather than ''perfect'' performance. In most physical education classes, the typical student does not have the time to develop skills beyond the level of advanced beginner. Therefore, *Teaching Basic Gymnastics* does not address true intermediate or advanced skills.

The events presented in the text include coeducational apparatus, individual and dual activities, pyramids, and modern rhythmic gymnastics. The level and number of skills presented in each teaching situation will depend on the amount of time available for the gymnastics unit and the instructor's expertise. Horizontal bar and uneven parallel bar skills are combined into Chapter 10 in that these beginning skills can be performed on both apparatus and the teaching and spotting techniques are identical.

Throughout the text attention is given to the importance of providing a safe learning environment by way of careful inspection and proper use and placement of mats and apparatus. Class organization is also discussed.

P.S.C.
M.T.

To The Teacher

Many skills presented in the text are analyzed to a particular side. They may be performed on the opposite side by reversing arm or leg movement.

Some spotting techniques are described from the left side, which is done to clarify hand placement on the performer. To spot on the right, the movements can be reversed. People generally develop a dominant side for spotting; however, even though it takes practice, it is advisable to learn to spot most skills from both sides.

The terms *inside* and *near hand* refer to the hand closest to the student or the hand that first touches the student during the initial phase of the skill. The terms *outside* and *far hand* refer to the hand farthest from the student or the hand that touches the student last.

Most skills are presented in a suggested progressive order for class presentation. However, the order given here may not always be suitable to class needs and instructors should use their own discretion.

The codes used throughout the book are as follows:

SL   Skill Level
PT   Performance Technique
SP   Spotting Technique
CE   Common Error
MO   Movement Out of Skill
VA   Variation

In each chapter a breakdown for grading skills is included. These grading sheets can be utilized in different ways, including:

1. Students can remove sheets to be placed in a teacher grading folder.
2. Grading sheets can be posted near the apparatus.
3. College/university students can use the grading sheets with each other as a pretest to teacher grading.

Test questions at the end of each chapter can be answered and used as study questions, or they can be used in conjunction with other test questions, depending on the focus of the class.

Contents

List of Illustrations

Chapter
1

Introduction

A PHILOSOPHY

When things are built on a solid foundation they last longer and the end results are more rewarding. Building a strong foundation in gymnastics begins by learning the fundamental skills well enough to be executed efficiently. When this is achieved, success comes often and frustration seldom occurs.

From the very beginning in gymnastics it is important to know where the body is at all times in relation to space (called kinesthetic sense). Some people are gifted with a great degree of kinesthetic awareness, whereas others must work harder to reach the same degree of awareness. Therefore, it is essential for students to *feel* their bodies in motion on the mat (e.g., while doing a forward roll) before attempting motion in the air without support of the hands or feet.

People are by nature different. Some are strong and some are weak; some are more flexible than others; some are agile whereas others move more slowly; and some have more interest and drive than others. All people cannot excel in gymnastics but all can obtain a certain degree of success. Therefore, gymnastics instructors must keep in mind that each student in a given group can do only what their mind and body will allow, and should be evaluated accordingly.

HISTORY

The word *gymnastics* was used by the ancient Greeks, and later by the Romans, to describe physical activity of any kind. Early Greek history indicates that gymnastics developed as systematic exercises to which great emphasis was given. The exercise system endorsed by Greek educators and philosophers thus became an integral part of their educational process. The Greeks were lovers of beauty, and as such they regarded gymnastics as a way of beautifying the human body. They also realized that by exercising the body's muscles they could also promote health, comfort, strength, and vigor. The Spartans maintained a rigid exercise system for male and female youths, and often participated in war dances, running, leaping, rope climbing, and balancing activities.

The Romans later adopted the Greek exercise system for their military training program. As the Greek and Roman civilizations declined, so did gymnastic activity; in fact, any form of physical activity was discouraged. This held true throughout the Middle Ages, except that knights were trained in horseback riding, swimming, archery, climbing, sword fighting, and jousting for tournaments during the age of chivalry.

It was not until Johann Basedow (1723–1790) opened a school in 1774 that physical training again became a part of the educational program. Christian Salzman (1744–1811), after teaching Basedow for three years, opened his own educational institution in Schnapfenthal, Germany. In 1788, the gymnastics and games program was directed by Friedrich Gutsmuths (1759–1839), often referred to today as the "grandfather of gymnastics." Gutsmuths taught gymnastics for almost fifty years, inventing endless games and apparatus for his students. He wrote many books, including *Gymnastics for Youth*, in which he called his system of teaching "natural gymnastics."

Friedrich Jahn (1778–1852), a sociologist and follower of Gutsmuths, then became known as "Vater John," the "father of gymnastics." Two years after Napoleon defeated the Prussians at Jena, Jahn published *German Nationality*, in which he argues that the rejuvenation and restoration of Germany would be possible through the country's youth. In it he strongly advocated a program of physical education made up of compulsory exercises, elective exercises, and games, which he called *turnen*. Jahn's system of physical education spread rapidly throughout Germany with the formation of Turner Societies (called *Turnvereins*), and he saw it as a way of unifying Germany by combining gymnastics training with nationalistic demonstrations. After Napoleon's defeat at the Battle of Waterloo, Turnvereins grew stronger until Metternich convinced the King of Prussia that they were preparatory schools for revolutionary training. The king ordered the societies closed and Jahn was imprisoned. The Turnvereins went underground for a time but later surfaced again.

Other early pioneers of gymnastics include Adolph Spiess (1810–1858), who introduced gymnastics in Switzerland's schools, and Pehr Ling (1776–1839) of Sweden, who was the first to appreciate the corrective value of gymnastics and who invented such equipment as the vaulting box and stall bars. Franz Nachtegall (1777–1847) initiated the first training school for gymnastics teachers in Copenhagen, Denmark.

After thousands of refugees fled Germany in 1848 because of the revolution, many of them founded German Turnvereins in the United States. The first to appear was in Cincinnati, Ohio, in November of 1848. Others followed in Boston and Philadelphia in 1849 and in New York and St. Louis in 1850. By 1885, there were eighty-nine Turner Societies in the United States, and their motto became "a sound mind in a sound body."

Systematic physical training was established in Czechoslovakia in 1843 at the Physical Institute in Praha (Prague) by German scholar Rudolph Steffany. His method of gymnastics was based on Spiess's, and from 1855 the institute was under the direction of gymnastics enthusiast Jan Malypar. In 1862, Miroslav Tyrs, a former student of Malypar's and a doctor of philosophy and fine art at Charles University at Prague, founded the "Sokol" gymnastic movement, which spread quickly throughout Czechoslovakia. The Sokol system was similar to the Turner Society in Germany. The first Sokol units established in the United States were in St. Louis, Missouri in 1865, Chicago in 1866, and New York in 1867.

There was a great move toward physical education both before and after the American Civil War in 1860. Military schools stressing physical fitness became prevalent by 1888. Schools that taught physical education began to flourish, and many colleges began to build gymnasiums. In 1865, the German Turners built the Normal College in Indianapolis, Indiana. Many YMCAs established gymnasiums, and physical education teachers were in great demand. Some teachers came to the United States from Germany and other Middle European countries, bringing with them their expertise and training in gymnastics.

About the same time, the Slavs, Swiss, Swedes, and others immigrating to the United States established their own gymnastics clubs with systems similar to that of the Germans. These organizations held social as well as gymnastics gatherings, which served to perpetuate the languages and customs of their native countries and to unite them as a group. In short, the Turners and Sokols had a profound influence on the development of gymnastics in the United States during the late 1880s.

Each club had its own rules governing competition. Eventually, with the inception of the Amateur Athletic Union (AAU) in 1885, athletes from different clubs met to promulgate rules and regulations for competition. Soon after the AAU was established, local and national championships were conducted.

In October of 1968 the AAU was replaced by the United States Gymnastics Federation (USGF). Since its inception, the USGF's responsibilities have grown. It is responsible for the standardization of judging gymnastic competitions, and it has created the local, regional, and national age-group competitive program and safety certification standards. The USGF has also developed a strong research program in an effort to enhance teaching, coaching, and performance techniques from both psychological and physiological perspectives.

GYMNASTICS IN THE SCHOOL CURRICULUM

Gymnastics should be an integral part of the physical education curriculum, offered in kindergarten through high school and college. The values derived from gymnastics participation are numerous, including increased strength, flexibility, balance, endurance, kinesthetics, agility, self-discipline, coordination, courage, self-confidence, social awareness, and perseverance. Although students need a certain amount of strength, coordination, kinesthetic awareness, and flexibility to perform gymnastic skills, gymnastics helps to develop these very same physical qualities. Any skill in gymnastics can serve as a self-testing activity for the student; that is, it can monitor his or her ability and progress. Gymnastics also allows for creativeness, small- and large-group interaction, and challenges to students at all levels. Other values derived from participation in gymnastics include appreciation for the skills of the elite gymnast, cooperation with peers and teachers, self-confidence obtained in mastering a skill, and the importance of being physically fit.

With increasing media coverage of the Olympics and other international gymnastics events, schools have been encouraged to develop or broaden existing programs in gymnastics. Ideally, gymnastics units should be offered for a minimum of four weeks for each grade level.

Students should not be expected to perform skills at an intermediate level without first mastering the basics. Provisions must be made each year or in each unit for students with inadequate backgrounds and physical abilities. On the other hand, it is not fair to limit the activities of gifted students. Although each chapter in the text includes basic skills, it also presents more challenging skills for the proficient student. **It is important not to under- or overestimate students' abilities. This can be avoided by using skill-progression charts and by not allowing students to attempt advanced skills before they master basic skills. If students cannot perform lead up skills, do not allow them to perform the skill itself.** Don't force a student to perform a skill they don't feel ready to do. Charts illustrating skill progressions will make students aware of the necessity to learn in this manner. A master check sheet can also be posted to ensure that students complete skills in a progressive order.

SPOTTING

Spotting is in itself an art. It does not always involve putting a student through an entire skill but rather giving assistance where it is most needed for success and for preventing injury. Spotting can be done through hand contact, mechanical devices, (e.g., spotting belt), and by being there to assist when necessary.

The primary responsibility of the spotter is to prevent the head from falling to the mat or striking the apparatus. Therefore, the most common contact points for spotting are the student's shoulders, upper arms, back, chest or ribcage, and wrists. In general, spotters must be close enough to students to effectively spot without hindering the student or themselves. Although the spotter's safety is sometimes sacrificed when assisting a student, the spotter is not in danger providing that correct spotting techniques are used.

A spotter should know the following about the skill being spotted:

1. Position of the body from the beginning throughout the entire skill.
2. What part of the body produces the force or momentum to initiate movement of the skill.
3. What parts of the body control the movement of the skill, such as the hands, hips, or feet.
4. In what part(s) of the skill are accidents most likely to occur, and what can be done to prevent accidents or to assist the performer at that point.

Remember giving proper assistance is most important to maintain students' interest in gymnastic skills and to create confidence in the student. Always be alert.

As a teacher or coach it is important for you to fully understand liability and the law for your school, club, or institution. This information can be obtained from your principal, department head, or manager. Plan all activities to adhere to all safety precautions.

DEALING WITH ATYPICAL STUDENTS

Atypical students can be grouped into the following categories:

1. Obese.
2. Obese and weak.
3. Weak.
4. Defeatist.
5. Apprehensive.
6. Audacious.
7. Self-conscious.
8. Kinesthetically inadequate.
9. Nonorthopedic handicapped.

The efficiency with which students learn and perform gymnastic skills is of increasing concern to physical educators. Serious efforts should be made to individualize instruction to ensure some degree of success for all students, especially the atypical student. A physical educator may take several approaches in dealing with classes; however, individual philosophies and those of the school govern the final decision. Developing realistic goals for the student is of utmost importance at the beginning of a gymnastic unit. Consider the student's present ability level and the number of class meetings or time to be spent in actual practice. The following suggestions for dealing with atypical students are made for use in individual situations. We encourage teachers to grade atypical students with spotting assistance or inanimate physical aids. Again, don't force a student to perform a skill they don't feel ready to do.

1. Designate one mat to be used with weights. List specific directions for exercises for various body parts including upper arms, abdomen, lower back, and legs. Allow students to exercise with weights during class in lieu of performing gymnastic skills for which they are not physically ready.

2. Encourage advanced students to work on various skills with their peers. However, do not deprive them totally of their practice time.

3. Designate an area for kinesthetic-awareness activities. These activities might include performing the following:

   a. Tripods.

   b. One-legged headstands.

   c. Roll from squat to back pike position, then return to squat.

d. From a pike on floor, extend hips and legs to vertical position.

e. Hang over bar (horizontal or uneven) in pike position, swing back and forth.

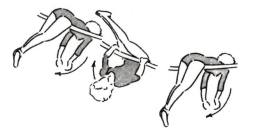

f. Single leg swing on bar.

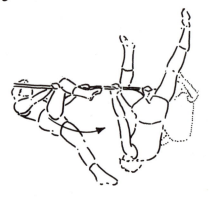

4. Build a solid inclined plane. Make the angle less than 45 degrees and cover with mats. Allow students to perform forward and backward rolls down the incline.

5. To curb actions of audacious students, demand rigid adherence to skill progression. Do not allow students to attempt skills without first passing the prerequisites.

6. *With chalk,* mark *X*s on mats where hands and feet make contact during performance of a cartwheel and other skills. *With tape,* make lines on mats for tumbling skills that may eventually be performed on the balance beam.

7. For handstand roll use **4- to 12-inch mats.** Have students place hands on tumbling mat just in front of landing mat as they kick to a handstand position, then roll onto landing mat. The higher mat should be used first. This will prevent hard falls due to initial arm weakness when lowering body to the mat or due to fear of being inverted.

8. Use stacked mats (two 6 by 12 folded). Have student lie on floor with hips close to mats. Place feet on top of mats, put hands under shoulders, and push up into backbend position, then kick over through a back walkover. Many students are afraid to go backward; this activity eliminates the backward portion of the back walkover, and allows a relatively nonflexible person to get the feeling of performing a back walkover. Progressively lower height of stacked mats.

9. Use stacked mats (two 6 by 12 folded). Have student stand at one end of stack. Lunge forward to place hands on other end of mat and perform handspring. The elevation gives students time to get their body around when there is inadequate kick-push action of legs. This activity should be spotted. Progressively lower height of stacked mats.

10. Use large square of foam covered with soft material. Have student stand at one side of foam and perform back handspring over foam. This alleviates fear of falling on the head. If the arms collapse, the head hits the foam instead of the mat. This technique prevents a student from undercutting the back handspring. A spotter should be used with this method.

GENERAL SAFETY PROCEDURES

Apparatus

The teacher should be concerned with the general condition, safe use, and maintenance of apparatus. The following safety procedures are recommended for the preservation and use of apparatus. It is advisable that a company representative check the equipment once a year.

Mats

1. Mats, whatever the surface, must be kept clean.
2. Carry, rather than drag, mats.
3. Do not allow students to walk on mats with street shoes.
4. Repair torn mats as soon as possible.
5. Do not tumble on mats that are ripped or torn.
6. When not in use, store mats where they will not be abused.
7. When using more than one mat, be sure no separation or overlapping exists between mats.

Horse

1. Check adjustment mechanisms before each use.
2. If using pommel horse for vaulting, use plugs or nonslip tape to cover holes.
3. Use saddle soap or appropriate cleaner for horse covering at least once a year or as needed.
4. When using pommel horse, be sure pommels are secure.
5. Sand any rough spots on the pommels. If major cracks appear and cannot be corrected, replace pommels.

Vaulting Board

1. Depending on the board, frequently check screws, bolts, and so on.
2. Due to the constant pounding of boards with coil or leaf springs, or air bags, visually inspect prior to use.
3. Replace slippery or torn surfaces.

Rings

1. Check wooden rings for cracks and replace if necessary.
2. Replace any strap or cable not in good condition.
3. Make sure rings hang evenly.
4. Keep rings out of reach while not in use.

Beam

1. Make sure beam supports are secure.
2. Check beam surface for cracks in wood or tears in suede or vinyl coverings. Replace if necessary. Some wooden beam cracks or rough spots can be sanded and filled with wood putty if necessary.
3. Do not allow students to use the beam as a seat or coat rack.
4. Store beam as-is or dismantled when not in use.
5. Move the beam on rollers or movers made for the beam. Do not shove one end at a time.

Parallel Bars

1. Check adjustment mechanisms to make sure that pistons are secured properly.
2. Occasionally uprights become loose in their base. Simply tighten bolts.
3. Inspect bars for rough spots and cracks. If defects cannot be repaired, replace bars.
4. If a bar becomes warped, replace it.

Horizontal Bar

1. Check floor plates periodically to be sure they are secure in floor.
2. Check uprights to make sure they are straight (plumb).
3. When changing height of horizontal bar, be sure to secure locking devices. Make adjustments in cable, chain, and turnbuckle when necessary.
4. Be sure locking device above floor plate is in proper working order.
5. When chalk buildup on bar is excessive, remove with steel wool or emery paper.

Uneven Parallel Bars

1. See 1–4 of parallel bars.
2. If bars are cabled, see 1–5 of horizontal bar.
3. If bars are portable, move with proper transporters rather than shoving across the floor.

Note: *Refer to USGF safety manuals for other safety tips.*

CLASS ORGANIZATION

Because tumbling is considered fundamental to all apparatus work, it is a good event with which to begin a gymnastic unit. If a floor exercise or wrestling mat is not available, mats can be placed end to end. Skills may be performed across the width or length of mat.

Tumbling may be taught as a separate unit or used as a station with selected pieces of apparatus. Students rotate from one station to another.

Teachers must use discretion concerning the number of stations and amount of apparatus that can be placed safely on the floor at one time. Class size, ability, and previous experience of the students must also be considered.

Students may be organized into ability groups or may be paired (the more advanced student with a less skilled student). Students may also be grouped randomly—six in group A, six in group B, and so on.

Students should be rotated from one type of apparatus to another keeping in mind usage of different muscle groups. For example, vaulting should not follow tumbling, nor should horizontal bar follow rings.

If the schematic drawings shown below cannot be adapted to your gymnasium, adhere to the following criteria:

1. Set up tumbling strips and vault runways along wall areas to prevent students from stepping into runway of an oncoming vaulter or into path of a tumbler.

2. Landing area and area adjacent to other apparatus must have sufficient clearance to prevent students from colliding with apparatus or each other.

3. Do not place apparatus near doors, windows, or walkways.

The following is a suggested arrangement of equipment for the gymnastic unit.

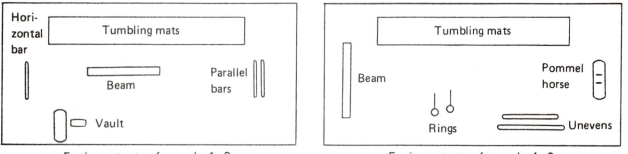

Equipment setup for weeks 1–3   Equipment setup for weeks 4–6

Ways to Organize Large Groups in Tumbling

1. Use cross-mat tumbling technique.

   a. Number off by fours and have every fourth student perform at one time with the person to the left acting as the spotter.

   b. File students: after one student has almost finished performing, the second starts, and so on.

12

   c. After students can perform skills well, give commands and have every other student perform.

   Example: Forward roll commands—step onto mat, squat, place hands on mat, roll.

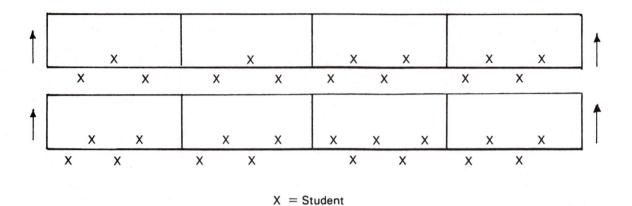

X = Student

2. Arrange mats in a semicircle.

   a. Apply same techniques as in number 1 above or work in groups of four if mats are of adequate size.

   b. Allow students to work in these groups at their own pace, with two performing and the other two acting as spotters.

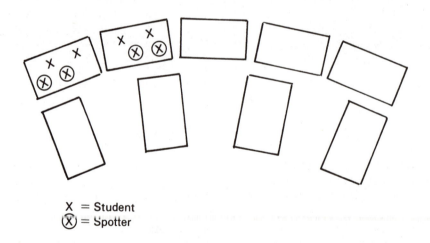

X = Student
Ⓧ = Spotter

The arrangements of mats shown in the accompanying figures allow for:

   1. Utilization of space.

   2. Ease of teacher monitoring of the entire group.

Chapter 2 Biomechanics

Too often in the learning process of teaching and spotting skills, one is confronted with many questions. Why did that happen? Why can't I get around? What am I doing wrong? To a novice these questions are often frustrating, and no matter what he or she may say, the student still fails to perform the skill properly. It is hoped that this chapter will help alleviate many problems for the novice by offering a basic understanding of the mechanical principles of movement by which skills can be taught and spotted more effectively and efficiently. Understanding movement is also the key to identifying performance errors, and spotting becomes a relatively easy job if one knows how, when, and where to apply force.

The following vocabulary discussed briefly below will be used:

Center of gravity—that point at which stability may occur (weight center of the body).
Base of support—body part or parts that support the body weight (and the space in between those body parts).
Motion—an observable change in position of the entire body or its parts.
   Sustained—slow movement.
   Percussive—quick or rapid movement.
   Translatory—movement through a continuing plane.
   Rotatory—movement about or around a central point.
   Curvilinear—movement as a whole in a circular path.
Axis—A line through the center of gravity around which rotation occurs.
Force—an influence that produces or tends to produce motion or a change of motion.
Friction—the resistance of one surface to that of another.
Gravity—the force of attraction that tends to pull bodies or weight downward toward the earth's center.
Newton's laws of motion—general principles governing the movement of objects through space.
   Inertia—properties remaining at rest or in motion unless acted upon by an outside force.
   Acceleration—resulting change in speed is directly proportional to the force producing it and inversely proportional to the mass.
   Action-reaction—for every action force there is an equal and opposite reaction force.

CENTER OF GRAVITY

Center of gravity (c of g) may be described as the center of body mass, or the point at which the body will revolve or rotate if spun by an outside force. On an individual standing erect with arms at the sides, the center of gravity lies between the hips and waist areas. Examples A–F illustrate how the center of gravity changes according to configuration of the body or body parts.

In order for motion to occur, force must be applied to displace the center of gravity past the base of support in the desired direction, thus overcoming inertia. Three basic principles to keep in mind regarding center of gravity are:

1. The closer the center of gravity is to the base of support, the more stable the object (A is more stable than C).

2. The closer the center of gravity is to the radius of rotation, the faster the object will move (D).

3. The higher the center of gravity upon landing on a vault, a tumbling skill, or a dismount, the lighter and more controlled the landing will be (F).

As a person stands erect, the feet are the base of support (A). If the body is to move forward with the feet stationary, then the upper body must lean forward, forcing the c of g forward of the feet.

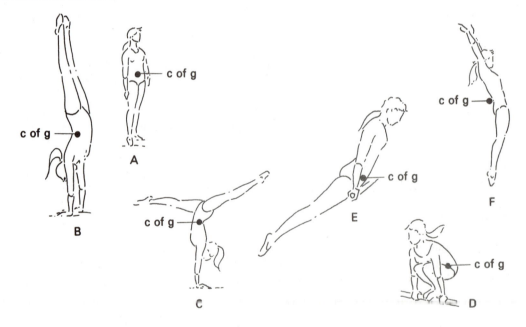

Walking is a series of events in which balance is lost and regained. The center of gravity is moved forward, distributing the stability of the body. As gravity pulls the body forward downward, the back foot pushes backward downward causing a forward upward force against the body. The back foot moves forward to form new base.

BASE OF SUPPORT

The *base of support* is the body part or parts that support the total body weight. In a normal standing position the feet are the base of support; in a handstand the hands are the base of support; and on the uneven bars in a front support position, the hands and hips on the bars are the bases of support. Understanding the relationship of the center of gravity to the base of support (also thought of as proper body alignment) is of utmost importance in teaching and spotting effectively.

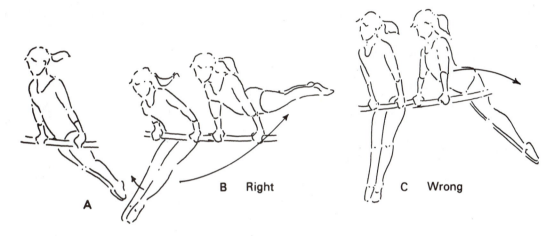

In a back hip circle (see page 219) the student starts in a front support position (A). In the process of moving the legs forward to prepare for the cast, the shoulders should remain forward (B). If the shoulders should move backward as the feet move forward and begin to cast, the body will be forced backward away from the bar (C). This is caused by moving the center of gravity past the base of support.

Completing a back walkover (refer to page 69) on the beam or floor is often a problem because of poor body alignment *or* relationship of c of g to base of support. In the initial stages the c of g is slightly above the hip area because the arms are raised (A). It should remain in this area throughout the skill because of the position of the arms. For stability throughout, the body must go from its first base of support (feet) to its second base of support (hands) to finish on the feet in one sustained movement. This can happen only if the split of the legs, flexibility of the back, and kick-push of the leg action is adequate for the particular individual's body weight. The body generally collapses or the spotter must push with a great deal of effort at the point when the hands contact the floor if the center of gravity is not directly over the base of support (hips and shoulders not over hands) (C). After the first foot contacts the floor, the second leg must remain straight (D) so that the line will not be broken at the hip area (E). The line from the fingertips to the toe of the second foot must remain straight until the final lunge (F) or low arabesque position has been reached.

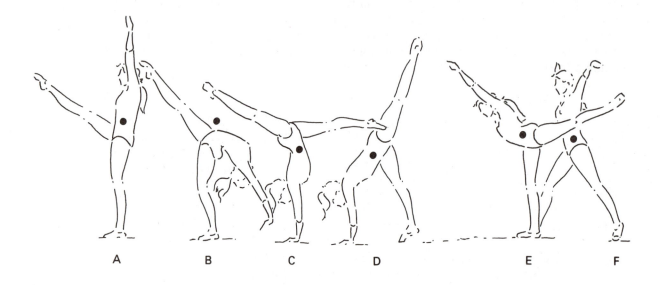

A   B   C   D   E   F

If the relationship of the c of g to the base of support is clearly understood and can be applied to performance, analyses, and spotting of gymnastics skills, then we can say that Newton's laws of motion have been observed and practiced.

MOTION

Motion is usually thought of as an observable change in position of the entire body or its parts. *Sustained motion* occurs when the body parts move slowly in a given direction or position (e.g., stretching upward to a stand from a forward roll; stretching of the body into the glide before a kip on the bars; or constant muscle tensing to maintain the vertical position in a handstand).

Percussive motion consists of a sharp or rapid movement of the body or its parts from one position to another (e.g., the kipping action of the hips and push of the arms on the back roll extension; or the immediate rebound [punch] from the reuther board before execution of a vault).

There are two basic types of motion, translatory (linear) and rotatory (angular). In *translatory motion* an object or body moves through a continuing plane at a constant rate. The best example of this is a body moving forward while seated in an automobile or the body moving in air off a ski jump. In *rotatory motion* an object or body moves about or around a central point or axis. This axis could be part of the body, such as when the body rotates around the bar on a back hip circle. A front or back somersault would be classified as a *curvilinear motion* as the object is moving as a whole in a circular path.

Rotatory motion may take place around one of three axes. The *longitudinal axis* (A) runs the length of the object; the *transverse axis* (B) runs across the object at any level in its entire length; and the *sagittal axis* (C) goes from front to back at any level of the body.

In a freely suspended body, the axis or axes of rotation pass through the center of gravity. In a supported object, one in contact with another surface, the axis is at the contact point or in a nearby articulation (joint).

In many movements a combination of linear and rotatory motion occurs (e.g., running for a vault). The leg action is rotatory while the body as a whole moves in a linear fashion.

Two factors determine the type of motion that will result when force is applied: (1) *the point at which force is applied,* and (2) *the movement pathway available for the object.* If force is applied through the center of gravity, translatory (linear) motion will result. If force is applied away from the center of gravity, rotatory (angular) motion will

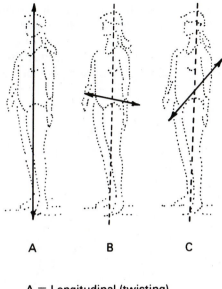

A = Longitudinal (twisting)
B = Transverse (cartwheeling)
C = Sagittal (rolling)

result. For example, a pencil resting on its side if pushed at midpoint should move directly forward. If force is applied at one end the movement would be in an arc. Therefore, the farther the force is applied from the center of gravity of an object, the greater the effectiveness of that force for rotation about the center (see example 1). This tendency of a force to produce rotation is called *moment of rotation* or *rotatory force*. Understanding this factor is of utmost importance to the spotter. If the spotter knows exactly at what point and in what direction to apply force, less physical effort will be required in assisting skill performance, and skills will be learned more efficiently (see example 2).

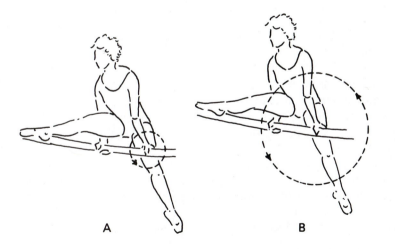

Example 1

Example 1   Mill circle on bars; (refer to page 231 for total skill). If the inside hand spots the upper arm (B) instead of the wrist area (A), the amount of force that can be developed is greater; therefore, the spotter can force the body around the bar with less effort.

Example 2 In a back sommie, if force is applied on the upper back in a forward direction at the same time force is applied to the hips in the direction of the turn, the movement would be constant and would result in a fall of the body downward (B). To be successful, force applied to the back should be upward (helping to gain height) while the force on the back of the legs and hip area should be up and rotating backward in the direction of the desired turn (A).

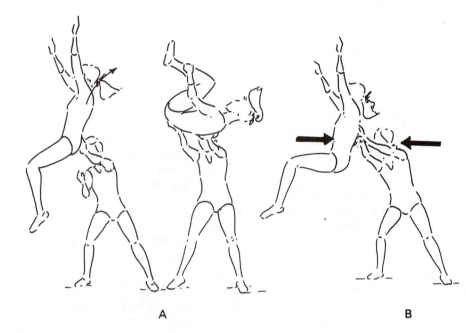

A   B

Example 2

FORCE

Force in some form is required to produce all motion. The word *force* is often used freely without any understanding of what it is, how it works, where it comes from, and how to control it. There are basically three types of force: *muscular, frictional, and gravitational.*

The forces needed to initiate and perform skills depend upon the muscularity and structure of the body. Muscle tension accounts for part of the difference over which the force is applied, speed developed, and the final outcome or performance of the skill. Therefore, if the muscles involved are brought into play at 50 percent, the skill will be executed at 50 percent of the performer's potential.

For example, the force needed to keep the body in a controlled handstand depends on fine muscular contraction in the fingers and hands to offset subtle shifts in the center of gravity.

Poor

Good

A fine degree of muscle contraction is necessary to assure a performer's smooth transition in and out of various movements.

An inadvertent loss of tension in the extensor muscle groups in performance of a back layout not only detracts aesthetically but also necessitates body flexion in order to land (A) rather than as in (B).

A

B

FRICTION

Friction comes into play mainly on the bars. Because most of the skills are performed with some type of hand grip, the degree of tension in the grip will directly affect the outcome of the skill being performed. Too much friction is a menace to the beginner, who tends to grip tightly so as not to fall off. In a mill circle, if the grip is too tight, the last third of the skill will be greatly affected.

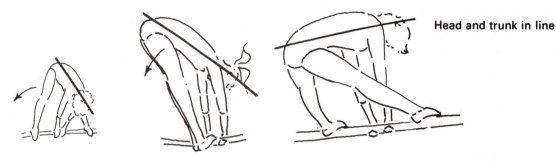

Head and trunk in line

For example in a sole circle, two points of friction work for the performer. If the legs are totally extended and pushing against the bar, the radius of rotation is increased (distance from hip to bar), and if the arms are totally extended and the grip controlled, the body will develop more momentum on the way down, therefore making it easier to complete the circle and transitional movements. Such a body position will also maximize the desired momentum.

GRAVITY

Gravity acts on all objects (including humans) at all times. The gravitational force is always exerted in a downward vertical direction. Thus, on some skills or parts of skills we can use gravity to our advantage. Gravity can assist on the first phase of skills such as mill circles, seat circles, and sole circles. The longer the radius of rotation (the higher the hips) and the more compressed the body (the closer the center of gravity to the base of support), the faster the movement on the first phase.

On the other hand, gravity can act against the last part of these same skills by trying to pull the body down after it has passed midpoint. If the body is not compressed sufficiently, the grip too tight, and the initial force forward inadequate, gravity can easily overcome the motion after midpoint.

Good compression   Too open

NEWTON'S LAWS OF MOTION

Inertia

A body at rest tends to remain at rest unless acted upon by an outside force. Likewise, a body in motion tends to remain in motion unless acted upon by an outside force. An outside force may be another person, object, gravity, or friction making contact with the body, or it may be muscular movement from within the body.

For instance, a body held in a stride position for a mill circle on the bars will remain in that position until the upper body and hip extend forward, moving the body weight forward (therefore moving c of g past the base of support).

A body spinning around the bars as in a mill circle could continue forward at the completion, unless the grip was tightened (friction) and the shoulders and chest were lifted upward at the completion of the skill to force the c of g directly over the base of support.

A body turning around the bar in a back hip circle could continue a second or third time (depending on momentum developed) unless the body moved from a pike to a layout (front support) position.

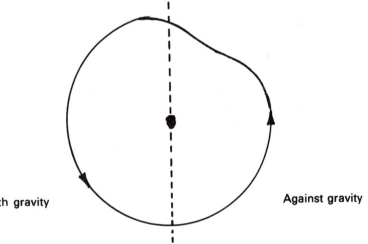

With gravity   Against gravity

Acceleration

When a body is acted upon by a force, its resulting change is speed. Acceleration is directly proportional to the force producing it and inversely proportional to the mass. Given an object of a certain weight, the greater the force applied to it the greater the speed of the object. Given a certain force applied, the greater the weight of an object, the less the speed of movement.

Therefore, the tighter the tuck the faster the spin (if equal force is applied), and the closer the c of g is to the radius of rotation, the faster the spin.

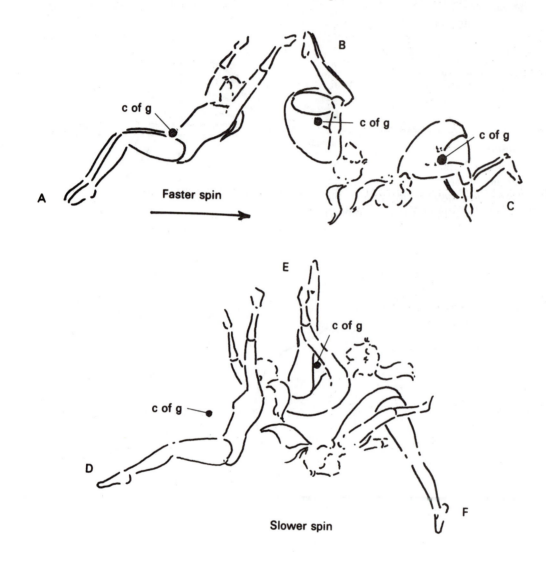

If two people punched the reuther board with equal force, the one weighing less would be projected farther.

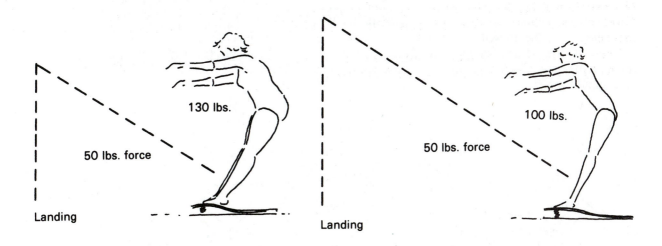

If two people weighing the same punched the board with different amounts of force, the one producing the greater force would be projected farther.

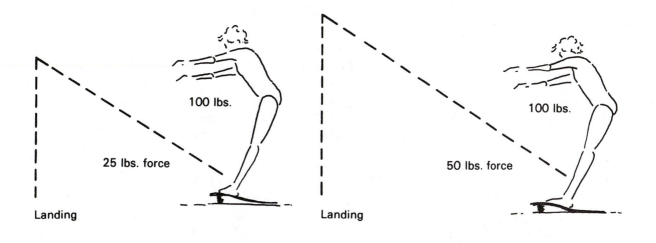

If force opposes the direction of motion, a decrease in acceleration will occur; and if the force is in line with the motion, there will be an increase in momentum. This could be applied to the handstand (A) and front handspring (B). From a standing position, the two skills have identical movement beginnings. The initial force (kick-push action of legs) for the handstand, of course, is less than for a handspring. When the vertical position is reached in the handstand, the muscles tighten and force the body upward in order to stop forward movement. If the force from the initial kick-push action is great enough, the body will pass through the vertical position, and with the secondary muscular force and hand push from the mat should return to an upright position.

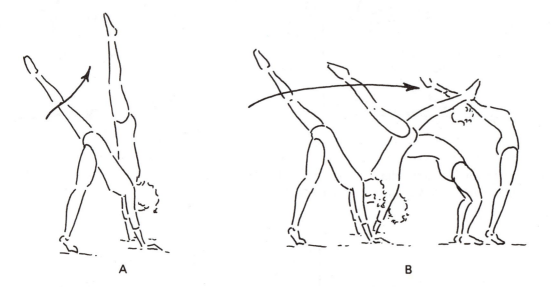

A   B

Action-Reaction

For every action force there is an equal and opposite reaction. In order to spring vertically for a sommie, the initial movement must be downward against the mat and floor. The more forceful the extension or lift from the floor, the higher the lift proportionate to body mass.

When the hip and upper body are extended forward in a mill circle, the center of gravity is pushed past the base of support; therefore, the body will move forward with proportional speed.

The body coming to a stand after a forward roll is the resultant force of pushing downward against the mat and floor by extending the legs and upper body in a vertical direction, providing the center of gravity passes over the base of support.

The position of the feet making contact with the mat out of a round-off is different for a back handspring and a back sommie or layout. (A) represents the proper position for a round-off back handspring.

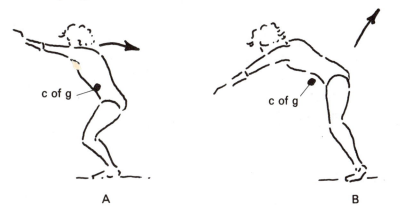

c of g

c of g

A   B

The feet come in closer to the hands for a back handspring than for a back sommie. The position of the feet out of a round-off for a back sommie should be farther away from the hands than for a back handspring (B). The object here is to hit or punch the mat slightly back, so that by the time the upper body has pushed from the mat, the total body can be in a vertical flight pattern with upward and backward momentum.

Notice below the angle of the body as feet hit the board; you can see why it is more efficient and effective to contact the reuther board with the feet slightly in front of the shoulders. At the angle of impact, if the arms are lifted forcefully to an overhead position and full body extension occurs, the body, being shot as a missile, will rebound on an upward inverted flight.

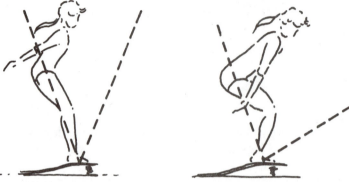

Body will be projected up and forward over or onto horse

Body will be projected forward into horse

In twisting and rotatory moves, once the body is free of the supporting surface it can no longer increase or decrease the initial force. However, a body can increase (by tucking) or decrease (by laying out) the speed of rotation. This is basically shortening or lengthening the radius of rotation.

On a front sommie, once the feet have left the floor the height gained in air will be equal to the push from the feet and legs. If the height is adequate and the performer proficient, the skill can be executed properly. If the height is adequate and the performer proficient, the skill can be performed with less amplitude, and landing might occur in a squat position.

For example, in all layout and twisting moves, the body must be totally extended on takeoff and remain totally extended throughout. The example below shows a very relaxed body throughout—a typical beginner, anxious to get the feet on the mat as quickly as possible.

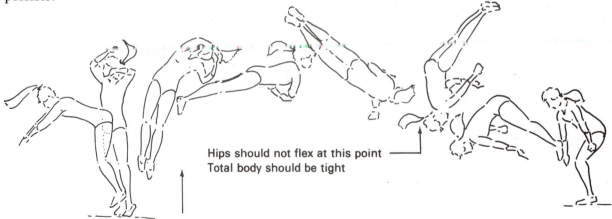

Hips should not flex at this point
Total body should be tight

Body not tight here at beginning

Chapter 3 — Conditioning

The purpose of any conditioning program is to prepare the body to perform skills effectively and efficiently as well as to encourage safety and confidence and to reduce the likelihood of injury. The suggested program is divided into component groups. Not all exercises in each group must be done; however, no group should be skipped in its entirety. Some exercises develop more than one component simultaneously, and may be varied weekly or daily to avoid boredom.

GROUP 1: CARDIOVASCULAR EXERCISES

The muscle tissues must have an adequate blood supply to perform efficiently. Exercises that enhance this body function are called *cardiovascular exercises* and generally involve moving the body parts quickly.

Suggested cardiovascular exercises:

1. *Jumping jacks* (Fig. C–1). Arm and leg movements may be varied from day to day.

Figure C–1

A grading sheet for conditioning skills appears at the end of this chapter.

2. *Running* (Fig. C–2). In place, running laps, or running a distance. Try to keep an even pace or rhythm and do not allow the upper body to sag.

Figure C–2

3. *Squat thrusts* (Fig. C–3). Generally, ten are sufficient to develop some degree of cardiovascular fitness if done daily.

Figure C–3

4. *Jump rope* (Fig. C–4). Jumping rope is an excellent form of cardiovascular exercise. You should start with one minute, then increase to ten. Ten minutes of jumping daily would almost insure that a student could complete a floor routine without vigorous breathing.

Figure C–4

5. *Locomotor skills* (Fig. C–5). Combine locomotor skills in a circular or line pattern. Perform at least five of each skill before going to next.

Figure C–5

GROUP II: STRENGTH

The student needs total body strength to maneuver through, in, on, under, and over the apparatus. Explosive power, a form of strength, is a definite asset for tumbling and vaulting. Strength is needed on the uneven bars as well as the beam—an individual must have sufficient strength to put and control the body through the many skills. Development of strength occurs when the student increases resistance or the number of repetitions with the same amount of resistance.

1. *Push-ups* (Figs. C–6a and C–6b). Keep body completely straight in both the push-up from a prone position and in a modified position.

Figure C–6a   **Figure C–6b**

2. *Pull-ups* (Fig. C–7). With hands in a forward grip (back of hand toward face), pull chin up above bar. Start with five, increase to fifteen. If assistance is needed in the beginning, have a partner lift with hands on legs above the knees.

Figure C–7

3. *Crunch* (Fig. C–8). Perform in supine position with knees bent, heels close to buttocks, and feet flat on mat. Keep arms bent with hands on side of head, on shoulders, or with arms crossed over chest. Raise head and chest (with chin up) 6 to 8 inches while pressing lower back to mat. Remember to contract abdominals during crunch. Hold three counts, repeat.

Figure C–8

4. *Leg lifts* (Fig. C–9). Hanging from a bar, lift the legs to a position parallel to the floor, hold two counts, then lower to a hanging position. On the next lift, raise the legs so the feet go above the head, hold two counts, then lower to hang. Repeat each sequence, starting with five and increasing to fifteen. Wearing heavy tennis shoes would add resistance and repetitions could be decreased.

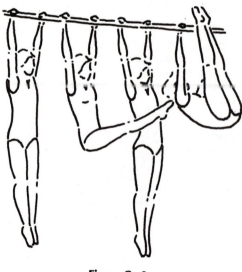

Figure C–9

5. *Leg tucks and extensions* (Fig. C–10). From a long hang position, bring the legs to a tuck position, then extend them forward to a horizontal position. Bring back to the tucked position, then extend to a long hang position. Start with five and work up to twenty.

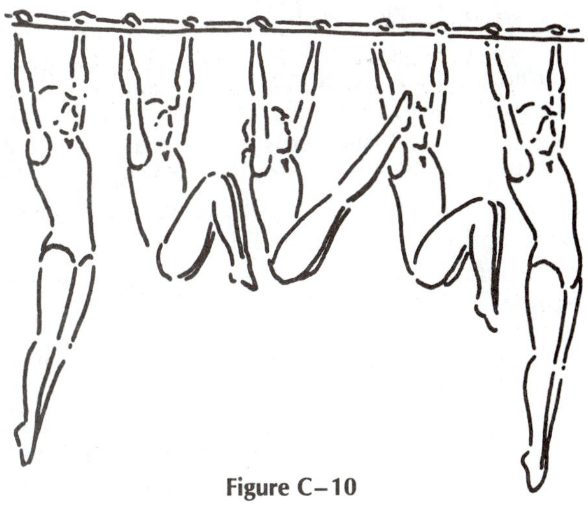

Figure C–10

6. *Parallel bar dips* (Fig. C–11). From a hand support position at the end of the bars facing in, bend the arms, lowering the shoulders to the bars. Extend the arms back to the starting position. Start with five and work to twenty.

Figure C–11

7. *Cast (push away and return to bar)* (Fig. C–12). From front support position with hands in a forward grip, flex hips, bring legs under bar (allow arms to slightly flex), and move shoulders forward of bar. Thrust legs backward-upward forcing body (except hands) away from bar, and extend arms. Return to bar in a fully extended (arched) position

Figure C–12

GROUP III: FLEXIBILITY

Flexibility, the range of movement for a specific joint, is important in gymnastics. When a student can perform a split, a walkover can be executed with greater ease, since the weight can be displaced and redistributed past the center of gravity more quickly. Stretching carefully is the best way to achieve greater flexibility. Many times it is advantageous to have partners, since they can produce more force or resistance. It is important to warm up the muscles prior to working on flexibility (running, jumping jacks, and so on). Partners should be encouraged to communicate during these exercises to prevent unnecessary pain and possible tearing of tissue.

1. *Splits* (Fig. C–13). Start by standing in a lunge position with hips and shoulders directly perpendicular to legs (this is referred to as *squaring* the hips and shoulders). Slide the legs gently away from each other and hold at the point where some discomfort occurs. If needed, the hands can be placed to the side of the body to hold some of the weight. Repeat procedure on both sides, five times a warm-up session depending on the present state of flexibility. If full splits have been attained, then the forward foot can be placed on a low bench or folded mat for added stretch. Reverse this procedure and have back foot resting on raised mat.

Figure C–13

2. *Splits with partner and other variations:*
   a. (Fig. C–14). Stand with back against wall. Lift one leg parallel to floor and place in partner's hand. Push down on partner's hand for thirty seconds, then allow partner to lift leg above head. This method allows antagonistic muscles to rest, then work at maximum during the stretch. Repeat with other leg, then switch partners.

Figure C–14

b. (Fig. C–15). Stand with back to wall, lean forward, and place hands on floor. Lift one leg vertically and push body to split position. Repeat on other side.

Figure C–15

c. (Fig. C–16). Sit in straddle position facing partner with soles of feet together. Grasp wrists and rock forward and backward while applying pressure through the feet. As flexibility increases, grasp at elbows, then at shoulders.

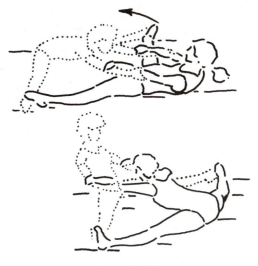

Figure C–16

3. *Lower back and shoulders* (Fig. C–17). Partner lies in prone position with arms by the head. While ankles are held, the partner lifts upward as high as possible, holding for three counts when reaching the stress point. Eventually, this exercise can be done with a twisting action upward.

Figure C–17

4. *Backbends* (Fig. C–18). For shoulder, back, and trunk flexibility. Start in a lying position (face up). Place heels by hips and hands under shoulders as for a backward roll. Push with hands and hips simultaneously to push body into a backbend position. Rock back and forth, gently keeping the head between the arms (look at fingers). When a good backbend can be performed, then put the legs together and try to force the shoulders past the hand position.

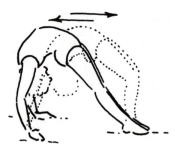

Figure C–18

5. *Knees to nose* (Fig. C–19). For flexibility in back of legs and lower back. Lie on floor on back with arms above head. Lift the legs upward and backward without bending legs and touch toes on floor behind the head. When this can be done without stress, flex the ankles, curl the toes under, and rock back and forth.

Figure C–19

6. *Trunk stretch and rotation* (Fig. C–20). Stand with feet just outside shoulders. Stretch slowly to the right, return to stand, stretch to left, return to stand, stretch forward, return to stand, and then stretch backward and return to the standing position. Hold each position for three counts. Each time stretch to the stress point.

Figure C–20

7. *Lower back and shoulders:*

   a. (Fig. C–21). Straddle partner in a squat position (do not sit on partner), grasp legs above the knees and lift. Lift only until hips begin to be pulled off the mat.

Figure C–21

   b. (Fig. C–22). Straddle partner in a kneeling position. Grasp upper arms and pull up and back gently until stress is felt. Hold a few seconds and lower gently. Do not raise hips off the mat.

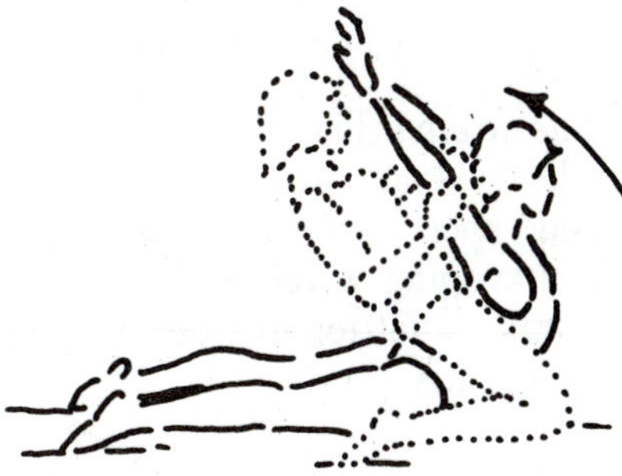

Figure C–22

8. *Trunk stretch* (Fig. C–23). On stall bar, lowered beam, or barre, lean forward with the body in an open pike or 90-degree position while grasping the object. Apply pressure (stretch) through the shoulders or have partner press gently on upper back and shoulder area. Stretch three seconds, relax three seconds. Repeat five times.

Figure C–23

9. *Trunk stretch in straddle sitting position* (Fig. C–24). Sitting in a wide straddle position, twist the trunk forward, leading with the right shoulder and swinging the right arm across the chest and the left arm overhead. Hold three counts and repeat movement to the left side.

Figure C–24

10. *Ankle stretch* (Fig. C–25). Kneel, then sit on heels. Place hands to side of the body beside knees. Lift the knees up toward the chest keeping weight on the ankles. Hold at stress point for five counts, then lower and repeat.

Figure C–25

11. *Front-to-back stretch* (Fig. C–26). Stand with feet about 18 inches apart. Bend forward to touch hands flat on floor in front of body, then stretch through the vertical and go backward to place the hands on the floor in a backbend position. Repeat five times. If student cannot get up from backbend alone, do with a partner and spot as if spotting for a limbre.

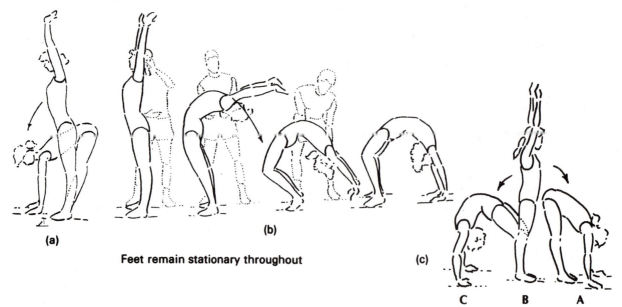

(a)

(b)

Feet remain stationary throughout

(c)

C B A

Figure C–26

GROUP IV: COORDINATION

Coordination is necessary to perform individual complex movements and series of movements in gymnastics. Coordination is the ability to put a body part in a certain position at the appropriate time. The best exercise to develop coordination is repetition of actual skills. Each skill has a specific rhythm; when this rhythm has been learned, the skill has been performed correctly. When the correct rhythm has been learned, coordination of the body parts has also occurred. In the process of repetition of exercises or specific skills, the mind and body are also learning concentration and discipline.

1. *Jumping jacks—8 count* (Fig. C–27):

   1–2 Jump with feet apart, hands overhead, return to starting position.

   3–4 Jump, lift right leg, clap under leg, then behind back.

   5–6 Jump, lift left leg, clap under leg, then behind back.

   7–8 Same as 1–2.

Jumping jacks aid in coordination in that they require concentration on putting the body parts in a specific position at a designated time.

Figure C–27

2. *Jumping jack variation—4 count* (Fig. C–28):

   1. Right foot forward, arms forward.
   2. Right foot sideward, arms sideward.
   3. Right foot forward, arms forward.
   4. Right foot beside left foot, arms at side.

   Repeat using left foot.

   Repeat having arms go in opposition.

Figure C–28

3. *Walking in backbend position* (Fig. C–29). Push up into backbend position and walk 20 feet, hop 20 feet, and then run 20 feet. To begin, have partner at side to help student move in the proper direction. After they are comfortable with walking forward, then they should hop and run forward. Well coordinated and flexible students should try walking, hopping, and running backward.

   a. Walking.
   b. Hopping.
   c. Running.

Figure C–29

4. *Inside outs* (Fig. C–30). Begin in pike position with both hands and feet on floor. Lift arm and leg of same side, force hips upward, place hand and foot on floor in backbend position and rotate hand that is still on floor. From backbend position lift leg followed by hand to continue to original position. Try to cover 20 feet.

Figure C–30

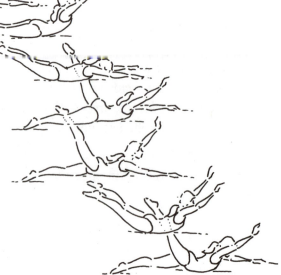

5. *Swan exercise—8 count* (Fig. C–31). Lie on mat in prone position; arms by head.

   1. Lift arms and upper body, lower.
   2. Lift legs together and straight, lower.
   3. Lift right arm and left leg, lower.
   4. Lift left arm and right leg, lower.
   5. Lift total body, lower.
   6. Lift right arm and right leg, lower.
   7. Lift left arm and left leg, lower.
   8. Lift total body, lower.

Repeat five times.

Figure C–31

6. *Arm circles* (Fig. C–32). Start in standing position with arms at side. Start with the right arm and have the left arm follow one step behind. Repeat, leading with left arm. Four count.

1. Right arm forward, left at side.
2. Right arm vertical, left arm forward.
3. Right arm to side parallel to floor, left arm vertical.
4. Right arm to side of body, left arm to side parallel to floor.

Repeat ten times.

Figure C–32

GROUP V: BALANCE

Good balance in gymnastics is necessary for success. Students must be able to balance in many positions—natural, inverted, horizontal forward (arabesque or scale), horizontal backward (back arabesques; beginning of back walkovers), and diagonal (various modern turns done on slant). Counterbalance is another factor one must be able to understand and perform for balance. Balance occurs only when body parts are equally distributed over the base of support, whether it be the feet, hands, seat, or other base. If one part extends past the base, moving the center of gravity, another part must counterbalance by extending in opposition (e.g., in an arabesque the chest moves forward and the leg lifts rearward).

1. *Leg lifts* (Fig. C–33). Stand without holding barre, beam, or other object. Lift foot forward parallel to the floor, move to the side, then move to the rear low arabesque, holding five counts in each position. Repeat with other leg. Perform four times on each side.

Figure C–33

2. *V-seat* (Fig. C–34). Sit on the floor, folded mat, or balance beam. Lift the legs forward to a V-seat position and hold for five counts. Arms can vary with each V-seat; they may be vertical, forward, sideward, or crossed over the chest.

Figure C–34

3. *Attitudes, arabesques, scales* (Fig. C–35). Assume any of the positions categorized here and hold for the count of ten. Vary the positions.

Figure C–35

4. *Balanced handstand* (Fig. C–36). Stretch into a straight body handstand and hold for ten counts. To begin, have partner stand to side and spot legs just above knees to help with balance.

Figure C–36

GROUP VI: PLYOMETRICS/EXPLOSIVE POWER

Plyometrics calls on the "body's natural stretch reflex." When a muscle is stretched quickly, the nerves respond by sending a message to the stretched muscle to immediately contract. This action aids to protect the muscle from being strained or torn and helps develop "explosive power." Plyometric drills speed up the stretch reflex so movement can become more forceful.

1. *Frog jump* (Fig. C–37). Start in a semisquat position, arms between knees. Explode straight up off the floor or mat, reaching up with arms, without arching back. Land back in a squat position. Jump six times, rest for thirty seconds. Repeat sequence twice.

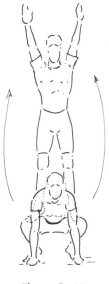

Figure C–37

2. *Standing long jump* (Fig. C–38). Start with feet 6 to 8 inches apart, knees bent and arms behind body. Swing arms forward as you jump forward, landing on both feet with knees slightly bent, then push off the floor or mat and land on both feet again. Go for distance, not height. Jump three times, rest thirty seconds. Repeat sequence three times.

Figure C–38

3. *Line jump sideward* (Fig. C–39). Stand to one side of a line or imaginary line on the floor. With feet together, jump from side to side for one minute. Repeat sequence again for one minute. As student improves strength and endurance, increase number of one minute repetitions.

Figure C–39

4. *Tuck jumps* (Fig. C–40). As rapidly as possible spring vertically and bring knees to the chest and extend before landing. Start with ten and work up to twenty-five.

Figure C–40

5. *Jump down and back up* (Fig. C–41). Use a stack of mats or a sturdy box. Begin jump training from a height of 12 inches, gradually work up to 18 inches. Jump down, jump one-half turn, jump back up and repeat. Jump three times, rest thirty seconds, repeat sequence three times.

Figure C–41

Conditioning Skills	Score	Dates									
Jumping jacks											
Running											
Squat thrusts											
Jump rope											
Locomotor skills											
Push-ups											
Pull-ups											
Crunch											
Leg lifts (1)											
Leg tucks and extensions											
Parallel bar dips											
Cast											
Splits											
Splits with partner											
Splits from wall											
Splits from straddle											
Lower back and shoulders (1)											
Backbends											
Knees to nose											
Trunk stretch and rotation											
Lower back and shoulders (2)											
Lower back and shoulders (3)											
Trunk stretch											
Trunk stretch in straddle											

(Continued)

Ankle stretch												
Front-to-back stretch												
Jumping jacks—8 count												
Jumping jacks—4 count												
Backbend walk												
Inside outs												
Swan exercise—8 count												
Arm circles												
Leg lifts (2)												
V-seat												
Attitudes, arabesques, scales												
Balanced handstand												
Frog jump												
Standing long jump												
Line jump sideward												
Tuck jumps												
Jump down and back up												

Tumbling

The values of tumbling in the physical education program are numerous. Tumbling challenges students to compete against themselves, as they do not have a teammate to help maneuver their bodies through intricate skills (except as a spotter). Lead up and tumbling skills, along with single and dual activities, develop coordination, flexibility, balance, strength, self-confidence, agility, kinesthetic perception, courage, and rhythm or timing.

If students are given a strong program in basic tumbling skills and are required to master those skills, chances for success on apparatus will be greater because learned tumbling movements can be transferred to other activities.

It is essential to have a definite skill progression for each group or individual and to have students master the fundamental skills before attempting more difficult ones.

The skills covered in this chapter are listed in a suggested progression sequence; however, other progressions may be used, depending on the ability and size of the group. To coordinate spotting techniques and variations, skills are not described in exact order. Some are oriented to the left or right. To perform skills to the other side, reverse directions.

SAFETY HINTS

1. Never allow students to tumble unless supervised.
2. Always tumble on mats.
3. Performers in a group should always work in the same direction to avoid collisions.
4. While others are performing, stay clear of mats unless acting as a spotter.
5. Remove all jewelry before tumbling.
6. Keep mats clean and in good condition. Avoid tumbling on mats with tears or mats covered with any type of dust.

A grading sheet for tumbling skills appears at the end of this chapter.

7. Use safety devices when necessary (e.g., spotting belts).

8. If mats are to be placed in succession, secure with tape or some other material that will keep them from slipping apart.

9. It is advisable to have student assistants if possible. They should be given special instruction (before or after school) on correct techniques.

10. Remind students to complete the attempted skill and not to "chicken out" in the middle of the skill.

11. Do not allow students to "goof off" at any time.

12. Advise students to keep eyes open at all times to develop kinesthetic awareness and to prevent accidents.

13. Do not allow students to tumble when fatigued.

14. Have a definite skill progression, and do not permit students to work above skill level.

15. Refer to the USGF's safety manuals for other safety tips.

16. Don't force a student to perform a skill they don't feel ready to do.

TEACHING SUGGESTIONS

A piece of uncooked spaghetti can be maneuvered through space more easily than a piece of cooked spaghetti. Students can understand and relate to this as they experiment with tight and relaxed bodies in a standing position.

The following hints should become an integral part of your teaching patterns and vocabulary.

1. The head in almost all skills remains between the shoulders (in a neutral position).

2. The arms are generally in three places:
   a. "Up"—overhead, covering ears.
   b. Close to body during twists.
   c. Close to ankle area during sommies.

3. When moving into handstands, walkovers, and so on, the hip of forward leg acts as the fulcrum of a seesaw and the extended leg and the rest of body as a seesaw (which does not bend at hip).

4. When moving out of back walkovers and cartwheels, the first foot that touches again acts as the fulcrum with the seesaw (straight leg to fingertips). When body has landed, the lunge looks like an empty seesaw.

5. When one body part is directly over the other, movement is more efficient and less stress occurs on the joints.

6. When in an inverted off-balance position, try to roll directly forward to avoid weight or stress being placed on one particular joint.

7. Teach students the fundamental principles of movements. Let them experiment in the basic skills with a small and large base for a headstand and discover why these analyses are necessary.

8. Students should learn tumbling skills from a step or step hurdle. Many skills may be later transferred to the beam. By doing skills from just one step, more explosive leg power is developed.

9. Just as it is easier to perform more efficiently as an uncooked piece of spaghetti, it is easier to manipulate or spot the person whose body is tight.

10. If students are taught correctly from the beginning and are ready for the next skill, they should need little spotting. Some of today's finest coaches spot very little because they provide a good foundation and safe environment for learning.

PROPER FALLING TECHNIQUES

Insufficient attention is generally given to proper falling techniques. Because of the potential risk involved in gymnastic activity, falling is a skill that should be learned. Falling exercises reduce injury, increase body awareness, and reduce students' fear.

The following points should be stressed before students actually perform the exercises.

1. Avoid exclusive use of hands to break a fall.
2. Incorporate rolling movements whenever possible.
3. Relax body after initial contact with mat, giving in to direction of fall with a rolling movement.
4. When initially breaking a fall with the hands, keep fingers extended and pointing forward.
5. Falls must be executed onto mats at all times. Mat thickness may vary from a 1½-inch mat to a 12-inch landing mat.

Exercise 1: Front Fall (Fig. FT–1)

The front fall technique is used to break a fall while falling directly forward when a rolling movement is not possible. Stand at edge of mat, bend hips, and fall forward while reaching forward with hands and arms outstretched toward mat. As hands initially contact the mat, arms are quickly flexed with a controlled resistive movement lowering body to a prone position.

The next four exercises are executed by jumping from an initial height of 8–12 inches. As students gain confidence, gradually increase height to at least 3 feet. One or two stacked mats make a good platform from which to "jump-fall."

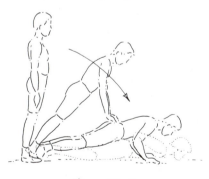

Figure FT–1

Exercise 2: Jump-Front Fall to Forward Roll (Fig. FT–2)

This exercise is used where a forward roll may be performed to help break a fall occurring in a forward direction. With platform placed in front of landing area, wait as long as possible before jumping forward so feet contact mat first, taking up the initial shock. Immediately following contact, with feet on mat, follow through with a forward roll.

Figure FT–2

Exercise 3: Jump-Front Fall to Shoulder Roll (Fig. FT–3)

Use same procedure described in exercise 2, except execute a forward shoulder roll. This variation allows students to use hands to a lesser degree in breaking the fall. Instead of rolling directly forward, turn body slightly to right and use left shoulder and upper arm to break the fall. Turn head to right with chin tucked down toward right armpit, and execute roll across upper back. Students should practice and master shoulder roll to both sides.

Figure FT–3

Exercise 4: Backward Fall-Backward Roll (Fig. FT—4)

This exercise is designed to develop safer falls while moving backward. Stand with back facing landing area. Allow body to start falling backward. Flex the hands with fingers pointing forward at sides of body. Flex hips, allowing upper body to bend forward. Begin to bend knees and reach backward with hands toward mat. Hands contact mat first. At this point, entire body is flexed and somewhat relaxed, with the chin on chest. Immediately move hands over shoulders and follow through with back roll. A shoulder roll will negate having to use the hands as much as is necessary with a good backward roll. Repeat exercise progressively faster and finally without using hands to break fall. The key to breaking the fall without using the hands at this point is flexing knees and hips maximally and immediately rolling backward.

Figure FT—4

Exercise 5: Jump Backward Fall to Shoulder Roll (Fig. FT—5)

Repeat the steps outlined in exercise 4 while falling and jumping backward from an initial height of 8—12 inches. Increase height gradually to 3 feet.

Figure FT—5

LEAD UP SKILLS

Students should master lead up skills before learning tumbling skills. Lead up skills develop better body awareness in space and can be done by almost everyone with little effort. Refer to the USGF's safety manual for other gymnastic readiness skills.

■ TRIPOD (Fig. T–1)

PT From kneeling position, place hands on mat at least shoulder width apart. Bend elbows and *spread fingers apart*. Place head on mat forward of hands to form triangular base. Lift hips upward by extending legs and place one knee at a time on elbows. Point toes toward ceiling. Hold for three seconds, then come down one leg at a time.

SP Place hands on hips and help lift knees to elbows.

CE 1. Triangle (base) too small or too large.

2. Top of head rather than hairline area on mat.

3. Elbows not stable while inverted (think about forcing them toward each other).

4. Trying to jump into position rather than controlling leg lift.

Figure T–1

■ TIP-UP (Fig. T–2)

PT From squat position with knees apart, place hands on mat between legs (fingers spread apart). Press knees forcefully against elbows, which are slightly bent, and shift body weight to hands. Keep head up. Hold for three seconds and then return to squat position.

SP Kneel beside student and assist by supporting shoulder and back of thigh.

CE 1. Failure to keep arms slightly bent.

2. Knees too far apart or too close.

3. Failure to keep head up.

4. Failure to elevate hips before tipping forward.

5. Failure to squeeze knees against elbows forcefully.

Figure T–2a   Side view

Figure T–2b   Front view

■ HEADSTAND (Fig. T–3)

PT Extend and join legs slowly to inverted position while shifting hips directly over head. Hold for three seconds, reverse procedure, and return to tripod.

SP For all variations of headstand: Stand to side of performer and assist with balance by grasping legs just above knee.

CE 1. Top of head rather than hairline area on mat.

2. Failure to maintain hips directly overhead.

3. Not keeping calf and thigh muscles tense.

4. Allowing arms to collapse or wobble.

5. Insufficient base of support (triangle).

Figure T–3

■ HEADSTAND FROM SQUAT OR LUNGE POSITION (Fig. T–4)

PT Form triangle with head and hands. Draw one leg close to chest, extend other leg to rear. Lift extended leg to inverted position while pushing with bent leg. Bring both legs together to inverted position; extend body with hips directly overhead. Hold three seconds and return to mat, one leg at a time.

CE 1. Same as 1–4 of tripod technique.

2. Insufficient lift of first leg and push with second leg.

Figure T–4

◼ HEADSTAND FROM PRONE POSITION (Fig. T–5)

PT Lift hips to allow hands and head to form triangle on mat. Draw (or walk) hips to overhead position. When hips are overhead, lift both legs (together and straight) to inverted position. Keep calf and thigh muscles taut.

CE 1. Same as 1–4 of tripod technique.

      2. Failure to lift hips to overhead position before extending legs vertically.

Figure T–5

TUMBLING SKILLS

◼ FORWARD ROLL (Fig. T–6)

SL Beginner.

PT From deep squat position with knees together, place hands on mat approximately 18 inches in front of toes. Push down backward with feet to extend legs and lift hips upward. Bend arms and lower upper shoulder area to mat (head tucks at last possible second before shoulder contact). Keeping legs extended, continue rolling, and as soon as hips have contacted mat, tuck legs and come to squat position reaching forward with hands. Eyes spot stationary object after returning to squat position to assist in maintaining balance and to prevent dizziness when doing several in a row.

   Hints 1. There should be a continuous motion from the squat position throughout the roll. If performer stops or pauses in any one phase, it will be more difficult to complete the roll successfully.

        2. The reason for keeping legs extended while on back in inverted pike position and then forcefully tucking them as hips contact mat is to develop extra momentum to return to squat position.

        3. Having students learn to use their feet for pushing from the very beginning enables them to learn other skills more rapidly.

        4. Have small, weak, or overweight students roll down an inclined plane covered with a mat. This plane should be no more than a foot high. A reuther board or a homemade plank (covered with a mat) could be used for this purpose.

SP Kneel to side of student. Place hand on back of head and neck to keep student from placing head on mat. If performer has difficulty returning to squat position after rolling, place hand on back and push to assist.

CE 1. Incorrect hand placement on mat. Hands should not be placed to side of knees.
2. Failure to push with feet to develop momentum.
3. Failure to bend arms, tuck head, and place shoulders on mat.
4. Tucking head too soon (results in back flopping on mat).
5. Failure to keep legs extended while rolling and then to tuck them forcefully as hips contact mat.
6. Placing hands on mat to assist body into squat position after rolling.

MO 1. Continuous forward rolls.
2. Forward roll to single leg squat and pose.
3. Forward roll to knee and pose.
4. Forward roll to V-sit.
5. Forward roll straddle to split.

Figure T–6

◼ VARIATIONS OF FORWARD ROLL

VA 1. *Remain in tuck position throughout* (Fig. T–7).

Figure T–7

2. *From stand to single leg squat* (Fig. T–8).

Figure T–8

3. *Forward roll to knee pose* (Fig. T–9).

Figure T–9

4. *From stand to knee to splits* (Fig. T–10).

Figure T–10

5. *From stoop position to stand* (Fig. T–11).

Figure T–11

6. *From straddle stand to straddle stand* (Fig. T–12). As hips contact floor, place hands between legs with fingers pointing forward to assist in pushing to straddle stand.

Figure T–12

7. *Without hands* (Fig. T–13). From deep lunge position, tuck head and roll onto upper back and shoulder area, allowing back of hand and arm to contact mat (out to side of body). End in any of the above variations.

Figure T–13

■DIVE ROLL (Fig. T–14)

SL Beginner.

PT Assume semisquat position with shoulders forward of feet and arms obliquely backward. Force arms forward and upward while simultaneously pushing with feet to extend legs and lift hips, causing body to leave mat and be suspended in air above mat momentarily. Place hands on mat and support body weight. Bend arms with control; tuck head and lower upper shoulder area to mat and continue rolling.

Hints: 1. Use 6- to 12-inch landing mats when first learning and when doing from a run.

2. Start from deep squat position and gradually raise body as confidence is gained. Eventually execute skill from a standing position, then a run with a 2-foot takeoff.

3. On all rolls forward, it is essential to keep head up until the last possible second. If this is mentioned in the beginning phases of learning, however, some students tend to collapse and fall on their head, especially those with weak arms. If your students are fairly strong, emphasize this point from the beginning.

4. Use a vaulting board and dive roll onto a landing mat.

SP Stand in front and to side. Place hand behind head and neck and assist in lowering body to mat without touching mat. A second spotter may assist by placing one hand on abdomen, the other on front of thigh to help lift legs above hips and control performer's body weight through rolling phase.

CE 1. Failure to push with feet and lift hips.

2. Failure to gain height as well as distance (not allowing body to be momentarily suspended).

3. Failure to tuck head after arms start to bend and just before placing shoulders on mat.

MO 1. Any of those skills mentioned for forward roll.

2. Dive roll, headspring combination.

3. Dive roll, spring immediately into some type of jump.

VA 1. Dive over people or rolled-up mats.

2. Dive through legs of person doing headstand with legs in straddle position.

3. Continuous dive rolls.

4. Dive through hula hoops.

5. Layout dive roll.

Figure T–14

◼ HANDSTAND

A good handstand position is an important skill to master because the body passes through this position in performing many skills. It is advisable to learn what it feels like partially upside down before attempting the handstand balanced position. One lead up to the handstand is to do a kick-up to a near-handstand position, switch legs, and come to a stand.

☐ Handstand Kick-Up (Fig. T−15)

SL Beginner.

PT Lift arms overhead while simultaneously lifting right leg. Step forward onto right foot (as if making a small lunge) and bend right knee. Place hands on mat, shoulder width apart. As hands contact mat, spread fingers, making sure arms are straight with shoulders behind hands (refer to third position in Fig. T−15). Swing left leg (straight) backward and upward. Immediately push with right foot. Eyes spot hands. As soon as body is almost inverted, switch legs and come to a stand on left foot.

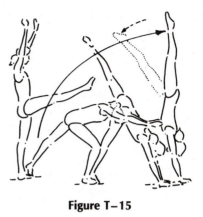

Figure T−15

> *Hint:* Practice kicking up to a handstand against a padded wall. Place hands approximately 6 inches from wall and keep head in a neutral position.

SP 1. Grasp above knee with both hands on one leg, stretch body to fullest.

2. Stand to side and forward of performer. Place inside arm across abdomen with other hand, palm up, under shoulder to keep student from collapsing.

CE 1. Failure to maintain straight arms.

2. Allowing shoulders to move forward of hand position.

3. Not keeping head in line with body.

4. Keeping head too high.

5. Placing hands too far away from or too close to feet.

6. Insufficient kick, push, or both.

☐ Balanced Handstand (Fig. T−16)

SL Beginner.

PT To achieve handstand or straight body position, many muscles in the body must work simultaneously. For a test of body tightness, stand in an erect position with feet together and try the following:

1. Inhale to feel chest lift.

2. Pull in abdominal muscles.

3. Squeeze gluteal muscles (rear end).

4. Squeeze knees and ankles together.

5. Extend ankles to raise on toes.

6. Lift arms overhead, elbows by ears.

7. Do 1−6 all at the same time.

Figure T−16

8. From a relaxed position, jump vertically to a relaxed body position.

9. From a relaxed position, jump vertically to an extended body position. (Note differences between 8 and 9; 9 is very similar to hitting the board for vaulting and springing vertically in a tight position.)

10. Kick to handstand, relax, then tighten. This tight position is what should be obtained immediately upon reaching handstand. There should be absolutely no sags.

Checkpoints for Balance

- Shoulders over hands.
- Hips over shoulders.
- Heels over head.
- Head in line with shoulders.

Hint: Use fingers (spread apart) to assist in balance by flexing them to feel as if they are trying to grasp mat.

SP Stand to side but forward of student. Grasp leg (swing leg) above knee as it reaches inverted position. After student can almost maintain balance, place arm (extended) toward back of legs in case of overbalance.

CE 1. Same as 1–5 in handstand kick-up.

2. Failure to extend shoulders and hips (body should be straight).

3. Allowing back to sag (body overarched).

☐Handstand Forward Roll (Fig. T–17)

SL Beginner.

PT Slightly overbalance handstand, bend arms slowly; flex hips and go into pike position. Tuck head, place shoulders on mat, and continue to roll.

SP Stand to side but forward of student. Grasp legs about knee level as they reach inverted position. Assist in lowering body to mat.

CE 1. Insufficient kick-push to inverted position.

2. Beginners have a tendency to keep arms straight too long, or tuck head too soon.

3. Failure to move body past head position (move center of gravity beyond base of support) before piking or bending arms.

4. Failure to place back of head then shoulders on mat.

Hint: To learn, use thick landing (crash) mat. Place hands close to crash mat. Roll onto mat from vertical position.

VA Handstand forward roll with straight arms.

Figure T–17

■BACKWARD ROLL (Fig. T–18)

SL Beginner.

PT Assume deep squat position with knees together (hands in front of body on mat partially supporting weight). Tuck head (chin to chest), push body backward off fingertips, and immediately transfer hands, palms up, to side of neck at shoulders. As hips contact mat, push downward on mat with feet and extend legs. Maintain straight legs until hands have contacted mat (palms down, fingertips toward hips). Place toes on mat overhead and simultaneously tuck legs. As hips go overhead, keep elbows close to head and neck area, extend arms (push with hands), and come to squat position.

SP Kneel to side of student; as hips are brought to overhead position, grasp waist to assist in lifting hips overhead to squat position.

CE 1. Not keeping back rounded on roll.

2. Incorrect placement of hands at shoulders (fingertips should point toward hips).

3. Late placement of hands.

4. Failure to push with hands (extend arms) as hips pass overhead.

5. Pushing with one hand more than the other (results in a crooked roll).

6. Allowing head to turn to side.

7. Allowing knees instead of toes to contact mat.

8. Failure to eye-spot when reaching squat position to assist in balance and prevent dizziness.

MO 1. Backward roll to standing position.

2. Backward roll to squat, then execute some type of jump.

3. Continuous backward rolls.

4. Backward roll, back roll extension.

Figure T–18

VA 1. *Backward roll to knee scale* (Fig. T–19).

Figure T–19

2. *Backward roll to straddle stand* (Fig. T–20).

Figure T–20

3. *Backward roll from straddle position to end in straddle position* (Fig. T–21).

Figure T–21

PT   Start from a straddle stand. As movement begins backward, place hands between legs on mat to help lower body to a straddle sitting position, then continue rolling backward using hands under shoulders to push hips overhead to return to a straddle stand.

■BACK SHOULDER ROLL (Over Right Shoulder) (Fig. T–22)

Note: *This particular variation of the backward roll is intended for use in a basic floor exercise routine; it is also for students who are weak, heavy, or fearful.*

SL   Beginner.

PT   From squat or sitting position, lower back to floor and lift legs upward straight and together. Have arms at side of body on floor. Continue moving legs over body until toes touch floor over right shoulder. Turn head with eyes looking toward knees. At this point bend knees; keep looking at knees; bring left arm off floor. Transfer remainder of body weight onto knees in sitting position.

CE   1. Stopping in middle of skill, thus losing momentum needed to get hips over shoulders.

      2. Not placing knees on floor close to shoulders.

MO 1. Toe rise.

2. Knee spin.

3. Forward roll.

Figure T–22

■BACK-ROLL EXTENSION (Fig. T–23)

SL Beginner.

PT Go through backward roll procedures to placing hands on mat under shoulders. As hips begin to pass over chest, thrust legs by extending hips upward while simultaneously pushing with hands (extend arms) against mat. Come to momentary handstand position. Snap down to standing position or lower one leg at a time.

Hint: Have spotter assist in performing this skill slowly so that student will know at what point in roll to extend hips and arms and what extending body to an inverted position feels like.

SP Stand to side and in front of student. As legs begin to thrust vertically, grasp above knee and assist in lifting body to handstand position.

CE 1. Thrusting legs too soon or too late.

2. Failure to thrust legs vertically and push with hands simultaneously.

3. Insufficient thrust of legs, insufficient push with hands, or both.

4. Failure to attain handstand position before returning to mat.

MO 1. Back extension, back roll.

2. Snap down, back handspring.

3. Back extension to split (covered in handstand variations).

4. Back extension straddle down (covered in handstand variations).

5. Back extension stoop through.

Figure T–23

VA *Back-roll extension, step out* (Fig. T–24).

   SL Advanced beginner.

   PT Performed the same as back roll extension, except when body reaches hand-stand position, one leg is lowered to mat before the other.

   SP Same as back roll extension.

Figure T–24

■CARTWHEEL (Left) (Fig. T–25)

SL Beginner.

PT Facing forward, lift arms overhead while lifting left leg. Step forward onto left foot (bend knee) while shifting weight to same foot. Place left hand on mat with fingers pointing to left side of body (hand placement to be directly in line with left foot). Forcefully swing right leg upward and immediately execute a strong push with left foot. (Legs maintain straddle position throughout entire skill.) As body executes a 90-degree turn, place right hand on mat about 14 inches directly in line with (and forward of) left hand. Push off mat (about 20 inches or more from left hand) with slightly bent knee. As left foot contacts mat, right leg is already in motion with a backward-upward swing. Right leg extends and upper body is raised. Entire body ends up facing the same as it did in starting position. Eyes spot hands as they are placed on mat.

SP *For left cartwheel:* Stand to left and slightly forward. As student places left hand on mat, grasp waist and assist in keeping hips over hands. If student has difficulty lifting second leg, slide right hand to thigh and force leg upward.

CE 1. Placing hands on mat simultaneously.

   2. Placing hands to left of body rather than directly forward in front of body.

   3. Placing left hand too close to or too far from left foot.

   4. Insufficient swing from right leg, insufficient push from left foot, or both.

   5. Allowing shoulders and upper body to turn before hands are placed on mat. This skill should be done in a straight line.

   6. Allowing legs to close while inverted.

   7. Failure to maintain straight arms and legs.

   8. Allowing right foot to contact mat before left hand leaves.

   9. Allowing hip to flex while inverted.

   10. Failure to eye-spot hands as they are placed on mat.

11. Failure to land with right leg slightly bent and to raise body as right leg is extending.

12. Failure to keep arms by head throughout skill.

MO 1. Quarter turn and second cartwheel.

2. Quarter turn and stop in handstand.

3. Quarter turn to any locomotor skill.

4. Quarter turn and cartwheel to opposite side.

Figure T–25

VA 1. *Cartwheel quarter turn* (Fig. T–26).

Figure T–26

2. *One-handed cartwheel near arm* (Fig. T–27).

Figure T–27

3. *One-handed cartwheel far arm* (Fig. T–28).

Figure T–28

4. *Dive cartwheel* (Fig. T–29).

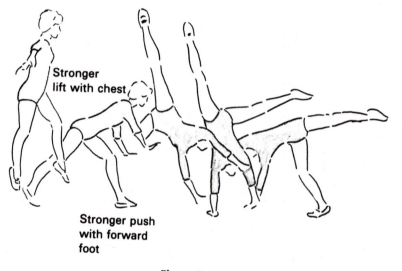

Stronger
lift with chest

Stronger push
with forward
foot

Figure T–29

SL Beginner.

PT Usually preceded by a hurdle. Same preparation as for cartwheel. Begin with a very strong kick-push action while lifting head and chest. Reach forward and upward before placing hands on mat. There should be a stronger push from the hands as they contact the mat almost simultaneously. This skill can also be performed with an underarm lift.

■LIMBRE (Fig. T–30)

SL Beginner.

PT Kick to momentary handstand with eyes looking at fingers. Extend shoulders behind hand placement (push in the direction opposite that in which skill is moving). As balance is lost, legs move in an arc; arch back and place feet on mat so that body is in momentary backbend position. As soon as feet are flat on mat, push with hands and force hips forward over feet to allow legs to extend (straighten knees). Arms are kept by head until standing position is achieved.

Hint: Head position is critical. The head must be kept in neutral position with arms stretched by head at all times. If head and arms are brought forward, body will collapse into sitting position. It is also important to extend shoulders fully to cause body to overbalance in order to go into backbend position.

SP Stand to side as student places hands on mat; grasp upper arm (with palm up and thumb to outside of arm) with inside hand. As body arches, place outside hand on lower back. As feet contact mat, outside hand forces hips forward so legs can extend and hand on arm assists in bringing body to erect position.

CE 1. Not keeping head between shoulders in neutral position throughout skill.

2. Not keeping arms straight throughout skill.

3. Failure to extend in shoulders after inverting.

4. Allowing feet to flop to mat rather than placing them on mat.

5. Failure to push with hands and to thrust hips forward to come to stand.

MO 1. Turns of any kind.

2. Any locomotor skill.

3. Walkover.

4. Handstand or handstand forward roll with variations.

Figure T–30

■FRONT WALKOVER (Fig. T–31)

SL Advanced beginner.

PT Lift arms over head while simultaneously lifting right leg. Step forward onto right foot (small lunge) shifting weight to right foot. Place hands on mat, shoulder width apart, and swing left leg upward to invert body; immediately push with right foot (extend leg). Extend in shoulders so that they go behind heel of hands. Keeping legs in wide stride position, allow back to arch and place left foot on mat (close to midline of body). Push with hands and thrust hips forward and straighten left knee. Come to erect position on left foot keeping head, arms, and shoulders in line until a controlled erect position is achieved. Keep right leg high so it can be placed down on mat. Keep right foot extended in front.

Hint: Think of stepping over a hurdle with right foot in order to keep it extended until erect position has been achieved.

SP Same as for limbre.

CE 1. Not keeping arms straight and by head throughout.
2. Failure to extend shoulders behind hands.
3. Not arching lower back.
4. Failure to place foot flat on mat.
5. Allowing legs to go over crooked (to side of body rather than in vertical plane).
6. Not pushing with hands and thrusting hips forward.
7. Allowing second leg to catch up to first leg and be placed on mat.

MO 1. Any locomotor skill.
2. Cartwheel.

Figure T–31

■BACK WALKOVER (Fig. T–32)

SL Beginner.

PT Stand on left foot with toes of right foot on mat and about 8–14 inches in front of left. Lift arms upward, stretch (extend) shoulders vertically, head between arms, and allow back to arch. (Keep hips over left foot until last possible moment to stretch shoulders more.) As hands contact mat (about shoulder width apart), lift right leg vigorously upward and overhead. Immediately push off mat with left foot to raise body to inverted position with left leg extended to rear. After skill is learned, start with forward leg parallel to floor or higher.

SP Stand to side; place inside hand on lower back and outside hand on back of upper thigh of front leg. Assist by supporting lower back and help lift forward leg to move hips directly over hands.

CE 1. Failure to start with weight on one foot.

2. Failure to extend shoulders and keep reaching backward.

3. Allowing hips to move forward of feet while going into backbend position.

4. Not maintaining straight arms.

5. Not lifting forward leg vigorously as hands contact mat.

6. Failure to push off with hands and lift upper body as first foot contacts mat.

7. Failure to keep legs in a wide stride position.

8. Allowing legs to go out to side of body rather than moving in vertical plane.

MO 1. Any locomotor skill.

2. Consecutive back walkovers.

3. Back walkover, back handspring. Bring second leg to mat beside first foot and immediately spring into back handspring.

Figure T–32

VA 1. *Back walkover to splits.* From inverted position with legs in wide stride position, slightly overbalance and extend shoulders. Lift chest and forcefully thrust lead leg (leg in rear) between arms.

2. *Back walkover to handstand straddle down* (Fig. T–33). Gain balance in handstand position from walkover. Allow shoulders to move slightly forward of hand position as legs move to wide straddle position. Flex hips and allow shoulders to move backward of hand position. Lower hips to floor with legs in wide straddle position.

Figure T–33

■KIP (Fig. T–34)

Note: The kip, a gross body movement of hip flexion and extension (with knees straight), is basic to many tumbling and apparatus skills (e.g., the back roll extension, headspring, and glide kip on bars).

SL Advanced beginner.

PT From supine position on mat, lift legs overhead by flexing hips. Keep legs together and straight, touching toes on mat behind head. Place hand under shoulders with fingertips pointing toward hips. Lower hips slightly; then simultaneously thrust legs forward, upward, and outward, and push forcefully with hands. Keeping arms straight and head neutral, come to stand with body fully extended (slight knee bend to absorb shock).

Hint: Learn to thrust legs first by extending hips vigorously. Then practice thrusting legs and pushing with arms to get into backbend (bridge) position.

SP Kneel (one knee) to side. Place inside hand on upper arm and outside hand on small of back as leg thrust begins.

CE 1. Failure to lower hips before thrusting legs and pushing with hands.

2. Insufficient thrust with legs, insufficient push with hands, or both.

3. Leg thrust and hand push not simultaneous.

4. Failure to keep head up and back until standing.

5. Failure to keep arms back overhead until standing.

Figure T–34

■ HEADSPRING (Fig. T–35)

SL Advanced beginner.

PT From squat position, place head and hands on mat forming triangle. Place toes on mat with slight knee bend. Push through toes, extending legs and forcing hips to overhead position. Keep body in pike position; as hips continue past head position and loss of balance occurs, force (heels first) legs forward-upward (extending hips) and simultaneously push forcefully with hands. Body is fully extended with arms overhead as feet contact mat (with slight knee bend).

Hint: Sometimes it is advantageous to learn this over a rolled-up mat.

SP Kneel (on one knee) beside performer. Grasp upper arm with inside hand and support lower back with outside hand; lift as performer extends hips and pushes with hands.

CE 1. Failure to allow hips to pass head position before thrusting legs and pushing with hands.

2. Failure to remain in tight pike as hips go to overhead position.

3. Same as 2–5 in kip.

MO 1. Any locomotor skill.

2. Another tumbling skill such as dive roll.

Figure T–35

■HURDLE (Fig. T–36)

The hurdle is an important and necessary skill that precedes any tumbling movement in which a one-foot takeoff is used, such as a round-off or front handspring (as opposed to a front sommie, which is executed via a two-foot takeoff). Students often feel a fast and lengthy run is needed to execute a round-off or front handspring. In reality, the important aspects of the hurdle are proper body, arm, and leg position during the hurdle and forceful aggressive use of the legs as a means of imparting speed and power to the tumbling skill. Generally, the leg that lunges forward out of the hurdle is the same as that used to execute other basic skills (handstand, cartwheel, and round-off) that start through the lunge position.

PT For clarity, the hurdle has been described to the side that coincides with the illustration. To practice the American hurdle (Fig. T–36), step left, step right, skip left, while swinging right leg forward with knee bent. At the same time, arms swing forward-upward with body inclined forward about 30 degrees. Step onto right foot in lunge position. Bring hands down toward mat well in front of right foot. Left leg is behind body ready to swing forcefully backward-upward. Right leg is forcefully extended joining left leg as body is inverted.

CE 1. Failure to coordinate skipping action.
2. Failure to incline forward.
3. Failure to reach well in front.
4. Diving rather than stretching forward.
5. Failure to forcefully kick-push with legs.
6. Failure to reach directly forward (some beginners tend to reach to side of foot).
7. Failure to immediately push off mat with hands and lift upper body for rebound.

Figure T–36

■FRONT HANDSPRING (Fig. T–37)

Note: *Basic tumbling skills such as front handspring, round-off, and round-off back handspring should be learned from a step without a hurdle. This forces the student to make maximum use of explosive power.*

SL Beginner.

PT Execute hurdle. Step onto right foot, bending knee. Place hands on mat in front of right foot (about 18 inches) while simultaneously swinging left leg backward-upward. Immediately execute a strong push with right leg (which is bent under body) so that legs meet as body passes through handstand position. Extend shoulders (block) prior to legs and hips passing over hands. Push body away from mat with hands and shoulders. Body is momentarily suspended in air in fully extended position. Reach for mat with toes. Body should be slightly arched upon landing, with head in neutral position, arms overhead, and knees slightly bent.

Hint: On front handspring, front handspring step out, and tinsica, legs are mainly responsible for inverting and rotating the body. Kick-push action of legs should be emphasized; also, if pushing action starts slightly before hands contact mat, body will invert faster. If kick-push action is quick and strong, hands will support entire body weight for a short time. Overbalancing from inverted position will occur much faster so that arms and hands do not push "dead weight."

SP Same as for front limbre.

CE 1. Uncoordinated hurdle and step.

2. Placing hands on mat before initial kick is made.

3. Placing hands too close or too far away from feet.

4. Insufficient thrust of right leg (extended leg); insufficient push from left bent leg.

5. Failure to extend shoulders, keep body stretched, and maintain arms overhead until feet make contact with mat (knees slightly bent to absorb shock and assist in maintaining balance).

Note: When head and arms come forward after hands leave mat, this usually causes hips to flex and body to fall backward or finish the skill in a squat position.

MO 1. Step into any locomotor skill.

2. Front handspring, handstand forward roll.

3. Front handspring, walkover.

4. Front handspring, squat jump, back roll extension.

5. Front handspring to straddle seat.

Figure T–37

VA *Front handspring step out* (Fig. T–38).

   SL Beginner.

   PT Executed on same principles as handspring, but keep legs in wide stride position throughout (as in walkover). There must be a very strong kick and push with foot of second leg and with hands so that body will return to mat with lead leg almost straight and hips forward of foot that contacts mat first. Keep head in neutral position at all times.

   CE 1. Same as 1–5 in handspring.

      2. Failure to keep legs in wide stride position throughout.

      3. Failure to land on lead foot with hips forward of that foot.

   MO 1. Any locomotor skill.

      2. Consecutive handspring step outs.

      3. Round-off.

      4. Aerial cartwheel or aerial walkover (front and side aerials).

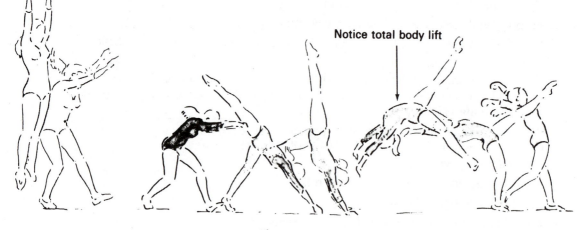

Notice total body lift

Figure T–38

■ ROUND-OFF (Fig. T–39)

The primary purpose of the round-off is to change forward direction into backward movement without loss of horizontal speed.

SL Beginner.

PT From hurdle, step onto left foot, bending knee. Swing right foot forcefully backward-upward, and begin pushing action with left foot as left hand contacts mat in direct line with body, with fingers pointing to side of body. Immediately place right hand on mat (about 5 inches in front of left) with fingers facing to left of body. As body passes through handstand position, it will complete a 180-degree (half) turn. Force legs together while inverted (before the turn), and as body is overbalanced, push hard with hands and shoulders. Flex hips, force feet close to hand placement, and lift upper body. As feet contact mat, immediately punch and lift vertically.

Hint: Go through the skill in slow motion without a hurdle to get the feeling of bringing the legs together and turning before snapping the legs down. Have students jump (spring up) immediately upon landing as if rebounding. This forces them to push with their hands and raise their heads and chests as their feet snap to the mat.

SP When going through the skill in slow motion, spot same as for a cartwheel. When performing from a hurdle, stand to the nonturning side and grasp hip area.

CE 1. Not placing hands on mat in direct line with body.

2. Insufficient kick, push, or both.

3. Failure to bring legs together and pass through vertical before completing half (180-degree) turn.

4. Failure to push hands and lift head and chest after feet have passed handstand position.

5. Failure to keep legs straight and together (slight knee bend when landing).

6. Failure to rebound vertically upon landing.

MO 1. Back roll extension.

2. Back handspring.

3. Back handspring series.

4. Back handspring, back sommie.

5. Back sommie.

6. Back aerial layout.

Figure T–39

76

■ BACK HANDSPRING (Fig. T–40)

SL Advanced beginner.

PT Stand with feet parallel and together. Keep arms at front of body and parallel to floor. Flex knees and hips, keeping shoulders over hips and begin to move backward as if to sit in a chair. As sitting movement begins, move arms downward-backward. When balance is lost, push vigorously with legs and simultaneously force arms forward-upward and overhead. Extend in shoulders and hips and reach for mat with hands. Body is suspended in air momentarily before hands contact mat (shoulder width apart and approximately 3 feet from foot placement on mat). Just after hands contact mat and body passes through handstand position, flex hips and force (snap) legs and feet to mat while simultaneously pushing from mat with hands and lifting head and upper body. Keep head in neutral position to prevent undercutting.

SP Stand to side. Place inside hand on back of upper thigh and outside hand on small of back. Use outside hand to assist student in maintaining a layout position and to keep from falling on head should arms collapse. Inside hand assists with leg thrust and snap down to stand.

> *Hint:* Some students find it helpful to start from a squat position, rock forward, then continue with above procedures from the squat position. Spotter is on one knee with hands in same position as above.

CE 1. Failure to maintain shoulders over hips when sitting backward to lose balance.

2. Insufficient thrust of arms backward.

3. Allowing arms to bend when hands contact mat.

4. Failure to keep legs together after takeoff.

5. Pushing with feet too soon or too late.

6. Insufficient push with feet and picking feet up from mat instead of allowing upper body to pull legs over.

7. Flexing hips too soon or too late (not allowing body to pass through handstand position).

8. Not extending shoulders, pushing away from mat with hands, and not lifting head and chest as feet are about to contact mat.

9. Allowing feet to flop to mat rather than being forced down.

MO 1. Continuous back handsprings.

2. Back sommie.

3. Back aerial layout.

4. Jump, then to any other locomotor skill.

5. Split.

Figure T–40

VA *Back handspring step out* (Fig. T–41).
  SL Advanced beginner.
  PT Same as beginning procedures for back handspring. Just before body passes
    through handstand position, split legs, then allow first foot to be placed on
    mat. Foot placement on mat is same as for back walkover.
  SP Same as for back handspring.

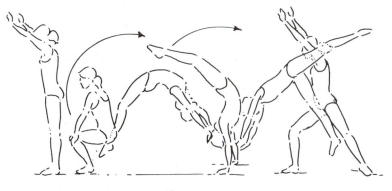

Figure T–41

■ROUND-OFF BACK HANDSPRING (Fig. T–42)

SL Intermediate.
PT The back handspring and the round-off are single skills, but they are difficult to
  perform together the first time. Fear is involved because a change of direction is
  required while upside down. Go through the first few in slow motion, but do not
  attempt to put the skills together until both are learned well. As feet are coming
  down in round-off, they should drive toward hands. (This is to get the body into
  position so that it can go immediately off balance backward.) As feet contact mat,
  knees are slightly bent with head neutral and chest up. Arms and upper body immediately extend upward and backward, and legs extend explosively to complete back
  handspring.
SP Have designated spot for student to start and for placement of hands on round-off.
  Stand about 2 feet beyond hand placement area. As soon as student comes down
  out of round-off, place outside hand on small of back and inside hand on back of
  upper thigh. Follow through as if spotting a standing back handspring.
  Hint: If students fear this skill during the learning process, have them do hand-
    stand, snap down, then back handspring. This technique develops more con-
    fidence.

CE 1. Inadequate leg thrust on round-off causing loss of momentum.
  2. Not driving legs under body enough in round-off.
  3. Stopping between the two skills.

MO 1. Series of back handsprings.
  2. Round-off back handspring, back sommie.
  3. Round-off back handspring, back layout, or full twist.

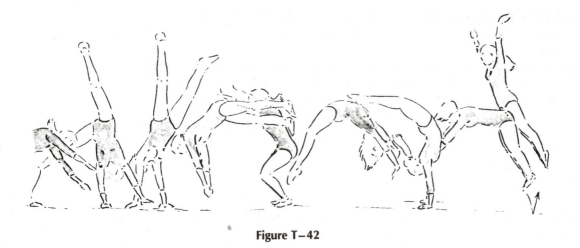

Figure T–42

■ TIMERS FOR BACK SOMMIES, LAYOUTS, AND TWISTS (Fig. T–43)

PT Punch out of round-off, directly vertical, and make total body as rigid as possible. Stay in this position until momentum has stopped and spotter assists in lowering.

SP As student punches out of round-off, place near hand on rump and back of thighs and other hand on shoulder. Direct total body upward, then lower as momentum slows down. Be sure to use legs to assist with lift.

Figure T–43

■BACK SOMMIE (from Standing Position) (Fig. T–44)

Note: *Before beginning back sommie, pick an object at eye level to keep looking for during rotation.*

SL Intermediate.

PT Bend knees slightly and spring vertically, swinging arms vigorously forward-upward to assist in gaining height. As maximum height is attained, drive knees to chest and rotate backward in tuck position. Drive knees toward hands—do not reach back down to grasp knees as this will impede backward rotation. As eyes contact spotting point, extend legs, keep raising upper body, and land on mat with knees slightly bent. Keep head in neutral position throughout.

SP 1. Use spotting belts.

2. One spotter should be at each side. Place inside hand on small of back (grasp garment if necessary) and lift or support throughout skill. Place outside hand on back of thigh as soon as possible after tuck position is attained and assist in rotating body. Never lose contact with performer.

Poor body position. Lift should be vertical rather than backward.

Figure T–44a

Figure T–44b

VA *Round-off sommie* (Fig. T–45).

SL Intermediate.

PT When performing back sommie or back layout out of a round-off, feet do not drive in toward hands as much as they do for back handspring, because on the sommie or layout the entire body must go directly upward before rotating. As feet contact mat from round-off, lift arm vertically as if jumping to reach the ceiling, with head in neutral position. The feet in essence "punch" the mat so the lift can be rapid and high. When reaching the peak of the lift, thrust knees toward chest, head in neutral position, and start rotating body. When three-fourths of the sommie has been completed, extend hips and legs and lift upper body.

SP Same as for round-off back handspring. Be sure contact is made on the round-off.

CE 1. Stopping after round-off; move must be continuous.

2. Not punching mat out of round-off to make vertical lift.

3. Throwing head and arms back immediately out of round-off.

4. Not tucking enough.

5. Opening tuck position too soon or too late.

Figure T–45

TUMBLING ROUTINES FOR CLASS, BEGINNING TO ADVANCED

The tumbling routines used in class will depend on the ability level of the students involved. Each class should be given routines that are challenging but can be performed with little difficulty. Performers should start and end routines at attention or other static position.

Suggested Routines

1. *Forward roll, dive forward roll, cartwheel* (Fig. T–46).

Back of head should make contact with mat

Figure T–46

2. *Handstand forward roll, limbre, cartwheel* (Fig. T–47).

Figure T–47

3. *Cartwheel quarter turnout, cartwheel quarter turnout, handstand forward roll* (Fig. T–48).

Figure T–48

4. *Right cartwheel, left cartwheel* (Fig. T–49).

Figure T–49

5. *Back roll, back straddle roll, back-roll extension* (Fig. T–50).

Figure T–50

6. *Back roll extension, back walkover* (Fig. T–51).

Figure T–51

7. *Front walkover, turn, back walkover* (Fig. T–52).

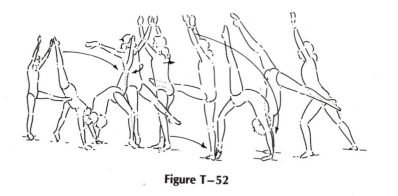

Figure T–52

8. *Fast cartwheels* (Fig. T–53).

Figure T–53

9. *Front walkover, cartwheel quarter turn inward, back walkover* (Fig. T–54).

Figure T–54

10. *Front limbre, front handspring* (Fig. T–55).

Figure T–55

11. *Front handspring step out series* (Fig. T–56).

Figure T–56

12. *Round-off, back handspring* (Fig. T–57).

Figure T–57

13. *Cartwheel, back handspring* (Fig. T–58).

Figure T–58

14. *Back walkover, back handspring* (Fig. T–59).

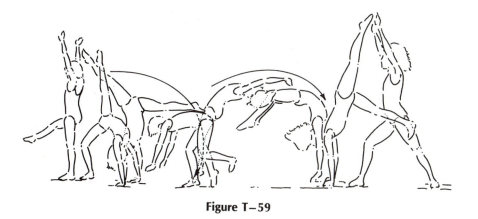

Figure T–59

15. *Front handspring step out, round-off, back handspring* (Fig. T–60).

Figure T–60

16. *Back handspring series* (Fig. T–61).

Figure T–61

▲ TEST QUESTIONS—*TUMBLING*

1. In any tumbling skill, forward momentum is developed
   a. when hands are placed on the mat.
   b. at the beginning of skill.
   c. when the skill is completed.
   d. when the center of gravity moves past the base of support.

2. At what angle in the diagram does the body begin lowering to the mat when completing a handstand roll?

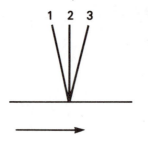

   a. angle 1.
   b. angle 2.
   c. angle 3.
   d. does not make a difference.

3. In performing a cartwheel, the hands are
   a. placed on the mat simultaneously.
   b. placed close to the lunge leg.
   c. alternatively placed directly forward in line with the lunge leg.
   d. placed more than shoulder width apart.

4. In the back walkover, the most common error for the beginner is
   a. allowing hips to move forward of feet at the beginning of skill.
   b. starting with the leg up.
   c. keeping the arms straight throughout.
   d. extending the shoulders in a vertical position.

5. The hips and arms extend forcefully in the back-roll extension as
   a. feet pass over the head.
   b. hips pass the head.
   c. knees pass over the chest.
   d. none of the above.

6. The spotting technique is the same for which of the following skills?
   a. handstand forward roll, back-roll extension, back handspring.
   b. limbre, front handspring step out, walkover.
   c. forward roll, backward roll.
   d. cartwheel, side aerial, back sommie.

7. Why do most beginners sit when landing on the front handspring?
   a. the head and arms are not kept in a neutral position.
   b. inadequate kick-push of the legs.
   c. the head is kept forward.
   d. all of the above.

8. The purpose of the round-off is to
   a. change direction.
   b. tumble forward.
   c. tumble sideward.
   d. learn rebounding techniques.

9. How much of a turn is made on the round-off?
   a. 360-degree turn.
   b. 90-degree turn.
   c. 75-degree turn.
   d. 180-degree turn.

10. In performing a back handspring, it is important to
    a. be balanced prior to springing backward.
    b. bend the arms when they contact the mat.
    c. flex the hips prior to reaching a vertical position.
    d. have forceful arm and leg thrusts.

TUMBLING

Name:

Tripod

Forehead on mat	_____
Triangle base sufficient for body size	_____
Hips lifted with control	_____
Knees *placed* on elbows	_____
Body steady in tripod	_____
Return to squat with control	_____
Score	_____

Headstand From Prone

Hip lift steady	_____
Legs together throughout	_____
Tight vertical position	_____
Lowers with control	_____
Score	_____

Tip Up

Hand position sufficient for body size	_____
Hip lift sufficient to allow knees on elbows	_____
Head up	_____
Position held momentarily	_____
Return to squat position with care	_____
Score	_____

Forward Roll—Piked

Hands extended forward	_____
Hips elevated	_____
Hip shift forward—back of head/shoulder contacts mat	_____
In pike on back	_____
Stands with control	_____
Score	_____

Headstand—Kick-Up

Tripod sufficient for body size	_____
Forehead on mat	_____
Smooth leg lift to vertical	_____
Body tight in vertical position	_____
Legs lowered with control	_____
Score	_____

Forward Roll—Tucked

Hands extended	_____
Hips elevated	_____
Tuck throughout	_____
Head tucked properly	_____
Stand with control	_____
Score	_____

Forward Roll to Single Leg Squat

Hands extended forward	_____
Hips elevated	_____
Head tucked—landing on back of head—shoulder	_____
Piked on back	_____
Arrives in single leg squat with control	_____
Score	_____

Handstand

Step to lunge sufficient	_____
Back leg kick sufficient	_____
Vertical position achieved	_____
Step down with control, arms by head	_____
Score	_____

(Continued)

TUMBLING *(Continued)*

Forward Roll—To Knee	***Handstand Forward Roll***
Hands extended forward _____	Vertical position achieved _____
Hips elevated _____	Vertical position passed with straight body _____
Piked on back _____	Arm bend, head tucked to land on upper shoulder _____
One leg bent to come to knee with control _____	Piked position on back _____
Piked position on back _____	Stand with control, arms up _____
Move to knees with control and chest up _____	Score _____
Score _____	
Forward Roll Stoop Position	***Backward Roll***
Hands extend in front of body _____	Body piked on back as toes touch the floor _____
Hips elevated _____	Hands push (extend) equally _____
In pike on back _____	Tuck from pike position _____
Back of head makes contact with mat _____	Stand with control, arms up _____
Stands with control, arms by head _____	Score _____
Score _____	
Dive Roll	***Back Roll Extension***
Sufficient push off from feet _____	Piked on back _____
Body stretched in dive _____	Explosive extension _____
Bend arms with control _____	Hips _____
Tuck head and land on upper shoulder area _____	Arms _____
Stand with control, arms by head _____	Reached vertical position _____
Score _____	Step down with control _____
	Score _____

(Continued)

TUMBLING *(Continued)*

Cartwheel

Step through lunge _____

Hand placement in line _____

Kick leg sufficient _____

Push leg extended to allow body
to reach vertical _____

Step down with rhythm and in
line _____

Quarter turn in—body in lunge _____

Quarter turn out _____

Score _____

Kip

Piked position _____

Hips lowered before kipping _____

Simultaneous extension of hips
and arms _____

Arms up by head after extension _____

Body extended to arrive in
standing position _____

Score _____

Limbre

Momentary handstand _____

Shoulders extended—back
arched _____

Feet placed on floor _____

Hip thrust forward, then arm
push to arrive in standing
position _____

Arms by head throughout _____

Score _____

Head Spring

From floor or folded mat _____

Head and hands in triangle _____

Sufficient push from feet to
lift hips _____

Hips past head before
simultaneous thrust of hips
and arms _____

Body extended before landing _____

Score _____

Front Walkover

Sufficient step to lunge _____

Continued extension of body and
hand placement _____

Adequate kick-push _____

Hip thrust and push with
hands adequate _____

Arrives at erect position with
arms up and leg extended _____

Score _____

Front Handspring

Stepped through lunge position _____

Kick-push simultaneous with
hand placement _____

Adequate kick-push _____

Body extended in flight _____

Arms by head throughout _____

Land upright on feet _____

Score _____

(Continued)

TUMBLING (*Continued*)

Back Walkover		**Round-Off**	
Hips over supporting foot	_____	Step through to lunge	_____
Arch back sufficient to allow hand placement under shoulders	_____	Hand placement simultaneous with kick-push action	_____
Adequate kick-push action to invert body	_____	Adequate kick-push	_____
Legs in split throughout	_____	Half turn (¼–¼ in air)	_____
Arrives at erect position with balance	_____	Legs together in vertical	_____
		Rebound with body stretched	_____
Score	_____	Score	_____
Back Handspring		**Final Score**	_____
Slight hip and knee flexion	_____	**Final Grade**	_____
Sufficient arm and leg thrust backward	_____		
Enough spring to enable shoulders to be over hands on landing	_____		
Body extended throughout	_____		
Rebound on contact with feet	_____		
Score	_____		

Comments:

Chapter
5

Pommel Horse

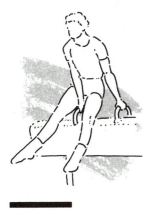

The pommel horse is considered by many to be the most difficult event for the novice. It is the only event with skills performed in a completely supportive position. Upper body strength, particularly in the back, arm, shoulder, and abdominal areas, is extremely important. Flexibility in shoulders, hips, and hamstrings is equally important.

Good pommel horse exercises are performed by connecting individual skills with swinging and circling movements of one or both legs. The student continually passes through front and rear support as well as stride leg support positions while releasing and regrasping pommels or end of horse with the hands. The novice must first learn these different positions statically, as well as how to transfer body weight from the shoulders, forward, backward, and side to side. As the student becomes stronger and develops proper timing and rhythmic swing, pommel horse exercises become enjoyable.

Due to the nature of pommel horse exercises, most skills need not or cannot be spotted, in that a spotter's presence would hinder performance of the skill.

HORSE NOMENCLATURE

Many skills performed with both hands supporting on the pommels can be performed at either end of the horse. Therefore, the student's position relative to the horse can be defined, as well as the three parts of the horse. As the student faces the horse, these parts are:

1. Neck—portion of horse between left end and left pommel.
2. Saddle—portion of horse between both pommels.
3. Croup—portion of horse between right end and right pommel.

A grading sheet for pommel horse skills appears at the end of this chapter.

To more clearly define leg movements relative to the horizontal axis of the horse, the terms *clockwise* and *counterclockwise* are used. The reader should imagine being able to look directly downward and see the top of the horse, as illustrated in the accompanying diagram.

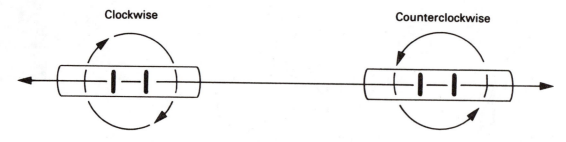

Note: *Practice all single leg cuts and single or double leg circles to both sides. The following mounts, skills, and dismounts are described to one side or in one direction only. Remember that each skill has a counterpart. Practice the skill to the opposite side with the opposite leg or legs moving in the opposite direction.*

SAFETY HINTS

1. Be sure the pommels are tightly fastened to the horse body.
2. Check that the horse body is secure in supports.
3. Surround the horse with mats. Be sure to cover any of the exposed metal base.
4. Use chalk on hands to prevent possible slipping.
5. Do not force students to perform a skill they don't feel ready to do.

POMMEL HORSE SKILLS

The following positions are basic to all pommel horse skills. They should be first mastered as static skills before introducing subsequent pommel horse exercises. Skills used to arrive at these positions are discussed later in the chapter.

1. *Front support* (Fig. PH–1).

Figure PH-1

2. *Stride leg support* (Fig. PH−2).

Figure PH-2

3. *Rear support* (Fig. PH−3).

Figure PH-3

4. *Feint support* (Fig. PH−4).

Figure PH-4

5. *Split leg support (straddle leg, one pommel support)* (Fig. PH-5).

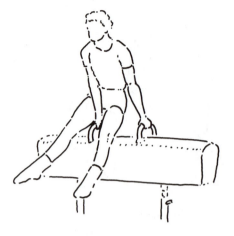

Figure PH-5

The following mounts originate from a stand at saddle with hands on pommels.

■ JUMP TO FRONT SUPPORT (Fig. PH-6)

PT Jump forward-upward. Press down on pommels locking arms at elbow. Good form should be stressed. Head should be in neutral position with arms and shoulders extended. To maintain balance on horse, shoulders must be forward of hands. Most of body weight is on hands. Part of body weight is taken on front of thighs since they will rest against horse.

CE 1. Failure to completely extend arms and shoulders.

2. Head down (chin on chest) or head up too high

3. Legs apart, knees bent.

4. Leaning too far forward or backward, causing loss of balance in either direction.

MO Single leg cut forward to stride leg support.

Figure PH-6

■JUMP TO REAR SUPPORT BY SQUATTING OVER HORSE (Fig. PH–7)

PT   Jump upward-forward lifting hips and flexing knees to chest (squat). Move shoulders forward of hands as legs pass over horse between hands. As feet clear horse, extend legs and hips downward. At the same time, move shoulders back to maintain balance in rear support position. Backs of thighs rest against horse, with most of body weight on hands. Hands maintain contact with pommels throughout entire movement.

CE   1. Failure to move shoulders forward while squatting over horse.

      2. Failure to clear horse with feet while squatting over.

      3. Failure to move shoulders back after squatting over horse.

      4. Failure to extend arms and shoulders in rear support position.

MO   1. Squat back to front support.

      2. Single leg cut backward to stride leg support.

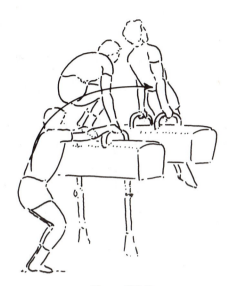

Figure PH-7

■SINGLE LEG CUT FORWARD WITH RIGHT LEG (Counterclockwise) TO STRIDE LEG SUPPORT (Fig. PH–8)

PT   Jump lifting both legs to right side. Transfer body weight to left arm. As right leg continues to move sideward and forward, release right hand, allowing right leg to pass over horse. Regrasp pommel and finish in stride leg support. Most of body weight is on hands; part of body weight will rest on front of left and back of right thighs. When lifting right hand from pommel, it is important to transfer weight to left arm by leaning toward left shoulder. Left arm should remain locked (straight) at all times.

CE   1. Failure to initially lift both legs to right side with body extended.

      2. Failure to transfer weight to left arm.

      3. Failure to keep left arm straight.

      4. Failure to keep legs straight.

MO 1. Single leg cut backward to front support (clockwise).

2. Single leg cut forward with left leg (clockwise) to rear support.

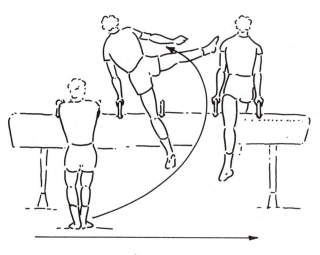

Figure PH-8

■SINGLE LEG CUT FORWARD WITH RIGHT LEG (Clockwise) TO STRIDE LEG SUPPORT (Fig. PH–9)

PT Jump, lifting both legs to left side. Transfer weight to right arm. Release left hand, allowing right leg to pass over horse and forward to stride leg support. Immediately regrasp left pommel and adjust weight to both hands.

CE 1. Failure to lift both legs to left side with body extended.

2. Failure to transfer weight to right arm.

3. Failure to keep right arm straight.

4. Failure to keep legs straight.

MO 1. Single leg cut backward to front support.

2. Back scissor to right.

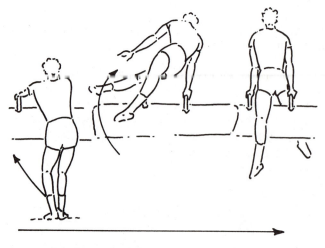

Figure PH-9

■SINGLE LEG CIRCLE WITH RIGHT LEG (Clockwise) (Fig. PH−10)

PT First half of this movement is the same procedure as for single leg cut forward (clockwise) to stride leg support. Just as stride leg support is completed, transfer weight to left hand and continue swinging both legs to right side. Right hand releases pommel allowing right leg to pass over right side of horse back to front support. Right hand regrasps right pommel with body weight equally distributed on both hands.

CE 1. Failure to transfer weight quickly from hand to hand.

2. Failure to keep arms and legs straight.

3. Failure to move both legs.

4. Failure to pass through stride leg support without hesitating.

MO 1. Single leg cut forward with left leg (clockwise) to stride leg support.

2. Single leg circle clockwise with left leg.

3. Half double leg circle clockwise to rear support.

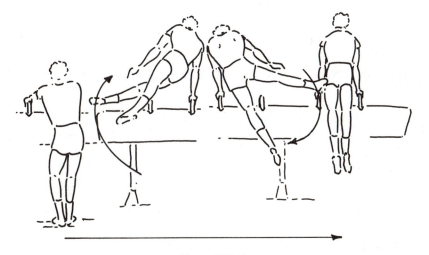

Figure PH-10

■FORWARD SINGLE LEG CIRCLE WITH RIGHT LEG (Counterclockwise) (Fig. PH−11)

PT First half of this movement is the same procedure as for single leg cut forward (counterclockwise) to stride leg support. Just as stride leg support is completed, transfer weight to right hand and continue swinging both legs to left side to lift hips as high as possible above horse. Left hand releases pommel and right leg continues to pass over left side of horse back to front support. Left hand regrasps left pommel with body weight equally distributed to both hands.

CE 1. Failure to transfer weight quickly from hand to hand.

2. Failure to keep arms and legs straight.

3. Allowing hips to turn to left over left side of horse; hips should face forward at all times.

4. Failure to swing both legs up to left side, which lifts hips higher on left side.

5. Failure to pass through stride leg support without excessive hesitation.

MO 1. Single leg cut forward with right leg.
2. Half double leg circle counterclockwise to rear support.

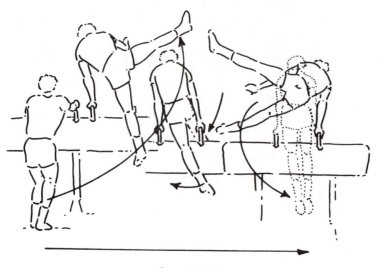

Figure PH-11

■HALF DOUBLE LEG CIRCLE (Counterclockwise) TO REAR SUPPORT (Fig. PH–12)

Note: All skills previously described as "mounts" are also performed as skills on the horse. Instead of jumping into the skill, the student performs it in a support position on the horse.

PT Jump lifting both legs to right side, body extended. Transfer weight to left hand, releasing right hand from pommel. Pass both legs over right side of horse. Regrasp right pommel transferring weight to both hands. At the same time, transfer weight backward from shoulders as rear support position is completed.

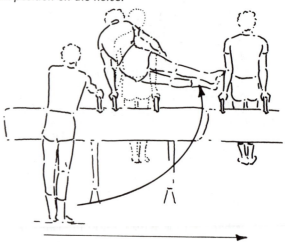

Figure PH-12

CE 1. Failure to keep body extended throughout movement.
2. Failure to keep arms straight.
3. Failure to transfer weight smoothly at proper times.
4. Failure to keep body extended and legs together and straight.
5. Sitting on horse instead of finishing in good rear support position.

MO Single leg cut backward with left leg counterclockwise to stride leg support.

Skills from Front Support Position

■SINGLE LEG CUTS, RIGHT AND LEFT (Fig. PH–13)

PT Swing both legs up to right side. Transfer body weight to left arm. Release right hand, allowing right leg to move over right side of horse and forward to stride leg support. Immediately regrasp right pommel and transfer weight to right arm. Swing both legs to left. As legs return toward stride leg position, transfer weight to left arm, continue swinging both legs up to right side. Release right hand to allow right leg to pass back over right side of horse. Regrasp right pommel and immediately transfer weight to right arm and swing both legs up toward left side of horse. Repeat entire exercise with left leg cutting over horse through a stride leg support and back to a front support position.

CE 1. Failure to keep arms and legs straight.

2. Failure to move both legs, not only cutting leg.

3. Failure to transfer weight from side to side at proper time, causing jerky movement.

4. Failure to swing and lift legs from hip joint, causing student to sit on horse in stride leg support position.

MO 1. Repeat exercise.

2. Alternating leg cut.

3. Single leg cut or circle counterclockwise with left leg.

Figure PH-13

■ALTERNATING LEG CUTS, RIGHT AND LEFT (Fig. PH–14)

PT   The basic single leg cut to stride leg support initiates this particular sequence. Students may start with either leg; however, for continuity and progression, leading with right leg has been chosen here. Cut right leg over right side of horse and regrasp right pommel with right hand. Immediately transfer weight to right arm, swing both legs up toward left side, release left hand, allow left leg to pass over left side of horse, and regrasp pommel with left hand. Ideally, at this point, both legs should be together, with most of weight still on right hand. As legs swing down through rear support position, quickly transfer weight to left arm. Force hips forward of pommels as body begins swinging to right side of horse. Release right hand to allow right leg to pass back over side of horse. Quickly transfer weight to right arm. Swing legs through stride leg support and toward left side of horse. Release left hand from left pommel to allow left leg to pass back over horse to front support. Quickly regrasp left pommel with left hand. Exercise may terminate at this point or be repeated. It is recommended that the exercise be repeated several times in succession. This is an excellent way to develop good rhythm and swing, which are important to progressive horse skills.

CE   1. Failure to keep arms and legs straight.

      2. Poor timing on weight transfers from arm to arm.

      3. Failure to keep hips extended and forward through rear support position.

      4. Failure to move both legs in all positions.

Figure PH-14

■SINGLE LEG MOORE (Fig. PH–15)

PT   This is a relatively simple skill used to turn 180 degrees while supporting on the pommels. Swing left leg to left side and over horse. At the same time, turn body 90 degrees to right. Transfer right hand to left pommel. At this phase of the skill both hands are gripping left pommel with palms facing away from body. Shoulders must be positioned over, or a bit forward of, hands with arms locked. (Student is facing length of horse while straddling neck.) Now transfer left hand to far pommel. At the same time, turn body 90 degrees to right again and bring right leg to join left in front support.

CE   1. Failure to keep arms and legs straight.

      2. Failure to transfer weight over hands when both hands grasp left pommel.

MO 1. Single leg cut with left leg clockwise.
2. Single leg circle with right leg clockwise.
3. Single leg circle with left leg clockwise.

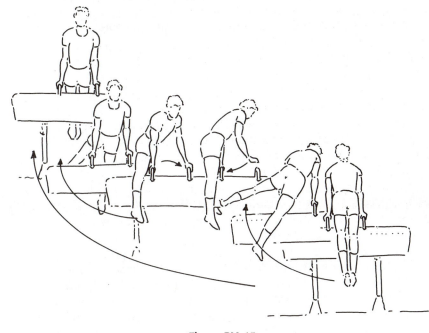

Figure PH-15

Skills from Stride Leg Support

■ FRONT SCISSOR (Fig. PH–16)

SL Advanced beginner.
PT Assume stride leg support with right leg in front. Swing both legs to left while transferring weight to right arm. Push down forcefully on right pommel while swinging both legs higher to left side of horse to raise hips as high as possible. Transfer body weight to right arm while simultaneously lifting left hand from left pommel. At this point, left leg cuts forward over left side of horse as right leg cuts backward under left leg. Regrasp left pommel as scissor is completed. Student is now in stride leg support with left leg in front. The front scissor may be preceded by a single leg cut with right leg counterclockwise. With proper timing and continuous fluid swing of both legs to left, the scissor will be easier to execute. The front scissor must also be practiced to right side.

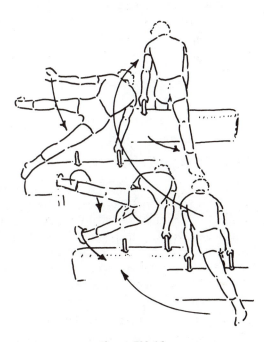

Figure PH-16

CE   1. Failure to keep arms and legs straight throughout movement.

       2. Failure to swing legs and hips high enough to left side.

       3. Failure to regrasp left pommel with left hand quickly, causing student to sit on horse.

MO 1. Single leg cut forward with right leg counterclockwise to rear support.

       2. Front scissor to right.

■BACK SCISSOR (Fig. PH–17)

SL   Advanced beginner.

PT   Assume stride leg support with left leg in front. Swing both legs to left while transferring body weight to right arm. Push down forcefully on right pommel while swinging both legs higher to left side of horse. Raise hips as high as possible. Transfer body weight to right arm while simultaneously lifting left hand from left pommel. At this point, right leg cuts forward as left leg cuts backward over left side of horse. Regrasp left pommel as scissor is completed. Student is now in stride leg support with right leg in front. The back scissor may be preceded by a single leg cut backward with right leg clockwise from a rear support. With proper timing and continuous fluid swing of both legs to left, the scissor will be easier to execute. The back scissor must also be practiced to right side.

CE   Same as 1–3 of front scissor.

MO 1. Single leg cut back with right leg clockwise to front support.

       2. Back scissor to right.

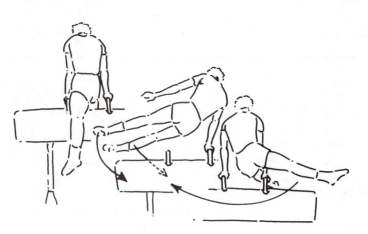

Figure PH-17

Dismounts from Stride Leg Support

■ SINGLE LEG SWING DISMOUNT FORWARD (Fig. PH–18)

SL Beginner.

PT Assume stride leg support with right leg in front. Swing both legs to left while transferring body weight to right arm. Lift left leg over left side of horse while simultaneously releasing left pommel and turning body 90 degrees to right. At this point, all body weight is on right arm. Press right leg against horse. As left leg clears horse and turn is almost completed, push right leg forcefully against horse. This action will help lift chest and push body away from horse to a good stand on mat. Student's right side is facing the horse now with right hand still gripping the right pommel.

CE 1. Failure to keep right arm straight.

2. Failure to keep legs straight throughout dismount.

3. Failure to turn to right aggressively.

Figure PH-18

■ SINGLE LEG SWING DISMOUNT BACKWARD (Fig. PH–19)

SL Beginner.

PT Assume stride leg support with right leg in front. Swing both legs to right while transferring body weight to left arm. Lift right leg over right side of horse while simultaneously releasing right pommel and turning body 90 degrees to left. Bring right leg back and together with left leg. Quickly release left pommel and regrasp with right hand (knuckles up). Lift chest while landing to a stand on mat. Right side of body faces horse with right hand gripping left pommel as dismount is completed.

CE 1. Failure to keep arms and legs straight throughout skill.

2. Failure to sharply turn body 90 degrees to left.

3. Failure to regrasp left pommel with right hand and lift chest for a good stand on mat.

Figure PH-19

Dismounts from Feint Support

■ FLANK DISMOUNT TO LEFT (Fig. PH–20)

SL Intermediate beginner.

PT From front support position, swing right leg over right side of horse; position in front of right pommel. With both hands, grip pommels with most of body weight on right arm. Twist hips slightly to left, and press lower abdomen against right forearm. Swing right leg forcefully backward over right side of horse keeping left leg pressed against horse. As right leg swings behind body, push off horse with left leg, bring legs together, and continue swinging both legs to left side (clockwise). At this point, lean forcefully toward right shoulder transferring body weight onto right arm. As both legs begin swinging over left side of horse, release left pommel. Extra effort must be made to extend hips completely as legs pass over and forward of horse. A final push with right arm backward is made to lift chest. Right pommel is released when student lands.

CE 1. Failure to keep arms and legs straight, especially right arm, which completely supports body as legs pass over left side of horse.

2. Failure to forcefully swing right leg behind horse.

3. Failure to press left leg against horse.

4. Failure to push off with left leg as right leg swings around and back over horse.

5. Failure to transfer body onto right arm as both legs pass over left side of horse.

6. Failure to push off horse with right arm and lift chest prior to landing on mat.

Figure PH-20

■FLANK DISMOUNT WITH 90-DEGREE TURN (Fig. PH–21)

SL Intermediate beginner.

PT Performance of this dismount is exactly the same as flank dismount up to the point when both legs begin swinging over left side of horse (clockwise). Just prior to releasing left pommel, begin to turn body to right toward right arm. Release left pommel, and continue pivoting body 90 degrees to right around right arm. Extend body, lift chest, and come to a stand with right hand still gripping right pommel. Right side of body is facing horse.

CE 1. Same as 1–5 of flank dismount.

2. Failure to extend body completely through 90-degree right turn.

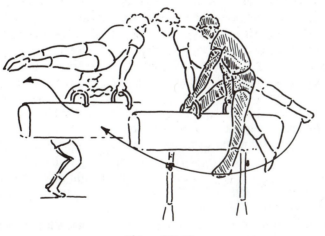

Figure PH-21

■REAR DISMOUNT (Fig. PH−22)

SL Intermediate beginner.

PT Performance of this dismount is exactly the same as flank dismount and flank dismount with 90-degree turn up to the point when both legs begin swinging over left side of horse. At this moment, begin turning hips forcefully 90 degrees to left and release left pommel. As backs of legs and buttocks pass over horse, quickly regrasp left pommel with left hand and release right pommel. Grip on left pommel is maintained until student comes to a stand with left side of body facing horse.

CE 1. Same as 1−5 of flank dismount with 90-degree right turn.

     2. Failure to sharply turn hips to left and lift legs.

     3. Failure to quickly regrasp left pommel with left hand.

Figure PH-22

Dismounts from Split Support

■SINGLE REAR DISMOUNT (Fig. PH−23)

SL Intermediate beginner.

PT From front support, execute single leg cut forward with left leg, clockwise, to stride leg support. Swing right leg up to right and over horse counterclockwise without releasing right pommel. Both legs are now forward of and splitting right pommel. Most of body weight is on right arm. Bring right leg back over right side (croup) of horse (clockwise). At the same time, release left pommel and begin turning body to right, pivoting around right arm. Place left hand on left end (croup) of horse. At this point, student has made a 180-degree turn to right and is in feint support position with right hand supinated on right pommel and left hand on left end or croup. The next phase of this dismount is exactly the same as executing a rear dismount.

With a little practice, student will be able to adjust to difference in left hand being lower than right, and not gripping a pommel when executing rear dismount from this variation of feint position. Keep in mind the feint support is an integral part of the total dismount.

CE 1. Turning 180 degrees to right too quickly from split support position.

2. Bringing right leg back too quickly from split support position.

3. Failure to keep right arm straight throughout entire dismount.

4. Same as 1 and 2 of rear dismount.

5. Failure to quickly place left hand back on croup when completing dismount.

Figure PH-23

■ DOUBLE REAR DISMOUNT (Fig. PH–24)

SL Advanced beginner.

PT Performance of this dismount is exactly the same as single rear dismount up to the point when student has made a 180-degree turn to right and is in feint support position with right hand supinated on right pommel and left hand on croup. Now execute a half double leg circle clockwise. While moving through rear support, release right pommel while turning 90 degrees to right. Body weight is supported on left hand and arm, which also serve as pivot point for 90-degree turn to right. Backs of legs and buttocks pass over horse during 90-degree turn. Left hand pushes down and away from horse and student lands standing with left side facing horse.

CE 1. Same as 1 and 2 of single rear dismount.
    2. Failure to keep leg and arms straight to maintain good high support.
    3. Stopping or sitting in rear support position.
    4. Leaning back too far while turning 90 degrees to right around left arm.
    5. Legs and buttocks too low while passing over horse during 90-degree turn to right.

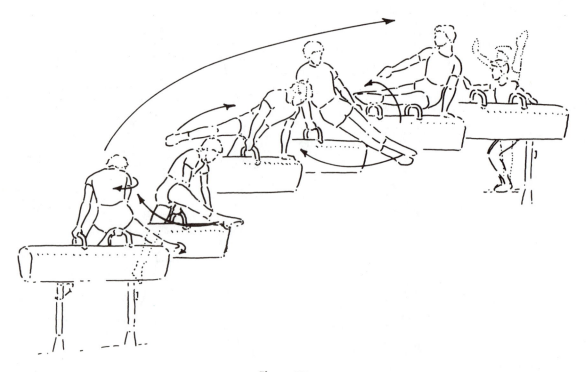

Figure PH-24

Beginning Routine for Pommel Horse (Fig. PH–25)

 1. Jump to rear support.
 2. Single leg cut back with left leg counterclockwise.
 3. Single leg cut back with right leg clockwise.
 4. Single leg circle with right leg clockwise.
 5. Single leg circle with left leg clockwise.
 6. Alternating leg cuts left and right leg.
 7. Single leg cut forward with left leg clockwise.
 8. Swing right leg over counterclockwise to split support on right pommel.
 9. Single leg cut back with left leg counterclockwise to feint support.
10. Flank dismount with 90-degree turn clockwise.

Figure PH-25

▲ TEST QUESTIONS—*POMMEL HORSE*

1. A front support position on the pommel horse requires the shoulders to be
   a. directly over the hands.
   b. forward of the hands.
   c. behind the hands.
   d. wherever they feel comfortable.

2. When executing a single leg cut forward counterclockwise,
   a. the leg passes under the right hand.
   b. the leg passes under the left hand.
   c. the leg passes over the right hand.
   d. the leg passes over the left hand.

3. A rear support position on the pommel horse requires the shoulders to be
   a. wherever they feel comfortable.
   b. behind the hands.
   c. forward of the hands.
   d. directly over the hands.

4. When executing a single left leg circle counterclockwise, the leg initially
   a. passes under the left hand.
   b. passes over the right hand.
   c. passes under the right hand.
   d. passes over the left hand.

5. When facing the horse at the saddle, the neck would be
   a. to your right.
   b. directly on the other side of horse.
   c. to your left.
   d. not seen.

6. When executing a half double leg circle counterclockwise,
   a. the right leg passes over right side of horse to a stride leg support.
   b. the left leg passes over left side of horse to a stride leg support.
   c. both legs pass over right side of horse to a rear support.
   d. both legs pass over left side of horse to a rear support.

7. Which of the following does *not* apply when performing pommel horse skills?
   a. keeping arms and legs straight.
   b. shifting body weight from side to side.
   c. keeping shoulders positioned directly over hands at all times.
   d. shifting body weight forward and backward from shoulders.

8. The feint position is used to initiate
   a. a flank dismount with a 90-degree turn.
   b. a flank dismount.
   c. a rear dismount.
   d. all of the above.

9. In a rear support position,
   a. the front of the legs are against the horse.
   b. the right leg is in front of and the left is in back of the horse.
   c. the back of both legs are against the horse.
   d. none of the above.

10. In a stride leg support on the horse,
    a. both legs are in front of the hands.
    b. both legs are in back of the hands.
    c. one leg is in front of and the other leg in back of the hands.
    d. none of the above.

POMMEL HORSE	Name:

Jump to Front Support

Jump sufficient _____

Arms locked—good body
    position _____

Held 3 seconds _____

             Score _____

Single Leg Cut Forward— Counterclockwise

Hips high on jump to side _____

Body extended _____

Good transfer to supporting arm _____

Leg straight on cut to stride
    leg support _____

Good position on finish of cut _____

             Score _____

Jump to Rear Support

Jump sufficient _____

Squat through clean—feet not
    touching _____

Arms locked—good body
    position _____

Held 3 seconds _____

             Score _____

Single Leg Circle—Clockwise

Hips high on jump to side _____

Body extended, good transfer of
    weight to supporting arm _____

Leg straight and smooth
    circling horse _____

Good front support position on
    completion of circle _____

             Score _____

Single Leg Cut Forward—Clockwise

Good transfer of weight to
    supporting arm _____

Leg straight on cut _____

Good position on finish to stride
    leg support _____

             Score _____

Single Leg Circle—Counterclockwise

Good transfer of weight to
    supporting arm _____

Leg straight and smooth
    circling horse _____

Hips high to side prior to
    completing circle _____

Good front support position on
    completion of circle _____

             Score _____

Half Double Leg Circle

Sufficient jump to lift hips high
    to side _____

Legs together and straight
    passing over horse _____

Smooth finish to rear support
    position _____

             Score _____

Front Scissor

Arms and legs straight
    throughout skill _____

Good transfer of weight to
    supporting arm _____

Hips high, smooth scissor, legs
    or feet not touching horse
    until scissor is completed _____

             Score _____

(Continued)

POMMEL HORSE *(Continued)*

Single Leg Cuts, Right and Left

Arms and legs straight
throughout _____

Smooth transfer of weight side
to side _____

Clean cuts forward and
backward _____

Feet not touching horse on cuts _____

Score _____

Back Scissor

Arms and legs straight
throughout skill _____

Good transfer of weight to
supporting arm _____

Hips high, smooth scissor, legs
or feet not touching horse
until scissor is completed _____

Score _____

Alternating Leg Cuts, Right and Left

Smooth transfer of weight left,
right, forward, and back _____

Legs and arms straight
throughout all cuts _____

Good front and rear support
positions _____

Score _____

Single Leg Swing Dismount Forward

Good transfer of weight to
supporting arm _____

Swinging leg lifted high with
knee straight _____

Smooth turn to controlled
landing _____

Score _____

Single Leg Moore

Arms and legs straight
throughout skill _____

Smooth transfer of weight _____

Finish in good front support
position _____

Held 3 seconds _____

Score _____

Single Leg Swing Dismount Backward

Good transfer of weight to
supporting arm _____

Hips high, with sufficient push
off from horse _____

Sharp turn to smooth controlled
landing _____

Score _____

Flank Dismount

Strong leg swing from feint leg
position _____

Arms and legs straight
throughout skill _____

Sufficient transfer of weight to
supporting arm _____

Body extended passing over
horse _____

Smooth controlled landing _____

Score _____

Single Rear Dismount

Arms and legs straight
throughout skill _____

Smooth transfer of weight from
arm to arm _____

Smooth turn from split support
through stride leg support _____

Sharp turn with good leg swing,
pass over end of horse to
smooth controlled landing _____

Score _____

(Continued)

POMMEL HORSE *(Continued)*

Flank Dismount with 90-Degree Turn

Strong leg swing from feint leg position _____

Arms and legs straight throughout skill _____

Sufficient transfer of weight to supporting arm _____

Body extended passing over horse _____

Smooth controlled landing _____

Score _____

Double Rear Dismount

Arms and legs straight throughout _____

Smooth transfer of weight from arm to arm _____

Smooth turn from split support through stride leg support _____

Sharp turn with good leg swing, pass over end of horse _____

Controlled landing _____

Score _____

Rear Dismount

Strong leg swing from feint leg position _____

Arms and legs straight throughout skill _____

Sufficient transfer of weight to supporting arm _____

Sharp turn of hips, legs parallel while passing over horse _____

Smooth controlled landing _____

Score _____

Final Score _____

Final Grade _____

Comments:

Chapter
6

Vaulting

Vaulting can be an exciting part of the gymnastics program if basics are taught and learned well. In most gymnastics programs, vaulting is performed across the width of the horse by both male and female students. At the beginning and intermediate levels, the techniques for side and long horse vaulting are similar.

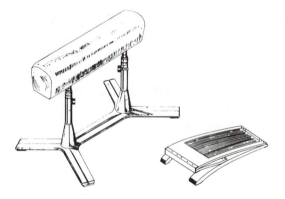

SAFETY HINTS

1. Runway should be free of obstructions.
2. If possible, use a vaulting runway made of rubber and similar to a fencing strip.
3. Use mats of double thickness or a landing mat on far side of horse where vaulters will land.
4. Use two or more spotters, especially for beginners.

A grading sheet for vaulting skills appears at the end of this chapter.

5. Make sure spotters know what vault is being performed.
6. If possible, use a trampoline for teaching on-horse and off-horse techniques. Place a folding mat on trampoline with a portion hanging over end where hands will make contact.
7. Have a definite skill progression for each class.
8. Never allow students to vault unsupervised.
9. Don't force students to perform a vault they don't feel ready for.
10. Adjust the height of the horse for the performance level of the student.

VAULTING TECHNIQUE

Vaulting is divided into three sections, preflight, on-horse and afterflight, and landing. For teaching, vaulting can be divided into as many as seven categories: approach, takeoff on board, preflight, on-horse, repulsion, afterflight, and landing. For ease of presentation, the vault is divided into approach (run), preflight (hurdle and flight to horse), on-horse contact, afterflight, and landing.

At the beginning level, major concern should be with the run and takeoff. The run can determine the performance for the vault so this motor skill must be mastered.

■ RUN (Fig. V–1)

PT
1. Slight forward lean with head held in neutral position.
2. Eyes focused on vaulting board (point of contact of feet).
3. Proper use of arms—forward and backward in opposition to legs.
4. Strong push downward and backward with balls of feet, never allowing heels to come in complete contact with floor.
5. Adequate knee lift so that when feet contact floor, push will be forceful enough to develop forward velocity.
6. Steady stride with increasing velocity, reaching maximum controllable speed midway to horse.

CE
1. Body leans too far forward or backward.
2. Run is flatfooted.
3. Arms not used properly.
4. Knees turned in or out during run.
5. Kicking heels up too high.
6. Run not forceful and speed not increased by midpoint of run.

Figure V-1

The distance or number of paces that each vaulter uses varies among individuals. To ensure reasonable consistency in contacting the board, carefully measure the distance by stepping off the number of feet or with a tape measure. The distance should be enough for students to reach maximum speed 3 to 4 steps before hurdle when performing beginning vaults and 20 meters for more difficult vaults.

The speed of the run also will vary with each student and, to some degree, will depend on the vault to be executed.

After students have learned to run properly, add the hurdle and contact with the vaulting board. It is advisable to learn the hurdle first from a step, then gradually add steps; from a slow run; and finally from a vaulting run. It is also important to practice using the board first without a run.

■ PREFLIGHT (Hurdle and Takeoff) (Figs. V–2 and V–3)

The preflight creates the *initial force* for performing any vault.

PT
1. Hurdle should be long and not too high so as not to lose forward velocity and to maintain balance. As hurdle step is taken, arms go down to sides of body.
2. Knee lift is only slight to allow both legs to come together quickly.
3. Balls of both feet must contact board parallel and simultaneously with slight knee bend. (Since action of vaulting board is very fast, a deep knee bend on contact would cause a long and sluggish takeoff.)
4. Shoulders and hips should be slightly behind toes when contact is made on board.
5. As feet contact board, arms reach forward and upward to assist on vertical lift and initial rotation.
6. Immediately extend knees explosively to ensure high vertical lift.
7. Ankle extension is also important; ankle should be extended fully to allow tips of toes to leave board last.
8. As hurdle step is taken, transfer eyes to horse or beyond, depending on type of vault being performed.

CE
1. Hurdle too high, too low, too short, or a combination of any of these.
2. Slowing run before hurdle.
3. Bending knees too much upon contacting board.
4. Landing flatfooted on board.
5. Allowing body to lean forward when feet contact board.
6. Little or no ankle or hip extension.
7. Poor arm direction or uncoordinated arm and leg action.

Note: A visible distinction (time lapse) from vaulting board to horse contact is essential.

Figure V-2   **Figure V-3**

■ ON-HORSE CONTACT

In order to develop or create a *secondary force* on any vault, the shoulders must be well behind hands as they contact the horse. This may be referred to as the "block." The shoulders are extended forcefully and simultaneously with hand contact.

PT 1. On most vaults, hands contact horse shoulder distance apart and in middle of top of horse.

      2. When hands contact horse, shoulders should be behind (never forward of) hands.

      3. Touch on horse should be short.

      4. Never allow shoulders to sag as hands contact horse.

CE 1. Hands on horse too long, usually resulting in downward slant after flight.

      2. Insufficient push off horse, or push poorly directed.

      3. Other faults due to poor takeoff, such as contacting horse on near side by leaning forward from board.

■ AFTERFLIGHT (Second Flight)

In general, the greater the preflight and push, the greater the afterflight. Body should be extended in air before landing; this mainly refers to squat and straddle vaults. Afterflight should be upward as well as outward. A higher afterflight allows more time to position the body for a good landing.

Afterflight is proportionally equal to the forces in preflight. This includes the speed of the run, angle of the body and force exerted as feet leave the takeoff board, and force exerted at on-horse contact.

■ LANDING

PT 1. Landing should be solid but light.

      2. Bend knees to absorb shock and to help maintain balance.

      3. Hold arms slightly forward for good body position and balance. After landing, move to normal side position.

      4. Bend hips so they are directly above heels.

CE 1. Allowing feet over horse before hands are removed causing shoulders to be well behind feet on contact with mat.

      2. Allowing upper body to collapse and fall forward when feet contact mat.

      3. Not bending knees and hips to absorb shock upon landing.

LEAD UP SKILLS

If a side horse is not available, other pieces of equipment can be used for teaching vaulting techniques, such as the following:

  1. Use a stack of mats (the kind that fold into sections), a Swedish box, or buck if available. Use with the following progression:

    a. From abbreviated run and small hurdle, jump to mats or box in squat position. Stand and jump off.

  b. Squat vault over apparatus.

  c. Jump to straddle stand, stand up, and jump off.

  d. Execute straddle vault from abbreviated run and hurdle.

2. Folding mats piled up (four mats) depending on skill level (Fig. V–4). Place board at end of mats and have students work on lifting their hips and performing a squat vault onto mats. Add another mat when students are capable of lifting and stretching in preparation for a layout position.

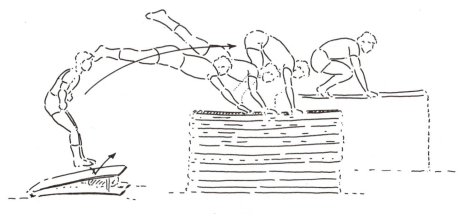

Figure V-4

3. Trampoline (Figs. V–5 and V–6). Two safety rules should always be enforced when using the trampoline for vaulting: a mat should be draped over end of trampoline so that no one falls through the shock cords or springs, and someone should always be at the opposite end and sides to assist a student who might lose balance upon landing.

Figure V-5

Figure V-6

If a horse and board are available from the beginning, be concerned with the height of the horse and the distance between the horse and the board. As quick success is a strong motivational factor in learning, lower the horse below standard height and place the board approximately 2 feet from the base of the horse.

■FLANK VAULT FROM ABBREVIATED RUN (Fig. V–7)

SL Beginner.

PT Take abbreviated run and hurdle. After vertical lift, quickly place hands on horse while simultaneously lifting hips and both legs to right side. As hips and legs approach horizontal level, shift weight to left arm. Lift right hand and arm off horse, extend body as hips and legs pass over horse. Push horse behind body as release of left hand is made just prior to landing with back to horse. Flex hips and knees slightly on landing.

SP Stand on far side of horse to nonflanking side of student. Reach across horse and grasp upper arm. Support until legs pass over horse and student has landed.

CE 1. Same as 1–7 for jump to squat stand (see following skill).

2. Not keeping shoulders over hands (leaning too far forward), making it difficult to keep body erect prior to and on landing.

3. Failure to maintain straight arms throughout skill.

4. Failure to extend hips when passing over horse.

5. Failure to keep knees straight and legs together throughout skill.

6. Failure to keep shoulders square, causing body to turn in direction of supporting arm and landing with side of body facing horse.

7. Keeping both arms or supporting arm on horse too long.

Figure V-7

■ JUMP TO SQUAT STAND ON HORSE (Fig. V-8)

SL Beginner.

PT Take abbreviated run and hurdle. After vertical lift from board, raise hips upward so that back is parallel to floor. Tuck knees to chest. Place hands on top of horse shoulder width apart, arms straight, and fingers spread slightly. Keeping hands on horse, lower hips and allow feet to come to rest on top of horse. Stand up and jump off. Be careful also to practice landing position each time.

SP Stand on far side of horse and to side of student. Reach across horse and grasp upper arm and wrist as performer places hands on horse. Be careful not to hinder student's movement.

CE 1. Poor run and hurdle.

2. Landing on board flatfooted.

3. Leaning forward on board.

4. Bending knees too much on board, causing forward momentum to be slowed down.

5. Insufficient vertical lift.

6. Poorly coordinated arms.

7. Failure to lift hips and bring knees to chest. Many beginners tend to bring hips under body rather than lift them backward-upward.

8. Failure to keep arms straight.

Figure V-8

124

■SQUAT VAULT FROM ABBREVIATED RUN (Fig. V–9)

SL Beginner.

PT After vertical lift, raise hips backward-upward and tuck knees to chest. After reaching forward-upward, place hands on top of horse. Immediately push downward on horse, lifting chest, then lift arms forward-upward. As feet pass over horse, extend legs and hips so that body is straight before landing. Then flex hips and knees slightly when feet contact mat. Look at board when running, horse when hurdling, and object at eye level when passing over horse.

SP Stand on far side of horse and to side of student. Reach across horse and grasp upper arm as performer places hands on horse. Maintain contact with student until balance is attained on landing, and move forward as student passes across horse.

CE 1. Same as 1–8 for jump to squat stand.

  2. Allowing hands to remain on horse as feet pass over horse.

  3. Failure to completely extend body before landing and then flex hips and knees on landing.

  4. Failure to lift head and chest after pushing off horse with hands.

  5. Allowing arms to go back overhead on landing. This causes many beginners to fall backward.

Figure V-9

■JUMP TO STRADDLE STAND (Fig. V–10)

SL Beginner.

PT From abbreviated run, hurdle, and vertical lift from board, lift hips, then move legs to wide straddle position. As hands contact horse, lift head and chest and place feet on horse in wide straddle position. When stopping in straddle stand on horse, shoulders will be forward of hands; however, in straddle vault, hands already will be reaching forward-upward at this point.

Figure V-10

SP Stand on far side of horse in front of student. Reach across horse and grasp upper arms as student puts them on horse. Assist by lifting and pulling to horse, if necessary, and help control straddle-stand position.

CE 1. Same as 1–7 of jump to squat stand.

2. Failure to lift hips high enough to allow feet to straddle onto horse.

3. Failure to straddle both legs.

4. Failure to lift head and chest when feet come to rest on horse.

5. Failure to maintain straight arms throughout skill.

■STRADDLE VAULT (Fig. V–11)

SL Beginner.

PT From abbreviated run, hurdle to board and immediately spring vertically, lifting hips backward-upward. Reach forward-upward with arms to place hands on top of horse (eyes look up at this point) while simultaneously straddling legs. Immediately push off horse with hands and lift upper body. As legs pass over horse, extend hips, lift chest, and bring legs together before landing. Land with knees and hips slightly flexed.

SP Stand in front of horse and student (one foot slightly in front of the other). As student places hands on horse, grasp upper arms. As student passes over horse, step back and help lift and pull to make sure horse is cleared. Maintain contact until proper landing.

CE 1. Same as 1–7 of jump to squat stand.

2. Failure to maintain straight arms throughout skill.

3. Failure to push off of horse and keep shoulders erect almost immediately after contact.

4. Failure to lift head and chest, extend hips, and bring legs together before landing.

Figure V-11

■ HANDSPRING VAULT (Fig. V–12)

SL Intermediate.

PT After running approach and punch from board, extend body as arms, which are by head, reach for horse. Think about driving heels forcefully toward ceiling or up and overhead. On contacting horse, body will be extended (to get a good block) slightly in front of the vertical position. As hands hit, immediately block or push to force body upward and outward into afterflight phase. Body must remain in layout position throughout vault. Reach toward mat with toes and as feet make contact, flex knees and hips slightly.

SP
1. Two spotters on near side of horse lift thighs as performer leaves board. Two spotters on far side grasp arm and hip area. Support hip area if needed to keep body extended and guide to landing position.

2. Spotter on near side of horse between vaulting board and horse. Make contact with hip area as student leaves board and lift vertically. (Bend knees and lift with legs rather than straining arms and back.) Spotter on far side of horse grasps arm and hip to help guide to landing position.

CE
1. Leaning forward on takeoff from board (not blocking).
2. Pike after punch from board.
3. Insufficient heel drive.
4. Failure to block shoulders on hand contact.
5. Allowing shoulders to move forward of hands on horse.
6. Failure to keep head in neutral position throughout.

Figure V-12

■ OFF TRAMPOLINE HANDSPRING (Fig. V–13)

SL Advanced beginner.

PT Place mat over most of trampoline top, with portion hanging over the end. Stand at opposite end directly on padded frame. Take one aggressive step forward, hurdle onto both feet landing approximately in center of trampoline. Using rebounding action of trampoline, reach forcefully forward while extending body and driving heels overhead. Body is at layout position at the time hands make contact with end of trampoline. Head is between arms. Push off with hands by forcefully extending shoulders without bending elbows. This action lifts body upward and then outward. Body must remain in layout position until landing. Arms remain overhead during afterflight, with head kept neutral. Toes should reach out toward mat. On contact, flex knees and hips slightly and move arms to oblique position. Using trampoline in this fashion enables students to concentrate on developing proper technique for a good handspring, specifically, the heel drive and lifting action from the shoulders with body extended. This also enables vaulter to practice the landing on "balance" with control.

SP Stand directly at end of trampoline to left side of student. As hands make contact, grasp upper left arm. Place left hand on lower back. This technique enables spotter to maintain contact with student and have control throughout skill and landing.

CE 1. Failure to "attack," that is, to be aggressive from beginning to end of handspring.
2. Failure to take advantage of rebounding action of trampoline to drive heels over head from takeoff.
3. Failure to keep arms straight and forcefully extend shoulders to lift body upward-outward.
4. Failure to keep head neutral during afterflight.
5. Failure to keep body extended and tight with arms overhead during afterflight.
6. Failure to concentrate on solid controlled landing.
7. Body too arched in flight phase.

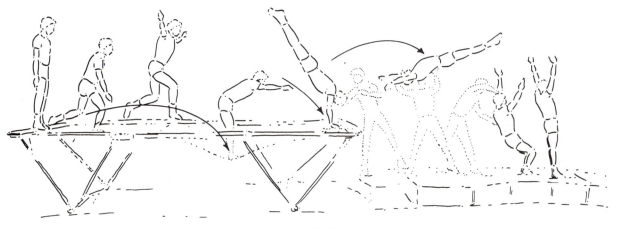

Figure V-13

LONG HORSE VAULTING

Once good side horse vaulting techniques are established on the approach, takeoff, on-horse contact, afterflight, and landing, the student is ready to vault over the long horse.

The mechanics of long horse vaulting are no different from those employed to vault over the side horse. The primary adjustment to be made is a psychological one. Often the student feels that vaulting over the horse lengthwise is extremely difficult but, in most cases, only needs to straddle over the long horse once or twice to establish confidence.

The trampoline as a vaulting aid is an excellent way to better psychological adjustment. The trampoline has size and length, which can help to break down the students' fear of the long horse.

■ LEAD UP FOR STRADDLE VAULT (Long Horse) (Fig. V–14)

SL Advanced beginner.

PT Approach horse with a short run at half speed. After vertical lift from board, reach forward with arms and place hands near middle of horse while simultaneously straddling legs. Keep hands firmly pushing down on horse. Arms and legs must be straight. Then lower legs down behind arms onto horse to finish in straddle sitting position. Repeat, each time increasing speed of run and reaching further forward onto horse. When hands can be placed on far end, push off and straddle over to stand on mat.

SP Stand close to and at the center of horse. As student's hands contact horse, grasp upper arms with (spotter's) right hand to left arm, left hand to right arm. Brace student's arms to prevent shoulders from leaning too far forward and arms from buckling. This will assist to lower straddled legs onto horse.

CE 1. Failure to be aggressive off board.

2. Failure to keep arms and legs straight.

3. Failure to keep body tight.

4. Failure to keep legs behind upper body.

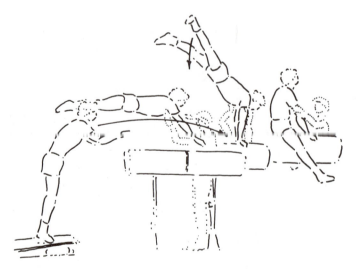

Figure V-14

■ STRADDLE VAULT (Long Horse) (Fig. V–15)

SL Advanced beginner.

PT The key to straddling over the long horse is aggressiveness. The student should run at a faster yet controlled speed, hurdle to the board, and immediately spring vertically, lifting hips backward-upward. Reach forward with arms to place hands on far end (neck) of horse. Look up at this point, and straddle legs. Immediately push forcefully off horse with hands and lift upper body. As legs pass to outside of horse, extend hips forward and bring legs together before landing to a stand on mat. Land with knees and hips slightly bent.

SP Stand close to the far end of horse. As student places hands on horse and pushes off, grasp left upper arm with both hands. Lift and pull arm forward. A second spotter on opposite side of horse may spot in the same manner with student's right arm.

CE 1. Poor run and hurdle.

2. Landing on the board flatfooted.

3. Leaning forward on board.

4. Bending knees too much on board.

5. Insufficient vertical lift.

6. Poorly coordinated arms.

7. Placement of hands too far from end of horse.

8. Failure to maintain straight arms and legs throughout vault.

9. Failure to push forcefully off horse and keep shoulders erect almost immediately after contact.

10. Failure to lift head and chest, extend hips, and bring legs together before landing on mat.

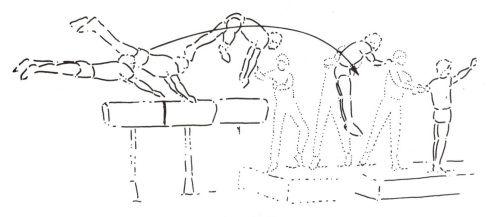

Figure V-15

■SQUAT VAULT (Long Horse) (Fig. V–16)

SL Advanced beginner.

PT After vertical lift and extending body (layout), bend knees sharply to chest as hands contact end of horse. Push forcefully off horse with hands, simultaneously lifting head and chest. As body passes over horse, force hips forward to extend body before landing.

SP Same as for straddle vault.

CE 1. Same as 1–7 for straddle vault.

    2. Failure to keep arms straight.

    3. Failure to push forcefully off horse and keep shoulders erect almost immediately after contact.

    4. Failure to lift head and chest and force hips forward to extend body before landing on mat.

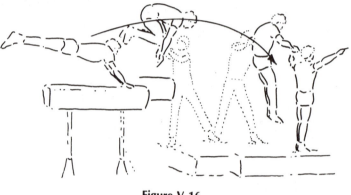

Figure V-16

▲ TEST QUESTIONS—*VAULTING*

1. What determines the space between the board and the horse?
   a. the type of vault being performed.
   b. the performer's ability and type of vault.
   c. the distance is always the same.
   d. the distance should be less than 5 feet.

2. In a squat vault, the hips pass over the horse
   a. before hands are released.
   b. with hands.
   c. after head and hands.
   d. before the hands touch.

3. In order to achieve the best lift, which area of the board should be contacted?
   a. the end.
   b. the curve.
   c. the front.
   d. it does not make a difference.

4. The most common reasons for hitting the horse with the knees on a squat vault is all but one of the following:
   a. lifting the hips high.
   b. poor hurdle.
   c. leaning forward from the board.
   d. the board is too close to the horse.

5. Where does the spotter stand for a straddle vault?
   a. to far side of horse.
   b. to near side of horse.
   c. to side of horse.
   d. between the board and horse.

6. If there is only one spotter on a handspring vault, where should he or she stand?
   a. far side of horse (to get arms and back).
   b. near side of horse (to lift total body).
   c. near side of horse (to lift legs).
   d. near side of horse, then run to far side.

7. When performing any type of vault, from where does the initial force come?
   a. hands on horse.
   b. layout position.
   c. push off horse.
   d. spring from board.

8. When performing any vault, from where does the secondary force come?
   a. body extension.
   b. run.
   c. hurdle.
   d. push off hands with shoulder extension.

9. Which of the following vaults should *not* be spotted from the side?
   a. straddle.
   b. squat.
   c. flank.
   d. handspring.

10. The trampoline is excellent as a teaching aide except for one of the following:
    a. on- and off-horse vaults can be learned separately.
    b. provide greater shock absorption from takeoff and landing.
    c. height of trampoline cannot be adjusted for smaller students.
    d. beginning through advanced vaults can be learned.

VAULTING

NAME: _____

Use of Vaulting Board

Takeoff 2–3 feet in front of board _____

Land on board on toes at curve _____

Vertical lift immediate _____

Total body stretch _____

Land solid with hip and knee slightly flexed _____

Score _____

Flank Vault

Spring from board sufficient to lift hips above horse level _____

Hand placement in center of top of horse _____

Hips extended to force body in horizontal layout as body passes over horse _____

Hand removed to allow body to pass _____

Landing with control—slight hip and knee flexion back to horse _____

Score _____

Squat onto Mats/Horse/Tramp

Sufficient push from board _____

Hips high enough _____

Arms extended forcefully forward and upward to horse _____

Hand placement center of mat and horse _____

Land on toes _____

Score _____

Jump to Straddle Stand

Sufficient punch from board _____

Hips lifted and legs straddled _____

Hands on center top of horse _____

Legs placed in straddle on top of horse _____

Score _____

Squat Vault

Takeoff sufficient, arm extension and lift of hips simultaneous _____

Hips high _____

Knees tucked _____

Hand push from horse before hips pass over horse _____

Score _____

Straddle Vault

Sufficient punch from board _____

Hip lift above horse _____

Legs straddled wide _____

Hand push from horse sufficient _____

Chest lift as straddled legs clear horse _____

Body extended—legs together before landing _____

Score _____

(Continued)

VAULTING *(Continued)*

Handspring Lead Up (Preflight)

Body straight in preflight _____

Arms straight on contact with
tramp _____

Body remains straight with
follow through to landing
on tramp _____

Score _____

Handspring

Sufficient takeoff on board _____

Body extended in preflight on
horse _____

Landing with control _____

Slight hip and knee flexion _____

Score _____

Long Horse—Lead Up Straddle

Sufficient takeoff from board _____

Hand placement in middle of
horse _____

Arms and legs straight _____

Legs straddled then lowered to
sitting position _____

Score _____

Straddle Vault (Long Horse)

Sufficient push off board _____

Vertical lift sufficient—body in
layout _____

Hand placement on neck of
horse _____

Forceful push off horse _____

Legs straddle horse as hips
extend forward _____

Land with legs together and
controlled _____

Score _____

Handspring Lead Up (Afterflight)

Coordinated step-hop, takeoff _____

Body extended _____

Hands push off tramp _____

Body straight in afterflight _____

Slight knee and hip flexion on
landing _____

Score _____

Long Horse Squat Vault

Sufficient push off board _____

Body in layout in vertical lift _____

Hand placement on neck of
horse _____

Hand push forceful _____

Legs tucked as body passes over
horse _____

Landing with control, hips and
knees flexed slightly _____

Score _____

Final Score _____

Final Grade _____

Comments:

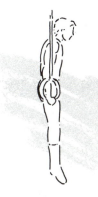

Chapter
7

Still Rings

Because rings hang freely from cables and straps and, therefore, are unstable, they are usually difficult for beginners. Learning to swing forward and backward while hanging "below" the rings becomes a unique experience and must be practiced to develop proficient swing technique. Skills performed "above" the rings, or in a support position, are also more difficult, in that students must not only support their body weight but control unstable movement of the rings. Good swing technique, referred to as *the basic swing,* is extremely important for successful performance of many skills executed with swing. Upper body and hip flexor strength and upper back and shoulder flexibility are necessary.

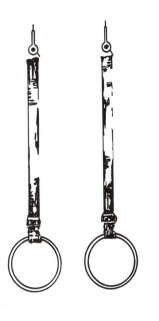

SAFETY HINTS

1. Use a 6- by 12-foot landing mat, at least 4 inches thick, under rings, or several thicknesses of 1-inch thick mats that are at least 12 feet long.
2. Students should apply chalk to hands each time before gripping rings.
3. Inspect rings periodically for cracks.
4. Inspect periodically straps, cables, and hardware from which rings are suspended for defects.
5. Do not use rings for long swings from point of suspension.
6. Don't force students to perform skills they don't feel ready to do.

A grading sheet for ring skills appears at the end of this chapter.

STILL RING SKILLS

This first group of skills is in the category of various static positions while student hangs from hands below rings. They are basic ring skills and aid the beginner to adapt to different body positions, which serve to test and develop the beginner's "spatial orientation" and upper body strength. To facilitate learning and ease of spotting, these and many support skills are taught with rings at head height, 5–6 feet above the mat so that student can grip rings without jumping to reach them. When possible, have two sets of rings: one at head height and another at regulation height, 8 feet above the mat.

Due to the nature of the event, jumping to a front hang position is the only way the rings are mounted. Generally, the first skill is considered the mount.

■ L HANG (Fig. R–1)

SL Beginner.
PT Grip rings, then straighten arms. On low rings, bend knees to allow arms to straighten. Then lift legs forward with knees straight and extended so that legs are horizontal to mat. This is an excellent self-testing skill indicative of hip flexor strength. If this position cannot be held for three to five seconds, students must exercise to strengthen this muscle group.
SP Spotter may help lift legs to proper position. If student has strength necessary to hold this position, a spotter is not required.
CE 1. Bending knees to lift legs.
    2. Flexing arms.
    3. Throwing head back and closing eyes.
MO Lift legs to pike position inverted hang.

Figure R–1

■ PIKE POSITION INVERTED HANG (Fig. R–2)

SL Beginner.
PT Grasp rings and lift legs forward toward face by flexing hips. Allow arms to straighten as upper body lowers backward. Hips should be flexed (tight pike position); back should be slightly rounded and parallel to the mat. Legs are between arms. Keep eyes open and look directly at knees.
SP Stand facing left side, close enough to adjust student's position if not correct. Place right hand under back and left hand on back of thighs.

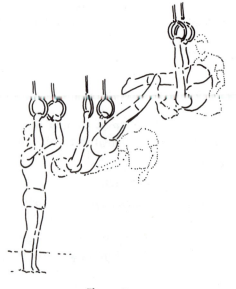

Figure R–2

CE 1. Looking back toward mat, losing orientation.

2. Allowing hips to get too low or too high, making it more difficult to hold position.

3. Pulling up by bending arms while in bent hip position.

4. Closing eyes. Eyes should be open, looking directly at knees.

MO 1. Cast forward to long hang swing through front hang.

2. Kip to support.

3. Dislocate backward.

◼ INVERTED HANG (Fig. R–3)

SL Beginner.

PT This position should be initiated from pike position inverted hang. Extend hips fully so that lower part of body, which is directly above head and shoulders, is inside and in line with ring straps. Rings may be pulled close to outside of thighs to feel position. Body should be straight with head dropped back so that student can see mat below.

SP Same as for pike position inverted hang. Again, if necessary adjust student's position and keep legs from falling forward or backward due to loss of orientation, reach up and reposition legs back between straps.

CE 1. Keeping chin on chest once position is checked.

2. Closing eyes.

3. Pulling body up by bending arms.

4. Knees or hips bent, or both bent.

MO 1. Pike position inverted hang.

2. Lower to rear hang.

3. Swing down through front hang on high rings.

VA Swing to inverted hang on high rings.

Figure R–3

◼ REAR HANG (Fig. R–4)

PT Same procedure as for inverted hang. Lower legs backward and fully extend shoulders and hips. Look toward mat. If toes and feet rest on mat because student is taller, perform on high rings or raise low rings. To complete rear hang, pull back to pike position inverted hang. This is a good indication of upper body strength.

SP Same as for inverted hang. If student is unable to pull back to pike position inverted hang, assist by placing left hand, palm up, on abdomen and right hand, palm up, on closest lower leg and impart lifting movement.

Figure R–4

CE 1. Not extending shoulders and hips completely.

2. Bending knees to pull back to pike position inverted hang.

3. Keeping chin on chest.

4. Closing eyes.

MO Release rings lifting head and chest to a stand.

VA Lower to rear hang from inverted hang when strong enough to do so.

Supporting above Rings

■FRONT HAND SUPPORT (Fig. R–5)

SL Beginner.

PT Grasp rings, palms facing in. Spring vertically from both feet while quickly pulling rings downward. As shoulders move above hands, turn rings out quickly and forcefully extend arms. Keep rings close to body throughout entire movement. Once above rings, lock elbows and hold rings close to outside of upper legs. This skill tests upper body strength. Student may experience difficulty keeping rings from moving uncontrollably. With practice and increase in strength, this movement can be controlled. Student should maintain grip on rings until controlled stand on mat is made.

Figure R–5

SP Standing directly behind student, lift at waist until student locks arms and has control of support position. At this point, move hands down to lower thighs and support lightly. Assist to standing position on mat should arms collapse.

CE 1. Failure to jump hard and pull rings downward.

2. Failure to turn rings out quickly once shoulders reach height of rings after jumping up.

3. Failure to keep rings close to body throughout movement, especially turning rings out as in 2 above.

4. Failure to extend arms and shoulders once in support position.

5. Failure to turn rings outward. Rings should be parallel to legs instead of being turned in.

6. Dropping chin down. Head should be erect, looking straight ahead.

7. Failure to keep body tight.

MO 1. L support.

2. Lower backward to pike position inverted hang.

■MUSCLE UP (Fig. R–6)

SL Intermediate beginner.

PT Perform the same as jumping to front hand support, with two exceptions. When performed on high rings, a dynamic arm flexion and extension action is used, since student cannot push off mat with feet. The key to this skill is the "false" or "high" overgrip the student must take when initially gripping the rings. It is easier to take the proper grip on the low rings and then simulate the pull-push action with the arms by not jumping up.

To simplify false grip, reach through rings, hands toward each other, and place wrists on top underside of rings. Then close hands around rings without letting rings slip down into palms. Grip rings from between base of thumb and as high as possible on heel of hand just below wrist. Pull rings down dynamically into chest rather than just to shoulders by maximally flexing arms. The critical point occurs at this phase. Quickly turn hands outward as shoulders reach level of rings. Flex hips slightly to lift feet forward to rock shoulders above rings. Once shoulders are above hands, the second "push-up" phase is usually done more easily.

SP Same as for front hand support.

CE 1. Failure to maintain false grip to at least turn out of rings phase.

2. Failure to raise shoulders high enough before turning rings out.

3. Failure to keep rings close to body throughout entire skill.

4. Failure to be dynamic throughout both phases of skill.

MO L support.

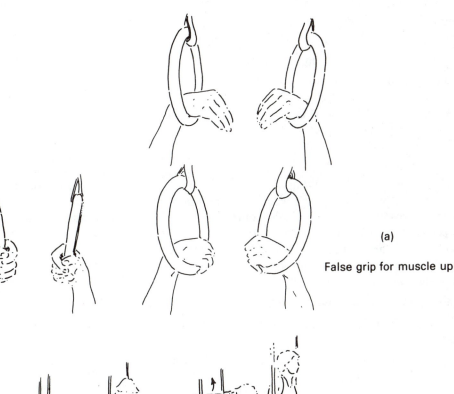

(a)

False grip for muscle up

(b)

Figure R–6

■ L SUPPORT (Fig. R–7)

SL Intermediate beginner.

PT From front hand support position, raise legs to position horizontal to mat at a 90-degree angle to upper body. Hold head erect, chest open.

Figure R–7

This position is considered a basic skill. However, it is used in most advanced routines and often precedes other movements involving greater strength. Student must be able to maintain support position and have good hip flexor and abdominal strength. This is an excellent exercise for strengthening these areas and developing a sense of balance in the support position.

SP Stand facing left side of student. Place left hand, palm up, under back of knees. Place right hand, palm up, on buttocks. Adjust legs to proper 90-degree angle; offer support if necessary by a lifting motion.

CE 1. Same as for front hand support.

2. Legs below a 90-degree angle, indicating a lack of hip flexor strength.

MO 1. Roll forward to pike position inverted hang.

2. Shoulder stand.

■ LOWER BACK TO PIKE POSITION INVERTED HANG (Fig. R–8)

SL Intermediate beginner.

PT From front hand support, lift legs by flexing hips and, at the same time, begin to bend arms and lower upper body backward. Continue flexing hips and lowering upper body backward smoothly. When legs are high enough, extend arms with control and finish in pike position inverted hang. Look at knees throughout entire movement. The key to this skill is a smooth, controlled movement while lowering back with arms first bending and then extending.

SP Stand facing left side of student. Place left hand, palm up, on back of thighs to help lift legs. Place right hand, palm up, on back and resist upper body lowering back too fast throughout entire movement.

CE 1. Bending knees while lowering back.

2. Dropping head back, losing orientation.

3. Falling back, instead of lowering back.

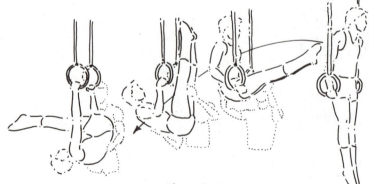

Figure R–8

■FORWARD ROLL TO PIKE POSITION HANG (Fig. R–9)

SL Intermediate beginner.

PT From L-seat position, begin to elevate hips overhead while bending arms, lowering shoulders to level of rings. Lower shoulders below rings as hips keep moving forward overhead. Hips must be tightly flexed throughout entire roll. At this point, smoothly and slowly straighten arms to keep lowering body below rings to pike position hang.

SP Standing to left side of student, place left hand on upper back to control roll forward and lowering through to pike position hang. Place right hand on back of left thigh and assist by lifting hips.

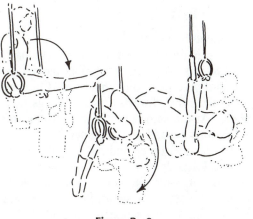

Figure R–9

CE 1. Failure to lift hips overhead sufficiently to continue rolling forward.

2. Bending knees causing possible loss of control.

3. Failure to keep rings close to body through entire roll.

4. Failure to lower body slowly, with control, to pike position hang.

■SHOULDER STAND (Fig. R–10)

SL Intermediate beginner.

PT From L-seat position, begin to elevate hips overhead while bending arms, lowering shoulders to level of rings. As shoulders settle in lowest position inside rings, fully extend hips with smoothly controlled motion. Hold head up slightly; look to mat below. Maintain balance by adjusting rings with arms and shoulders. It is helpful if student has mastered shoulder stand on parallel bars.

SP Standing to left side of student, place left hand on upper back or shoulder. Place right hand on front of left thigh. Assist to a vertical position, feet over head. Move left hand up to back of thigh to position and "feel" the balance, if necessary. Spotter may stand on stacked mats, bench, or similar object if unable to reach student's legs.

CE 1. Body too arched or hips bent.

2. Chin on chest, causing overbalance.

3. Placing shoulders on top of rings, instead of placing rings in a position outside shoulders. All body weight should be on hands.

4. Pulling hands in toward chest, rings should be pushed outward.

MO 1. Lower vertically to inverted hang.

2. Push back to support, and lower back to pike position inverted hang.

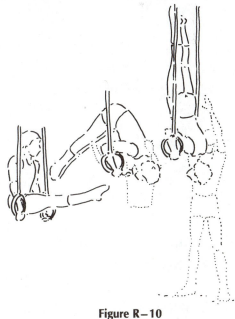

Figure R–10

■ KIP (Fig. R-11)

SL Advanced beginner.

PT The kip is an important universal gymnastic movement. On the rings, the kip is used to raise the body to a front hand support from a pike position inverted hang.

 From pike position hang, extend hips slightly and quickly "compress" back into tight pike, then forcefully extend legs forward-upward at approximately a 45-degree angle. At the same time, begin pulling rings dynamically down toward hips. This action raises head and shoulders above rings. At this point, forcefully push downward on rings by extending arms to finish in front hand support.

SP Facing left side, place left hand on back of thighs and right hand in small of back. As student compresses to tight pike and begins hip extension, push up with right hand, use left hand in similar manner, and be ready to give more support with left hand as support position is completed.

CE 1. Extending hips too slowly from pike position inverted hang.

 2. Extending hips above or too far below 45-degree angle.

 3. Not actively pulling on rings with hands as hips extend.

 4. Not forcefully pushing down on rings near completion of support position.

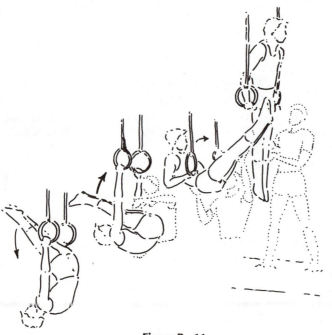

Figure R-11

High Ring Skills

■ BASIC SWING (Fig. R-12)

SL Beginner.

PT From front hang position, tense hip, abdominal, and gluteal muscles to initiate pendulum swing. Flex hips, raising feet forward-upward as rings are pulled behind head. (Pull is initiated from shoulder joint.) This action starts body swing.

Just prior to peak of forward swing, extend hips and shoulders forcefully, but smoothly, "opening up body." This action raises center of gravity. As body swings downward-forward from hang (vertical position), flex hips slightly while passing through vertical position. As body begins to swing backward-upward, again forcefully extend hips to raise body higher. At this point, it is extremely important not to bend knees. Shoulder and upper back flexibility is significant in this segment of the swing. Also exert downward push on rings in conjunction with hip extension to again raise center of gravity higher on this backward-upward phase of swing. As body begins downward-forward swing, flex hips just after vertical (front hang) position is passed and pull rings behind head to accelerate forward-upward phase of swing.

When this technique is perfected, each succeeding swing will raise the center of gravity. Practice basic swing to develop a smooth, controlled swing with good elevation both forward and backward. This should be used as a warm-up exercise, swinging four to six times at least three separate times during the start of each ring practice session.

SP Stand facing left side, close enough to allow enough room for student to swing by. If necessary, help forward swing by placing right hand on small of back, left hand on back of left thigh, and impart lifting movement to left as body swings forward. For backward phase of swing, place left hand on abdomen, right hand on front of left thigh, and impart lifting movement to right during backward swing.

CE 1. Failure to keep head in neutral position, between shoulders, through entire phase of swing.

2. Bending knees and not keeping body tight throughout swing.

3. Pulling or pushing unevenly with arms, causing swing to go sideward.

4. Bending arms at either end of swing.

MO 1. Flyaway dismount.

2. Back straddle dismount.

3. Front uprise.

4. Inlocate.

5. Back uprise.

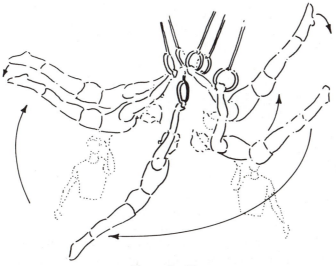

Figure R–12

■DISLOCATE DISMOUNT (Fig. R–13)

SL Beginner.

PO Initiate this skill from pike position inverted hang. Extend hips forcefully with legs moving directly backward, slightly upward, approximately at 30-degree angle. At the same time, thrust arms forcefully to side, along with downward push on rings. Originate this arm movement from shoulders, so arms remain straight. Do not jerk head backward. Instead, as body begins to turn over, look for mat below. As arms begin to move forward from sideward thrust, release rings and land on feet.

SP Stand to left, place left hand, palm up, on student's chest just after rings are released to make sure upper body keeps rotating to upright position. Right hand may be placed on upper back just before student lands on feet to assist balanced landing.

CE 1. Failure to extend hips forcefully or not at proper angle.

2. Failure to keep arms straight throughout sideward thrust to point of release.

MO Dislocate to front swing.

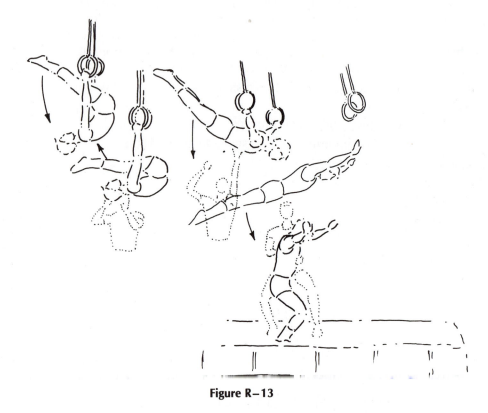

Figure R–13

■BACK FLYAWAY DISMOUNT (Fig. R–14)

SL Intermediate beginner.

PT After basic swing is mastered, back flyaway dismount may be taught. As body passes the vertical and begins to swing forward-upward, flex hips slightly to increase speed of forward swing. Bend arms to lift body higher. As body rotates upward and reaches close to vertical position, release rings with body fully extended. Lift head and chest before feet contact mat.

SP Stand at left side, actively aid the forward-upward swing by placing left hand on back and pushing. Do this just as student passes vertical phase of swing. As rings are released, reach up with right hand to chest to make sure that the chest lifts to complete rotation. Place right hand on the back to aid in a secure landing, and to prevent possible over-rotation.

CE 1. Releasing rings too soon can cause possible under-rotation, or releasing too late can cause over-rotation.

2. Not fully extending body after release of rings.

3. Not enough swing prior to releasing rings.

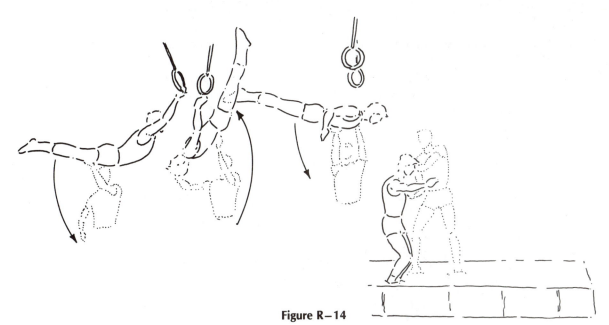

Figure R–14

VA *Back flyaway, pike* (Fig. R–15). Use as a lead up to get feel of flyaway.

PT Swing need not be great; student can flex hips more tightly on upward phase of swing and swing through bent hip inverted hang still gripping rings. As soon as student sees mat, release rings and land on feet. This technique leaves little margin for error. It is not a "true" flyaway but can serve as a lead up to the flyaway.

SP Same as for flyaway.

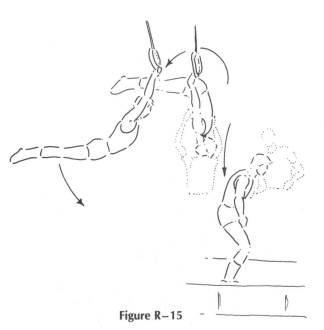

Figure R–15

■STRADDLE CUT BACKWARD DISMOUNT (Fig. R–16)

SL Intermediate beginner.

PT For the novice, this dismount is performed in the same manner as lead up to fly-away. The only difference is a reasonably strong forward-upward swing. Flex hips at point of release. Straddle legs and release rings when legs come in contact with lower arms. In this position, look at mat and keep rotating backward, closing legs before landing on feet.

SP Same as for flyaway.

CE 1. Failure to develop enough forward-upward swing.

2. Failure to "watch" legs swinging forward-upward toward hands by looking back too soon.

3. Releasing rings too soon on forward-upward swing, causing possible under-rotation.

4. Failure to release rings just as, or just prior to, inside of thighs contacting lower arms. This will stop most rotation backward developed by the swing.

5. Bending knees.

Figure R–16

■STRADDLE CUT FORWARD DISMOUNT (Fig. R–17)

SL Intermediate beginner.

PT This skill is best taught from a pike position inverted hang, and may be taught on either the high or low rings due to the ease of spotting. The initial action of this dismount is similar to the kip. Rock chest forward by pulling with arms and at the same time straddle legs. Back of knees will momentarily be across lower arms. The most important part of this skill is to forcefully rock chest forward so that, at the point of release, upper body is as vertical as possible. Release rings and forcefully drive legs forward-downward toward mat.

SP Stand directly behind and under student who assumes pike position hang. Place both hands on either side of upper back ("lats"). As student rocks forward, pulling with arms and straddling legs, push forward, then support upper body until student lands on mat.

CE 1. Performing entire movement too slowly.

2. Failure to position chest erect prior to release.

3. Failure to keep knees straight.

4. Failure to forcefully place feet down on mat after release.

5. Failure to keep bringing chest forward after releasing rings.

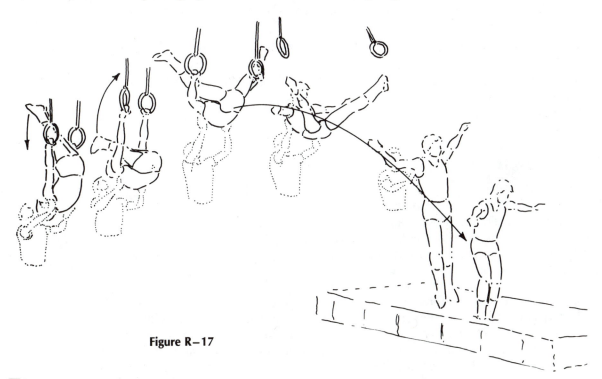

Figure R−17

■ INLOCATE (Fig. R−18)

SL Intermediate beginner.

PT This movement is performed as the body reaches horizontal position on back swing. Flex hips forcefully into tight pike. Think of "lifting" as well as flexing hips. At the same time, move arms directly from in front of head out to side and behind hips to an inverted hang in a piked position.

SP Stand to left, place left hand, palm up, on abdomen; place right hand, palm up, on front of left thigh. Impart lifting action as student lifts and flexes hips at peak of backswing. Make contact just as body passes vertical phase of swing and is swinging backward-upward.

CE 1. Failure to generate sufficient backswing.

2. Failure to be aggressive with hip lift and sideward movement of arms.

3. Bending arms.

4. Failure to drop chin toward chest as hips are lifted.

MO 1. Straddle cut forward dismount.

2. Kip to hand support.

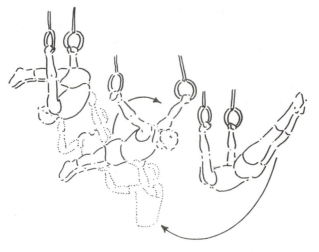

Figure R–18

■DISLOCATE (Fig. R–19)

SL Advanced beginner.

PT The term *dislocate* is misleading in that the skill does not involve any abnormal movement. Therefore, teacher and student should not have any apprehension about the skill. It is, however, complex and must be treated accordingly.

From pike position inverted hang, extend body from hips forcefully with legs shooting backward at approximately a 45-degree angle. At the same time, extend arms directly sideward and continue circling forward and together in line with head and body. Complete before downward-forward swing to avoid jerky movement of body passing through vertical phase of swing. Do not jerk head back. Actually, head should remain in neutral position between shoulders and arms throughout dislocate. It is also extremely important to keep tension on rings by pushing down on rings with hands throughout dislocate. This will reduce or eliminate any unnecessary pull on shoulders. Follow through by swinging to bent hip hang.

SP Stand to left, place left hand, palm up, on chest. Place right hand, palm up, on front of right thigh immediately after body is extended and arms are thrust sideward. Actively help lower body through downward swing toward vertical. How much or how little will depend on how well skill is performed. On first attempt, spotter should give maximum assistance.

CE 1. Extending hips with legs shooting too much below or above 45-degree angle.

2. Failure to keep arms straight throughout movement.

3. Jerking head back causing arms not to continue circling forward.

4. Not finishing entire movement before vertical position is reached, causing too much pull on shoulders.

5. Failure to maintain tension on rings throughout entire movement.

MO Front uprise.

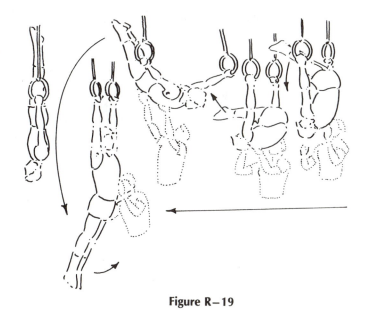

Figure R–19

■FRONT UPRISE (Fig. R–20)

SL Intermediate beginner.

PT A good basic swing is a prerequisite to front uprise. It is used to move the body into front hand support via forward swing.

When first learning this skill, practice from two to three basic swings. Just after vertical phase of swing, as body begins forward-upward swing, flex hips, lifting body higher. At this point, extend body forward forcefully at hips. At the same time, pull on rings. This action raises shoulders above rings at which moment arms extend quickly, pushing down on rings. This action raises body to front hand support position. Think of this as a pull-push action with arms. Keep hands close to body throughout entire uprise.

SP Stand to left, place right hand in small of back. Place left hand, palm up, on back of upper left thigh. Contact should be made just after student passes vertical phase of swing. Push up with right hand and lift with left. Follow through by supporting body to front support. Spotter may stand on stacked mats or similar device to maintain contact throughout skill.

CE 1. Failure to develop sufficient forward-upward swing.

2. Failure to forcefully thrust hip upward, causing body to stay too piked making it difficult to elevate chest above rings.

3. Failure to forcefully pull-push with arms.

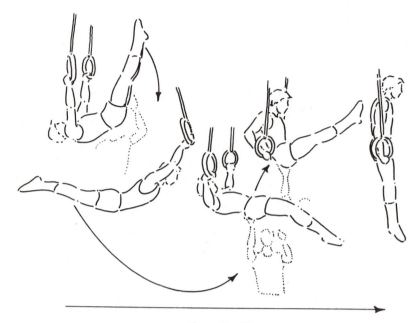

Figure R–20

■ BACK UPRISE (Fig. R–21)

SL Advanced beginner.

PT A good basic swing is necessary to perform this skill and is used to get the body into front hand support via back swing.

   When first attempting back uprise, practice from two to three basic swings. As vertical phase of swing is passed, extend body forcefully backward along with backward-upward swing. Think of "lifting heels," keeping knees straight. At peak of backswing, which should reach a horizontal position, forcefully pull down on rings. In conjunction with backswing, this action raises shoulders above rings. At this point, forcefully push down on rings by extending arms. Think of this as a pull-push action with arms. At completion of uprise, hands should be alongside hips in front hand support position. Body remains extended throughout uprise.

SP Stand to left, place left hand, palm up, on abdomen. Place right hand, palm up, on front of left thigh and lift through to support position. Spotter may stand on stacked mats or similar device to keep lifting throughout uprise. Hand contact should be made just as body passes vertical phase of swing.

CE 1. Failure to generate good backswing.

   2. Failure to keep arms close to body throughout uprise (pull-push action).

   3. Bending knees and/or hips on backswing.

   4. Failure to be dynamic throughout movement.

MO L support.

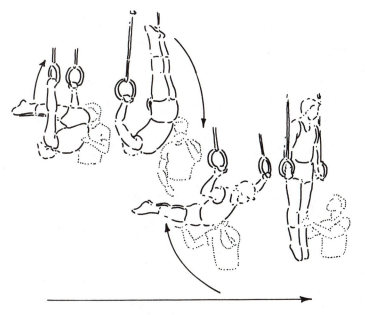

Figure R—21

Beginning Routine for Rings (Fig. R—22)

1. Basic swing through pike position hang.
2. To rear hang.
3. Pull back to pike position hang.
4. Cast forward back uprise.
5. L-seat hold.
6. Forward roll to pike position hang.
7. Inverted hang.
8. Dislocate dismount.

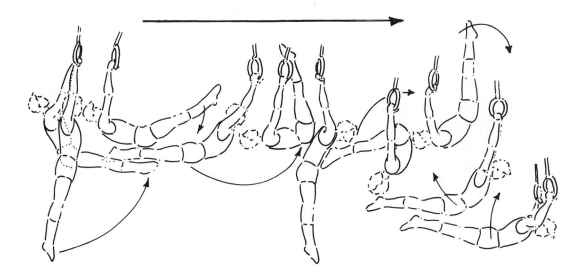

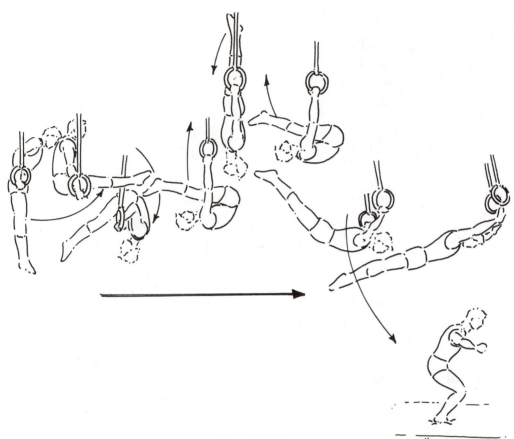

Figure R—22

▲ TEST QUESTIONS—*STILL RINGS*

1. An L hang position is performed with the
   a. arms and hips bent.
   b. arms straight and knees bent.
   c. arms straight and hips bent.
   d. arms straight, hips and knees bent.

2. An inverted hang position is performed with the
   a. hips above the shoulders and flexed.
   b. hips above the shoulders and straight.
   c. hips above the shoulders and knees bent.
   d. hips above the shoulders and arms bent.

3. To execute a muscle up, which grip is used?
   a. overgrip.
   b. undergrip.
   c. full grip.
   d. false grip.

4. An L-seat on the rings requires which of the following?
   a. arm and shoulder strength.
   b. arm, hip flexor, and abdominal strength.
   c. good shoulder flexibility.
   d. good hip flexibility.

5. The basic swing is essentially
   a. a pendulum swing forward and backward.
   b. a pendulum swing from side to side.
   c. the rings swinging forward and backward from the point of suspension.
   d. none of the above.

6. Which of the following skills may *not* be performed from a swing?
   a. pike position hang.
   b. flyaway dismount.
   c. muscle up.
   d. back uprise.

7. A good flyaway is performed with the
   a. hips bent.
   b. body straight and knees bent.
   c. arms slightly bent and the body fully extended.
   d. arms straight and the body tucked.

8. A front uprise is performed
   a. with a strong swing and knees bent.
   b. with a false grip.
   c. at the forward end of a strong swing.
   d. at the rearward end of a strong swing.

9. A good basic swing is used for which of the following?
   a. dismount.
   b. as a warm-up exercise.
   c. uprises.
   d. all of the above.

10. An inlocate requires
    a. extreme hip flexibility.
    b. a good swing.
    c. average shoulder flexibility.
    d. b and c.

STILL RINGS	Name:

L Hang

Arms straight _____

Legs extended in L _____

Held position 3 seconds _____

Score _____

Rear Hang

Legs lowered backward from
inverted hang with control _____

Arms and legs straight
throughout _____

Shoulders and hips extended
completely _____

Score _____

Bent Hip Inverted Hang

Legs lifted upward with control _____

Arms straight as body moves
into pike _____

Back rounded slightly _____

Eyes spotting knees _____

Score _____

Front Hand Support

Palms facing in _____

Sufficient spring upward _____

Rings turned out as shoulders
pass hands _____

Arms extended _____

Rings kept close to body
throughout skill _____

Held support position 3 seconds _____

Score _____

Inverted Hang

Legs extended upward as chest
moves downward _____

Body straight in vertical position _____

Eyes looking at mat _____

Score _____

Muscle Up

Explosive action of arm flexion
and extension _____

Rings turned out as shoulders
pass hands _____

Arms extended _____

Rings kept close to body
throughout skill _____

Held support position 3 seconds _____

Score _____

L Support

Arms and legs straight
throughout _____

Legs parallel to floor (mat) _____

Held position 3 seconds _____

Score _____

Kip

Sufficient hip extension and
pull-push with arms from
bent hip hand position _____

Locked arms and good support
position at completion of kip,
held 3 seconds _____

Score _____

(Continued)

STILL RINGS *(Continued)*

Lower Back to Bent Hip Inverted Hang

Legs together and straight _____

Upper body lowered with control _____

Leg lift sufficient to finish in bent hip inverted hang _____

Score _____

Basic Swing

Smooth swing with control _____

Body reaching close to or parallel to mat at either end of swing _____

Legs together and straight throughout _____

Score _____

Forward Roll to Bent Hip

Good L-seat position _____

Knees straight through roll _____

Controlled roll with finish in good bent hip hang _____

L-seat and bent hip hang held 3 seconds _____

Score _____

Dislocate Dismount

Aggressive hip extension at proper angle _____

Arms straight throughout thrust to side _____

Body completely extended prior to releasing rings _____

Controlled stand on landing _____

Score _____

Shoulder Stand

Legs together and straight throughout _____

Controlled press to vertical position _____

Eyes looking toward mat _____

Body vertical between straps _____

Held position 3 seconds _____

Score _____

Back Flyaway Dismount

Good swing, smooth and high _____

Early release of rings for complete follow through of sommie _____

Body extended throughout (may be flexed as in lead up) _____

Legs straight together to good controlled landing _____

Score _____

Straddle Cut Backward Dismount

Good swing, smooth and high _____

Release rings when body about vertical _____

Legs apart, knees straight as release is made _____

Body extended after release, to smooth controlled landing _____

Score _____

Inlocate

Good swing, smooth and high _____

Arms and legs straight throughout inlocate _____

Finish in a good bent hip hang position _____

Score _____

(Continued)

STILL RINGS (Continued)

Straddle Cut Forward		Final Score	_____
Good tight bent hip hang position	_____	Final Grade	_____
Good pull with arms to rock chest forward	_____		
Straddle legs with relatively straight knees	_____		
Feet under body to controlled landing	_____		
Score	_____		

Comments:

Chapter 8 Balance Beam

Unlimited imagination and creativity enhance balance beam performance. This 4-inch-wide, 16-foot-long apparatus presents a challenge because much body control and courage must be exhibited to maneuver the body through the intricacies of skills and routines performed on the beam.

Students should first practice all skills on the floor (preferably on a line) to develop proper technique. Next, they should practice skills on a low beam to develop confidence, and finally on a regulation height beam. In a class with many body types and levels of ability, students should work and be graded on a *low* beam. This eliminates much fear, and students with lesser abilities will achieve greater success. The low beam is also safer. Skills on the beam are divided into the following categories:

> Mounts
> Locomotor skills
> Turns and pirouettes
> Static positions
> Tumbling and acrobatic moves
> Dismounts

SAFETY HINTS

1. Do not allow students on equipment without supervision.
2. Surround beam with mats.
3. Prior to each class period, make sure beam supports are secure.
4. Use safety aids, such as beam training pads, if available.
5. Spotters should be alert at all times to avoid accidents. Whenever possible, teach students spotting techniques along with performance techniques.

A grading sheet for balance beam skills appears at the end of this chapter.

6. Avoid mounting beam near supports (except when mounts are performed at end of beam).

7. Keep fatigued students off beam.

8. When a board is used to mount beam, remove as soon as performer is on beam and out of the way. If students are practicing mounts, the board does not need to be moved each time.

9. Wear nonrestrictive clothing and proper footwear.

10. Provide definite skill progression for each class.

Note: In the following skills, parts of the body are designated (e.g., "the right foot") for clarity.

TEACHING SUGGESTIONS

Working on the beam requires balance adjustment for the student. Therefore, the following suggestions are offered.

1. Keep beam(s) as low as possible. Use benches or bleachers. Have students stand on beam to attain straight body position. Ask them to move right or left shoulder out of line, and then correct imbalance. Have students move other body parts until awareness of the importance of a straight body is learned.

2. Mark areas on walls for students to spot while working on turns. Eye-spot is important for balance.

3. Turns are generally done on toe. Body should be in correct alignment and total body should lift at time of turn.

4. Concentration is a must; distractions must not be allowed.

5. Students with adequate training can mount and walk the beam slowly—then hop, run, and leap. Skills should never be performed without orientation to space first.

6. One end of beam can be used for mounts while other is used for dismounts.

7. Several students can practice turns at the same time.

Mounts

■FRONT SUPPORT TO STRADDLE SEAT (Fig. B–1)

SL Beginner.

PT Stand facing beam (toward middle); place both hands across beam with fingertips facing away from body. Jump to front support with straight arms, upper thighs resting on beam. As right leg is lifted sideways, up and across beam to straddle position, shift weight to left hand and turn right hand across beam so that heels of hands are together. Then lift left leg to complete straddle position on beam.

    Hint: To learn, allow legs to lower to side of beam and move directly into straddle sitting position. When more abdominal strength is developed and confidence is gained, maintain legs in wide straddle position as above.

SP Stand on opposite side of beam; hold upper arms while in front support to help support and control performer.

CE 1. Failure to allow shoulders to move forward of hand position on beam.

    2. Failure to maintain straight arm and leg position throughout mount.

    3. Failure to shift weight to one hand when going into straddle position.

MO 1. V-seat: Place both hands on beam behind body and lift legs forward. Do not allow head and shoulders to slump.

    2. To squat position: While leaning forward and shifting weight to hands, swing legs downward-backward, then upward to squat position on beam with one foot slightly in front of other. Eyes spot end of beam throughout movement.

Figure B–1

    CE a. Failure to keep arms straight on backswing of legs before feet are placed on beam in squat position.

        b. Failure to lean forward (shoulders over hands) throughout backswing.

        c. Failure to lift heels higher than hips on the backswing before squat position.

■ KNEE-SCALE MOUNT (Fig. B–2)

SL Beginner.

PT Stand facing beam; place both hands across beam. Jump to straight-arm support while simultaneously placing right knee (not shin) on beam. Extend left leg to rear. When springing upward to straight-arm support, allow shoulders to be forward of hand position. For full extension of the knee scale, change hands to opposite grip (fingers pointing toward feet), keep shoulders and head up, and fully extend left leg to rear.

SP Stand to opposite side of beam. Support upper arm and hip area.

CE 1. Failure to use spring from legs for getting into knee position on beam.

    2. Failure to allow shoulders to lean forward of hands on jump to straight-arm support.

    3. Failure to maintain straight arms in knee-scale position.

    4. Failure to keep head and shoulders up.

MO Quarter (90-degree) turn right or left on knee to knee scale parallel to length of beam; pose, then stand.

VA Use vaulting board placed perpendicular to beam. Take running approach into knee-scale mount.

Figure B–2

■SQUAT MOUNT (Fig. B–3)

SL Beginner.

PT Stand facing beam with hands across top of beam. Jump to straight-arm support allowing shoulders to move slightly forward of hand position. Lift knees to chest, then land on beam with both feet between hands in deep squat position. Hold head up at all times.

SP Stand on opposite side of beam and support upper arms, or stand to side of student and grasp upper arm with inside hand and back of upper leg during squatting action.

CE 1. Failure to maintain straight-arm position.

2. Jumping into rather than up and onto beam.

3. Failure to keep hips low when squatting.

MO 1. Quarter (90-degree) turn right or left into pose.

2. Quarter (90-degree) turn right or left into forward roll.

3. Stand, quarter (90-degree) turn right or left into a pose or other locomotor skill.

VA Single leg squat mount.

Figure B–3

■STRADDLE MOUNT (Fig. B–4)

SL Beginner.

PT Jump to straight-arm support, allowing shoulders to move slightly forward of hand position while simultaneously extending legs sideways in wide straddle position. Hold head up and forward.

SP Stand on opposite side of beam and support upper arms.

CE 1. Failure to keep arms straight.

2. Failure to allow shoulders to lean forward of hand position.

3. Failure to lift hips high enough to allow legs to remain straight and for placement on beam.

MO Quarter (90-degree) turn right or left into lunge position; then stand or go into forward roll.

VA 1. Use board placed perpendicular to beam.

    2. Free aerial straddle.

SL Advanced beginner.

PT Same procedures as for straddle mount except that feet do not touch beam; instead, allow them to pass over beam and maintain straddle position across it.

SP One spotter on opposite side of beam to support upper arms. Second spotter steps in from behind performer to make sure performer does not fall backward as legs straddle.

MO Quarter (90-degree) turn maintaining straddle position; sit, go into V-seat, then into backward roll, or swing legs downward-backward and upward to squat position on beam.

Figure B–4

■SINGLE LEG SHOOT THROUGH TO STRIDE LEG POSITION (Fig. B–5)

SL Beginner.

PT Place hands across beam. Jump to straight-arm support while simultaneously lifting hips high enough to allow one leg to bend. Bring knee to chest, then extend leg forward across beam. Other leg remains straight at all times. Keep head and shoulders forward and up.

SP Stand beside student's non-shoot-through leg, grasp upper arm, and support throughout skill.

CE 1. Failure to maintain straight arms.

    2. Failure to allow shoulders to move forward of hand position.

    3. Failure to elevate hips high enough to allow one leg to bend and pass over beam.

    4. Failure to follow through with shoot-through leg (extend knee and thrust leg forward).

5. Allowing shoot-through knee to turn outward rather than lifting directly toward chest.

MO 1. Rest on beam in stride position, quarter (90-degree) turn to V-seat.

2. Rest on beam, quarter (90-degree) turn, backward roll.

3. Rest on beam, quarter (90-degree) turn, swing legs downward-backward and upward to squat position on beam.

Figure B–5

▪ FORWARD-ROLL MOUNT (Usually Done with Vaulting Board Placed at End of Beam) (Fig. B–6)

SL Beginner.

PT At end of beam, place both hands on beam with heels of hands facing each other. While springing from feet, extend arms; elevate hips high enough to tuck head and to place back of neck and upper back on beam. When neck and upper back have contacted beam, immediately shift hands to bottom of beam. Keep elbows close to head and pull with hands to maintain balance. Keep body in piked position and lower body to beam as if trying to make each vertebra contact beam, one after the other.

SP One spotter on each side of beam. Spotter standing beside student lifts thighs to move hips overhead to inverted position. Second spotter helps lower body to beam by grasping student's waist. Second spotter stands to back of student during roll.

CE 1. Failure to maintain straight-arm support and to allow hips to get high enough to tuck head.

2. Not tucking head soon enough.

3. Failure to transfer hands to bottom of beam and to pull to help maintain balance.

4. Failure to remain in pike position while lowering body to beam.

MO 1. To V-seat position.

2. Roll to squat stand; immediately stand.

3. Roll to crotch (straddle) seat position; swing legs downward-backward and upward to squat stand on beam.

4. Roll to squat stand, pose, then stand.

Hips not up high enough

Figure B–6

■ STEP-ON MOUNT (Usually Done Obliquely to or at End of Beam) (Fig. B–7)

SL Beginner.

PT After approaching beam from angle, swing inside leg forward-upward onto beam, followed by outside leg. (Leg action is similar to scissors kick in high jump.) Put second foot on beam slightly in front of first. Extend legs when kicking but immediately tuck to land in squat position. Upper body must be slightly forward to allow momentum to carry body up onto beam. Keep eyes focused forward and upward.

    Hint: To learn this, use hand closest to beam for support until in squat position. Eventually hand should not come in contact with beam.

SP 1. Hold outside hand and run with student, giving added assistance on jump.

    2. Stand on opposite side of beam and reach across beam to grasp student's inside hand and upper arms.

CE 1. Failure to use one-foot takeoff.

    2. Failure to swing inside leg vigorously forward-upward.

    3. Failure to keep momentum going forward by slightly leaning into jump.

    4. Trying to stand too soon on beam after reaching squat position.

MO 1. Immediately stand after balance is attained in squat position.

    2. Pose, then stand.

    3. Forward roll.

    4. High squat jump.

Figure B–7

LOCOMOTOR SKILLS

Locomotor skills are a major part of balance beam performance; however, they are mainly used as transitional and contrasting moves. These skills must be practiced individually starting on a line on the floor, then transferred to a low beam. Spotting for most locomotor skills is usually done to the side of the beam. The spotter walks along or stands by the student and offers an outstretched hand at all times to assist in maintaining balance or preventing a fall. It is important for the spotter to know what skill is being performed and to be alert at all times.

Walks

Both forward and backward walks should be done with an erect body and with abdominals tense and hips tucked under. Lead with the toe to avoid walking flatfooted. Small steps with arms put at a definite position are better than giant steps with arms dangling. Eyes spot end of beam or object at eye level, never down at feet.

Variations of rhythm in walking are important to learn. The walk can start high on toes, then with knees bent slightly for two steps at a lower level. The same steps could be done slow, fast, fast. As confidence is gained with various walks, increase speed gradually into a run.

Hops, Leaps, Jumps

Learn these locomotor skills on the floor first because they require the body to be momentarily lifted above the beam. Toes leave beam last when taking off and contact beam first when landing. These skills are always started in a demi-plié position (slight knee bend with heel off beam) and ended in a demi-plié or some other position that allows for flexion of knees to absorb shock and a smooth landing, and assists in maintaining balance. Upper body is almost always held erect except in skills used to convey certain body lines. Arms are relaxed at shoulders and are also used to assist in gaining the impression of attained height. When the leg goes backwards, turn out is from the hips.

It is important that hops, leaps, and jumps be explosive and show maximum height and full body extension. If skills are for height, movement must start and end in the same vertical plane; if for distance, loss of balance forward occurs before movement is taken forward and upward.

When spotting, stand to side of beam and offer outstretched hand to student at all times. The following are suggested combinations of locomotor skills (reverse foot and arm positions so student does not become one-sided):

1. Step, step hop, run, run, jump into deep squat.
   l   l   r   l   slightly in front of l

2. Grand battement forward, changement, slide, step, cat walk.
             r   r in front   l   l   start with r

3. Run, run, regular leap, run, run, stag leap.
   l   r   l   r   l   r

4. Step, cat walk, step hop, extended forward leg, two steps backward, squat jump.
   r   start l   r   l   l, r

TURNS AND PIROUETTES

Turns are used on the balance beam to change direction and add variety to a routine. Do turns high on balls of feet except in variations. Hold body erect, with head up and shoulders relaxed. Turns should convey a feeling of lightness and continual motion. For balance, the center of gravity must always be over the base of support (feet). Use small steps. Hold arms in definite position and use them to help lift the body to balls of feet when turning. When the leg is lifted in a turn, such as a kick turn, lift it at least parallel to beam. Eye-spotting is important in turning for balance and to prevent dizziness.

Spotting for turns: Stand at side of beam and assist with outstretched hand.

■SQUAT TURN (Fig. B–8)

SL Beginner.

PT Assume deep squat position on balls of feet with one foot slightly in front of other and hips directly above feet. Keep shoulders and head up with slight arch in back. Hold arms out at sides. Lift body slightly and pivot half turn (180 degrees) on balls of feet. Eyes spot other end of beam after turn.

Figure B–8

CE 1. Failure to squat with hips over heels and to maintain this position throughout turn.

2. Failure to keep shoulders directly over hips.

3. Allowing head to tilt forward and down.

4. Failure to eye-spot.

MO 1. Pose, then stand.

2. Forward roll.

3. Squat jump.

4. Immediately stand.

VA *Semisquat turn* (Fig. B–9)

    SL Beginner.

    PT Be careful that upper body does not sag forward. Be conscious of body lines in this position.

Figure B–9

■PIVOT TURN ON TOES (Fig. B–10)

SL Beginner.

PT Stand with one foot slightly in front of other on balls of feet. Keep body erect, head up, and shoulders relaxed. Initiate turn with hips and shoulders and squeeze inner thighs or knees together for balance. Pivot, making half (180-degree) turn, and end facing opposite direction. Arms may be held sideways throughout turn, or hold one arm forward in opposition to front foot and other arm sideways. Eyes spot other end of beam or some object at eye level after turn.

CE 1. Failure to maintain body erect through-
        out turn (if body leans forward, back-
        ward, or sideward, loss of balance
        occurs).

    2. Failure to eye-spot.

    3. Allowing feet to be too far apart on
        turn.

MO 1. Go into any locomotor skill.

    2. Pose.

    3. Step, kick into English handstand, exe-
        cute cartwheel or another tumbling skill.

    4. Go into deep squat position and perform
        arch jump (for distance).

Figure B–10

■BATTEMENT TOURNEY KICK TURN (Fig. B–11)

SL Beginner.
PT Kick right leg forward and upward; twist body to left and pivot on ball of left foot
    making half (180-degree) turn. As turn is completed, carry right leg up high behind
    body. Keep shoulders directly over left foot throughout turn for balance; during
    twisting action, arch back to allow shoulders to remain over foot. End in low ara-
    besque or high arabesque, or go directly into another locomotor skill or some other
    move such as forward roll. Arms may be in second position or go from a natural
    hanging position to fifth position as body twists. Eyes spot stationary object or end
    of beam.

*Note: This turn is usually preceded by a step, chassé,
or glissade.*

CE 1. Allowing shoulders to move backward
        on kick forward and upward.

    2. Allowing shoulders to drop forward after
        turn is completed.

    3. Failure to lift body and turn on toes.

Figure B–11

■LUNGE TURN—JAPANESE TURN—WOLF TURN (Fig. B–12)

SL Intermediate.
PT With one leg squat under body, other leg extended sideways, and arms to side, ex-
    tend leg in opposite direction of turn. Lift body slightly as arms and leg swing in
    direction of turn. Arms vary here depending on body build. Most people, however,
    succeed if arms go to curved overhead position. Others need them at sides of body.

Hips and shoulders must remain balanced over turning foot. To end, place extended leg on beam to side or end in squat position.

CE 1. Allowing shoulders to move forward, backward, or sideward of turning foot.

   2. Not lifting body slightly in initial turn action.

VA 1. Full turn, one-and-a-half turn.

   2. Turn to squat position, three-quarter turn, and stand.

   3. Turn to split.

Figure B—12

STATIC POSITIONS (Fig. B—13)

Poses are held only long enough to show that balance has been achieved in that position. A few of the many static positions are shown below.

Figure B—13

Tumbling and Acrobatic Moves

■FORWARD ROLL (Fig. B-14)

SL Beginner.

PT With one foot slightly in front of other, stretch forward and place both hands across beam (thumb and heel of hand on top of beam, fingers down side of beam). Shift weight to hands while lifting hips above head. Keeping hips forward and upward, start bending elbows, tuck head, and lower to beam to place back of neck and upper shoulder on beam. *Head must go between arms.* As neck and upper shoulder area contact beam, immediately shift hands to grasp under beam and squeeze elbows together (pulling with hands to keep body on beam). Continue rolling forward slowly, maintaining pike position as long as possible (should feel as if each vertebra contacts beam one after the other). Once this skill is learned, hands need not grasp bottom of beam.

Hint: 1. Some students find success starting from knees on beam and then going directly into roll. 2. Do forward roll to position on back. Practice standing up as a separate skill.

SP Stand at side of beam and face student. As arms are bending and head is tucked, grasp hip and waist area and help lower back and hips to beam.

CE 1. Failure to lift hips high enough to allow head to be tucked and placed between arms on the beam.

2. Failure to keep elbows close together and to pull on bottom of beam after shoulders have been placed on beam and hands switched to bottom of beam.

3. Failure to maintain pike position when rolling on back.

4. Rolling too fast.

MO 1. Straddle beam and swing legs downward-backward and upward to squat position, or land in knee scale and go into pose.

2. To V-seat.

3. To single leg squat, pose, then stand.

4. To squat position, pose, then stand.

VA Forward roll from stoop position. In general, requires better than average flexibility.

Figure B-14

■BACKWARD ROLL TO SQUAT (Fig. B-15)

SL Beginner.

PT Maintain balance in supine position. Place thumbs on top of beam under neck, with fingers on side of beam. Some people prefer both hands on bottom of beam in front of head; others prefer one hand on top and other hand on bottom of beam. Lift legs in tuck or pike position (should be straight knees eventually) to overhead position. As hips pass over head, extend arms (push with thumbs and grasp beam with fingers); place foot or feet on beam and finish in squat position, or immediately stand. As soon as head can be lifted, eye-spot end of beam.

SP Two spotters at first, one on each side of beam. Assist student by grasping at waist or hips, or lifting as hips pass over head. May also assist placement of foot or knee on beam before roll is completed.

CE 1. Failure to maintain tuck or pike position when rolling.

2. Failure to push with hands as hips pass over head.

3. Failure to eye-spot end of beam to assist in maintaining balance.

MO 1. End in squat position, pose.

2. End in squat position, half (180-degree) turn, and pose.

3. End in knee scale, sit back on heel, then stand.

4. End in single leg squat position, stand. (Fig. B-15b.)

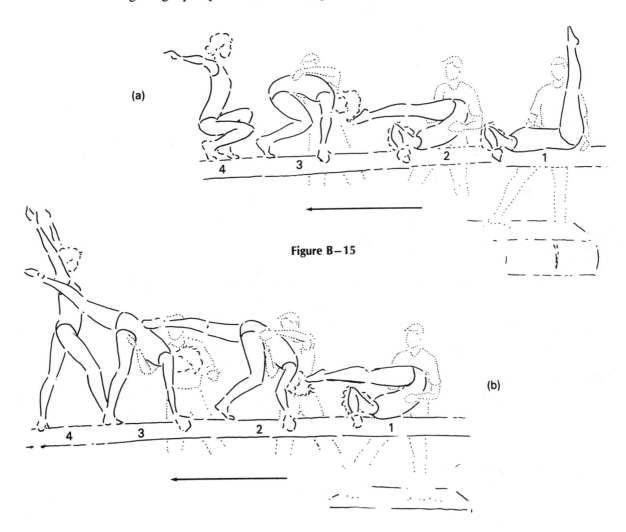

Figure B-15

■BACK SHOULDER ROLL (Fig. B–16)

SL Beginner.

PT From supine position, place head to side of beam so that right shoulder is on beam; adjust balance. Place left hand on top of beam (fingers to side of beam, thumb on top), left arm across neck, and right hand on bottom of beam. Some people prefer to have both hands on top of beam. Lift legs to chest in tuck or pike position and continue rolling over shoulder until head and torso can be lifted upward. Right knee should contact beam, and right hand should be shifted to top of beam. Eyes spot end of beam toward shoulder during roll and shift to other end of beam as roll is completed.

SP Same as for backward roll.

CE 1. Failure to stay in tuck or pike position while rolling backward.

2. Failure to use hands in a push-and-pull fashion to maintain body on beam (bottom hand pulls, top hand pushes).

3. Failure to constantly eye-spot.

MO Same as backward roll.

Figure B–16

■ENGLISH HANDSTAND (Fig. B–17)

SL Beginner.

PT Lift arms overhead while lifting left leg parallel to (or above) beam. Step forward onto left foot, bending knee slightly and supporting majority of body weight. Place hands on beam (heel of hands together, fingers to side of beam) about 18 inches in front of left foot. Shift weight to hands, swing right leg up immediately, then push with second leg. When body reaches inverted position, legs are together and straight, shoulders and hips are fully extended. Eyes spot hands.

SP Spotters on each side of beam. One spotter supports upper arms; other grasps hips to support and control student. If handstand is not attained, tell student to keep arms straight and shift body weight slightly to one side of beam and allow feet to be lowered to floor by spotter.

CE 1. Failure to maintain straight-arm support.

2. Failure to squeeze beam with hands.

3. Too much arch in back.

4. Insufficient swing with first leg, insufficient push with second leg, or both.
5. Failure to extend body fully in inverted position.

Figure B–17

■HANDSTAND FORWARD ROLL (Fig. B–18)

SL Advanced beginner.

PT After attaining full body extension and balance in English handstand, shift hips and shoulders, overbalancing, and pike at last possible moment. Control elbow bend and lower body to beam; tuck head and place back of neck and upper shoulder area on beam between arms. As soon as upper shoulder area contacts beam, transfer hands to bottom of beam. Maintain pike position and continue to roll.

SP Grasp hips to support and maintain control while student lowers to beam and rolls.

CE 1. Failure to shift hips and shoulders slightly backward when beginning to lower body to beam.

2. Failure to lower body to beam in same vertical plane that handstand was in (shoulders should not move forward of hands).

3. Failure to keep legs well behind head (tight pike) momentarily after upper back contacts beam.

4. Failure to control elbow bend (either too fast or too slow).

MO Same as for forward roll.

Figure B–18

■CARTWHEEL (Left) (Fig. B–19)

SL Advanced beginner.

PT Lift arms overhead while simultaneously lifting left leg at least parallel to beam. Step forward onto left foot, bending knee slightly and shifting body weight to that leg. Begin swinging right leg up and immediately place left hand across beam (heel of hand toward center of beam). Push off beam with left leg. Just before body reaches inverted position, place right hand on beam, shoulder width apart from left. Right foot should contact beam closer to right hand than in a regular cartwheel on the floor. Right leg should bend slightly upon landing. Left hand should push off beam slightly before right foot lands on beam. Left leg continues as right leg extends (straighten knee) and right hand is removed from beam. After completion of skill, entire body should be facing toward end of beam. Eyes spot hands on beam when inverting and look at end of beam or stationary object at eye level as body is raised.

SP Stand on stacked mats (if necessary) to reach hips and help student complete cartwheel successfully.

CE 1. Placing hands on beam before beginning kicking action.

2. Failure to kick legs through vertical plane (many tend to pike).

3. Failure to step forward and shift weight to bent forward leg after preparatory leg and arm lift.

4. Failure to place hands fairly close together (when learning).

5. Failure to straighten up immediately after first foot contacts beam. (Students tend to feel that they can maintain balance by staying low and delaying hand releases from the beam; however, their center of gravity is too high to maintain balance, so it is more advantageous to raise upper body as soon as possible.)

MO 1. Go into lunge position.

2. Bring back leg forward and continue walking, or pose, or turn on toes.

3. Go into pose.

Figure B–19

■BACK WALKOVER (Fig. B–20)

SL Low intermediate.

PT (For details refer to tumbling section in Chapter 4.) Master on floor first. The back walkover seems to be easier to learn than the front walkover because the eyes can spot beam and students can see where they are going.

SP Stand with back to student's back. With palms up, grasp hip area with thumbs pointing toward each other and fingers grasping outer hip area. As hands contact beam and hips are passing over hands, force wrists in opposite direction to assist in shifting weight past the hands.

Figure B–20

DISMOUNTS

Landing for all dismounts should be with slight hip, knee, and ankle flexion to absorb shock and to maintain balance. Land first on balls of feet. For safety reasons, it is advisable to have two spotters when first learning most dismounts. Make sure there are sufficient mats beside or at the end of the beam where dismounts will be performed. For more difficult dismounts, use a landing mat.

■ARCH JUMP DISMOUNT (Fig. B–21)

SL Beginner.

PT Stand sideways on beam. Bend knees and spring up and forward. While suspended, keep upper body erect. Keep head up and eye-spot stationary object at eye level throughout skill.

SP Stand beside beam and student. Have outstretched hand ready to grasp student's hand if assistance is needed.

CE 1. Failure to keep upper body erect.

2. Failure to push off balls of feet to gain maximum elevation.

3. Jumping out too far or not far enough.

4. Failure to keep body fairly straight while in air.

5. Not landing in steady position with feet shoulder distance apart, hips and knees slightly flexed.

Figure B–21 Land with feet directly under hips and shoulders, knees, hips, and ankles flexed to absorb the shock of landing

■ ROUND-OFF DISMOUNT (End of Beam) (Fig. B–22)

SL Beginner.

PT Stand about 2½ feet from end of beam, facing end. Lift right leg upward as arms go overhead. Step onto right foot, shifting weight to that foot, and begin swinging left leg backward-upward. Place both hands together on beam with fingers (of both hands) going down right side of beam. Push with right foot and bring both legs together in inverted position. Make half turn with entire body, pike at hips

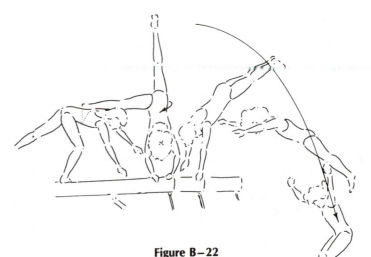

Figure B–22

slightly, and push off beam with both hands. As feet contact mat, bend knees and hips slightly, eye-spot end of beam. When skill has been learned, there should be a total lift of body off beam before landing.

SP Stand to lunge leg side of student, grasp upper arms as they are placed on beam, and maintain contact until feet are on mat.

CE 1. Failure to maintain straight arms throughout skill.

    2. Not achieving handstand position before turning.

    3. Failure to push off beam with hands.

■ CARTWHEEL QUARTER-TURN DISMOUNT (Fig. B–23)

SL Beginner.

PT Stand approximately 3 feet from end of beam. Lift arms and right leg. Lunge forward on right bent leg, and place hands on beam to right side (close together) while kicking left leg. Immediately push with right leg to get body to handstand position. When body is sideways and vertical, bring legs together. As body continues past vertical plane, push and release right hand, turn head to right, and push off with left hand, keeping both arms overhead. Land with back to beam, bending knees and hips slightly to absorb shock.

SP Stand to back of student and grasp rib cage to waist area as body is in inverted position ready to make quarter turn. Another spotting technique is to grasp wrist of second hand placed on beam (that near the end) and spot hip area with other hand.

CE 1. Too much momentum developed from leg kick-push action, causing lack of control and falling forward on landing.

    2. Failure to pass through vertical position, causing landing to be off to side of beam.

    3. Allowing head and upper body to drop forward on landing.

Figure B–23

Beginning Routine for Balance Beam (Fig. B—24)

1. Squat mount, quarter-turn body wave.
2. Step hop, pose.
3. Run run leap.
4. Pivot turn, pose.
5. Forward roll to squat.
6. Stand, side lunge.
7. Pose, quarter-turn.
8. Round-off dismount.

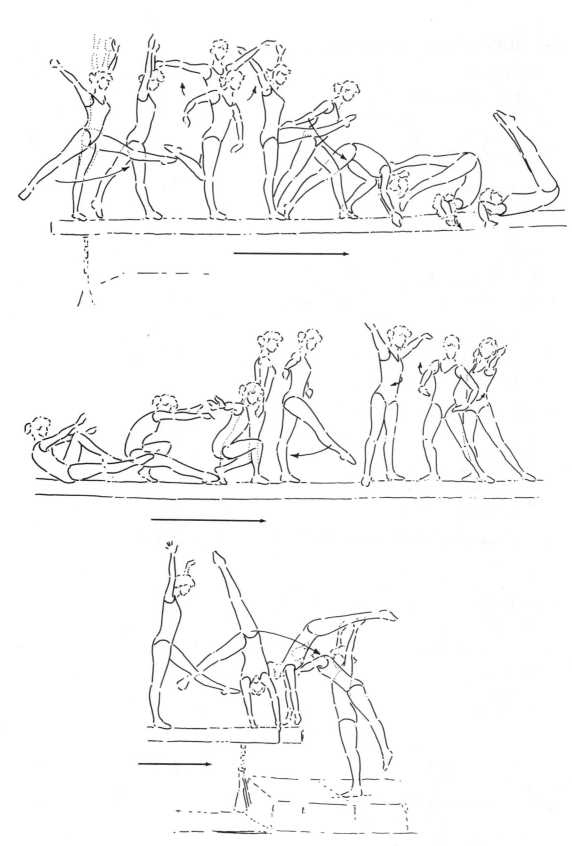

Figure B-24

178

▲ TEST QUESTIONS—*BALANCE BEAM*

1. Which of the following would *not* be considered a basic mount on the beam?
   a. front support to straddle seat.
   b. step-on.
   c. forward roll.
   d. handstand.

2. Locomotor skills include all but one of the following?
   a. step hop.
   b. leap.
   c. chainé.
   d. walks.

3. Which of the following best describes spotting for a forward roll?
   a. face performer, grasp hip area.
   b. behind performer, grasp hip area.
   c. to side, grasp neck and back.
   d. to side, grasp arm and hip.

4. Which of the following dismounts require the least amount of control by the performer?
   a. cartwheel.
   b. arch jump.
   c. round-off.
   d. cartwheel, quarter turn.

5. When working on the beam, it is most important for the spotter to be
   a. friendly.
   b. strong.
   c. passive.
   d. alert.

6. Which of the following walks is used on the beam?
   a. dance.
   b. fast.
   c. flatfooted.
   d. ordinary.

7. Successful turns on the beam are the result of all but one of the following:
   a. hips over feet.
   b. counterbalance of arms and legs on open turns.
   c. shoulders in front of feet.
   d. total body alignment.

8. Momentum is developed on the forward roll when the
   a. hands touch the beam.
   b. arms stretch forward.
   c. hips are raised.
   d. head is tucked between the arms on the beam.

9. We are concerned with proper body alignments on the beam because
   a. the spotter will not have to assist.
   b. of aesthetic beauty.
   c. skills can be performed efficiently.
   d. Proper body alignment is not a concern.

10. Which of the following mounts does *not* require the same beginning foot position on takeoff?
    a. squat on.
    b. single leg squat.
    c. front support.
    d. step-on from oblique.

BALANCE BEAM	Name:

Front Support to Straddle Seat

Sufficient hip lift _____

Arms straight _____

Thighs resting on beam with control _____

Leg lifted straight to sit in straddle on beam _____

Score _____

Straddle Mount

Sufficient vertical jump _____

Hips high before straddle attained _____

Place feet on beam in straddle _____

Arms straight, shoulders forward _____

Head up throughout _____

Score _____

Knee-Scale Mount

Sufficient vertical jump to place knee on beam _____

Arms straight, shoulder forward of hands _____

Leg extended to rear _____

Head and shoulders up _____

Hand grasp reversed _____

Score _____

Shoot Through to Stride

Sufficient vertical jump _____

Hip lift sufficient to allow one leg to extend over beam _____

Arms straight throughout extension _____

Head and shoulders extend forward and up _____

Score _____

Squat Mount

Sufficient vertical jump _____

Hips high before squatting _____

Arms straight _____

Feet placed on beam simultaneously _____

Hips lowered as feet contact beam _____

Head up throughout _____

Score _____

Forward Roll Mount

Hand placement on end of beam _____

Hip lift adequate to allow for head tuck _____

Hands grasp bottom of beam simultaneous with body pike _____

Elbows close to head _____

Score _____

Step-on Mount

Adequate push off from board _____

Step up continual _____

Upper body lift forward and continual _____

Legs extended _____

Balance maintained _____

Score _____

Chassé (Gallop)

Lead leg remains front _____

Slight plié when legs together _____

Vertical lift of both feet _____

Landing with control _____

Body with slight lean forward _____

Score _____

(Continued)

BALANCE BEAM *(Continued)*

Forward Walk	**Squat Turn**
Body erect, hips tucked under _____	On toes _____
Toe lead _____	Chest erect _____
Walk with rhythm _____	Turn with continual motion _____
Score _____	Head up throughout _____
	Score _____
Backward Walk	**Pivot Turn**
Body erect _____	On toes _____
Hips tucked under _____	Body erect _____
Toe touches beam first _____	Turn continual _____
Walk with rhythm _____	Score _____
Score _____	
Step Hop (Skip)	**English Handstand**
Step with toe lead _____	Body extended in step through to lunge _____
Slight knee bend before extension _____	Hand placement adequate distance from feet _____
Bent leg with toe pointed in hop _____	Kick-push to vertical with control _____
Rhythm continual _____	Return to lunge position _____
Score _____	Arms by head throughout _____
	Score _____
Wolf Turn	**Battement Tourney**
Body lifted slightly as turn initiated _____	Body erect during leg lift _____
Swing leg straight throughout _____	Chest erect during half turn _____
Chest and head up _____	Arabesque position attained _____
Hips balanced over squat leg _____	Score _____
Score _____	
Forward Roll	**Handstand Forward Roll**
Hands placed on beam sufficiently forward of feet _____	Body extended in step through to lunge _____
Hips elevated, legs extended _____	Hand placement adequate distance from feet _____
Head tucked between arms _____	Kick-push to vertical adequate _____
Hand shift to bottom, elbows in _____	Elbow bend, body lowered to beam with control _____
Body move to pike on back with control _____	Body in pike on beam _____
Stand with control _____	Score _____
Score _____	

(Continued)

BALANCE BEAM *(Continued)*

Backward Roll	*Cartwheel*
Body piked on back _____	Body extended in step through to lunge _____
Hands on top of beam _____	Hands placed to side on beam _____
Legs move to piked position with control _____	Adequate kick-push to pass through vertical _____
As toes touch beam, arm pushed and extended _____	Chest lift and leg lowered simultaneously _____
Finish in squat position _____	
Score _____	Score _____
Back Shoulder Roll	*Back Walkover*
Proper hand grasp _____	Body extended before backward movement _____
Body piked on back _____	Hips held over base foot _____
Knee on beam simultaneous with leg extension upward _____	Lead leg vertical as hands make contact _____
Arms extended _____	Stretch in shoulders in vertical _____
Head and chest lifted _____	End in stretched lunge _____
Score _____	Score _____
Round-off Dismount	*Cartwheel, Quarter Turn Dismount*
Step through to lunge allows for extended body into hand placement on beam _____	Step through to lunge allows for extended body into hand placement on beam _____
Explosive kick-push of legs _____	Kick-push adequate _____
Arms straight in vertical _____	Arms straight _____
Body extended in afterflight _____	Push off supporting arm _____
Landing with control, slight knee and hip flexion _____	Quarter turn out in air _____
	Landing with control _____
Score _____	Score _____
Jump Dismount	*Final Score* _____
Body stretched before landing _____	*Final Grade* _____
Landing light with slight hip and knee flexion _____	
Score _____	

Comments:

Chapter
9

Parallel Bars

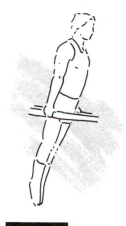

Parallel bars offer the student a great variety of movements. Swinging and static skills while in various support and hang positions are executed at the ends and in the center of the bars. Some skills move forward and backward along the length of the bars.

Upper body strength is extremely important, as are shoulder, hip, and hamstring flexibility. Students should engage in daily conditioning exercises to develop these areas.

_____

A grading sheet for parallel bar skills appears at the end of this chapter.

SAFETY HINTS

1. Prior to each use, check the bar supports to make sure they are secure.

2. Surround the bars with mats; cover all exposed metal base areas, making sure to cover an area adequate for mounts and dismounts.

3. Students should apply chalk to their hands before mounting the bars.

4. Adjust the width of the bars each time to accommodate the student. Generally, the distance between student's elbow and middle finger is correct. This is simply and quickly accomplished by holding either arm between the bars and adjusting accordingly.

5. Basic skills, and many advanced skills, should be mastered on the low parallel bars for safety and ease of spotting.

To become acquainted with basic parallel bar skills, the beginning student must be able to support his or her body weight comfortably in the following positions:

Support Position Skills

PB-1   Straddle seat.
PB-2   Front hand support.
PB-3   L support.
PB-4   Upper arm support.
PB-5   Bent hip, upper arm support.

As an added safety measure, students should master basic skills on the parallel bars set low, approximately waist high. To accommodate shorter students, stacked mats can be placed between the bars so that the bars are at waist height.

▇STRADDLE SEAT (Fig. PB–1)

SL Beginner.

PT Stand between bars near center, grip bars, jump up straightening arms (lock elbows), and swing legs forward by flexing hips. As legs swing above bar level, straddle legs, placing back of thighs on bars. Keep knees straight with body erect. Most of body weight is supported by back and inner part of thighs. Hands are mainly used for balance. This can be considered a rest position.

SP Spotting is not critical with bars set low. This is a relatively simple position to assume. Verbal correction may be made, such as "straighten knees."

CE 1. Failure to keep knees straight and toes pointed.

2. Failure to keep arms locked and body erect.

MO 1. Forward shoulder roll.

2. Shoulder stand.

Figure PB–1

■ FRONT HAND SUPPORT (Fig. PB–2)

SL Beginner.

PT This position may be assumed at either end or any portion between ends of bars. Standing at center or end of bars, grip bars, jump up, and straighten arms, extending elbows and shoulders. Body is in vertical position supported by arms.

SP Same as for straddle seat.

CE 1. Failure to keep elbows locked.

2. Failure to keep shoulders extended, causing poor posture and making it difficult to maintain position.

Figure PB–2

■ L SUPPORT (Fig. PB–3)

SL Beginner.

PT From front hand support, raise legs by flexing hips while keeping arms and shoulders extended. Legs should be parallel to length of bars, knees straight with toes pointed. Maintain this position three to five seconds comfortably.

SP Same as for straddle seat. Verbal correction may be needed for proper positioning. If there is insufficient hip flexor and abdominal strength, legs will simply return to vertical position. If arms collapse, student will come to stand between bars. The movement itself will help strengthen the hip flexors.

CE Same as 1–2 of front hand support.

MO Straddle seat.

Figure PB–3

■ UPPER ARM SUPPORT (Fig. PB–4)

SL Beginner.

PT Stand between bars, jump up, swing arms forward-upward. Land on under part of upper arms (biceps) with elbows bent, gripping bars firmly with hands. Push elbows down to keep shoulders from shrugging. Body is in vertical position below bars.

SP Spotting, again, is not critical. For shorter students, bars may be lowered.

CE   1. Failure to push elbows down toward mat, causing difficulty in maintaining position.

   2. Failure to fully grip bars with hands.

   3. Failure to keep head and body erect.

   4. Poor form.

MO   1. Swing.

   2. Swing to bent hip upper arm support.

Figure PB–4

■ UPPER ARM SUPPORT IN PIKE POSITION (Fig. PB–5)

SL Beginner.

PT From upper arm support position, swing legs forward-upward elevating hips above bars by flexing hips. At same time, forcefully push downward with hands on bars from shoulders. Look directly at knees. This will keep head in proper position.

SP Stand to left side, place left hand on lower back, right hand on upper back, palms up. As legs swing forward and upward, push upward with left hand to keep student's hips overhead. Right hand supports upper back.

CE   1. Failure to push down on bars with hands and force elbows toward mat. This action helps to lift hips above bars and prevents shoulders from sagging.

   2. Allowing head to drop back, which causes loss of orientation.

   3. Failure to lift hips above bars, which requires more strength to maintain position.

MO   1. Kip to straddle seat or hand support.

   2. Cast to upper arm support and swing to back uprise.

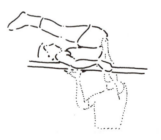

Figure PB–5

Low Parallel Bars Skills

■ HAND TRAVEL FORWARD (Fig. PB–6a) AND BACKWARD (Fig. PB–6b)

SL Beginner.

PT This skill is an excellent exercise to test and develop supportive strength. It also acquaints beginner with moving along length of bars forward and backward. Assume front support position just inside uprights. Move forward along bars by shifting body weight from hand to hand while reaching forward. Transfer weight from side to side with body held in tight vertical position. After reaching far uprights of bars, move backward in same manner. Movement backward may be performed separately if rest is needed.

SP Spotting is not necessary with this particular skill as bars are low. If arms collapse, student should jump to standing position while moving arms overhead so that arms do not hit bars.

CE 1. Failure to maintain good front hand support position.

2. Failure to keep elbows locked.

3. Trying to move forward and backward too quickly, causing loss of control.

4. Looking back when traveling backward.

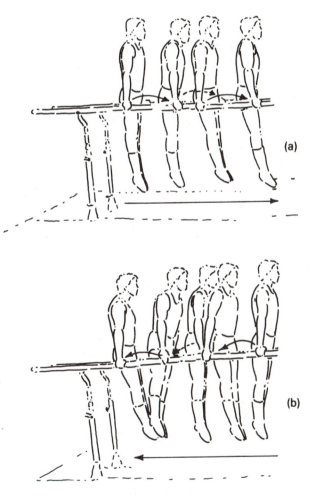

Figure PB–6

■STRADDLE TRAVEL FORWARD (Fig. PB–7a) AND BACKWARD (Fig. PB–7b)

SL   Beginner.

PT   Stand at end of bars. Grip bars, jump to hand support, and swing legs forward to straddle seat. Reach forward and grip bars while leaning forward from shoulders. At the same time, tense gluteal muscles, lift legs behind body, and bring legs together. Swing legs forward again to straddle seat, and repeat. Usually three straddle travels in either direction bring student from one end of bars to other.

    The straddle travel backward is initiated by gripping bars behind body, lifting legs from bars, and bringing feet together. As legs swing down, lean forward from shoulders and swing legs back. Student must "feel" when legs are high enough on backswing to clear bars and should then straddle legs. Inner thighs contact bar first. Regrip bars behind body, repeat movement.

CE   1. Failure to keep elbows locked for maximum body support.

     2. Failure to keep knees straight at all times.

     3. Failure to look forward at all times.

Figure PB–7

■ FORWARD SHOULDER ROLL—STRADDLE SEAT TO STRADDLE SEAT (Fig. PB-8)

SL Beginner.

PT From straddle seat in center of bars, grip bars directly in front of thighs. Bend forward, bringing shoulders down to bars. At the same time, lift hips overhead, keeping legs straddled. At this point, thighs should clear bars. Force elbows out from body as roll forward is slowly begun across uppermost part of arms. When hips start to drop, release bars and reach forward gripping bars again before thighs contact bars. As thighs touch bars, push down with hands to finish in straddle seat position. Keep body in tight pike position, legs straddled with knees straight throughout entire roll.

SP Stand at left side, place right hand, palm up, on lower left thigh and push up to lift hips. As student begins to roll across upper arms, reach under bars with both hands, palms up, on student's back to momentarily support body through roll and release and regrasp student's hands.

CE 1. Failure to maintain legs straddled and hips in tight pike position throughout roll.

2. Failure to force elbows out from body during roll causing shoulders to slip through bars.

3. Failure to lift hips sufficiently to initiate roll forward.

Figure PB-8

■ BACKWARD SHOULDER ROLL—STRADDLE SEAT TO STRADDLE SEAT (Fig. PB-9)

SL Beginner.

PT From straddle seat, grip bars directly behind thighs. Lower upper body backward slowly to rest on upper arms. Elbows must be away from body. At the same time, lift legs overhead by pushing down on bars with hands and flexing hips maximally. At this point, body is actually in bent hip upper arm support with legs straddled. Keep forcing legs and hips behind head. When student feels hips dropping further behind head, release bars and reach directly behind shoulders to regrasp bars. Most of body weight is momentarily on hands now. As inner thighs contact bars, forcefully extend arms by pushing down on bars, lifting head and chest, and finish in straddle seat position.

SP Stand at left, reach under bars with both hands, palms up. As upper body lowers backward, place left hand on lower back, right hand on upper back. Spotter now is able to help lift hips to initiate backward roll by pushing up. This hand placement also allows spotter to support and control student throughout entire roll backward.

CE 1. Failure to lift hips overhead to initiate roll backward.

2. Failure to maintain tight pike position with straight knees throughout roll.

3. Releasing hands too soon, causing hips to fall forward.

4. Dropping head back too soon, causing loss of orientation.

Figure PB—9

■SHOULDER STAND (Fig. PB—10)

SL Beginner.

PT Same preparation as for forward shoulder roll. When hips are directly overhead with most of body weight on shoulders, extend hips and bring legs together overhead. Hands gripping bars are used primarily to maintain balance. Look directly at mat below.

SP Stand on stacked mats or similar device, if necessary. Standing to left, place right hand, palm up, on left thigh to lift and position hips overhead. As legs come together, place left hand with right hand around left thigh to help achieve balance. Spotter will also prevent overbalancing causing too fast a roll forward, or underbalancing causing student to fall back toward bars.

CE 1. Failure to keep hips directly overhead.

2. Failure to keep elbows out from body making balancing more difficult and placing too much weight on hands instead of shoulders.

3. Allowing body to sag (body over-arched).

MO 1. Roll forward to straddle seat.

2. Forward shoulder roll.

3. Push up to front hand support position.

Figure PB—10

■SWING TO SHOULDER STAND (Fig. PB–11)

SL Beginner.

PT From basic swing in hand support, just prior to peak of backswing, bend arms, lowering shoulders, forward of hands, to bars. Keep body tight and hips extended. Feet should be directly overhead as shoulders contact bars and settle. Balancing is the same as for shoulder stand from straddle seat. With most of body weight on shoulders, hands are used to maintain balance.

SP Stand to left side on stacked mats or similar equipment. As student's legs swing back and arms bend, place right hand on front of left thigh. Place left hand on back of left thigh and elevate hips overhead to maintain balance once shoulders settle on bars.

CE 1. Failure to generate a sufficient backswing.

2. Lowering shoulders to bars too soon.

3. Bending hips while lowering shoulders to bars.

4. Placing shoulders on bars too close to hands.

5. Too much backswing, causing student to roll forward through a shoulder stand.

Figure PB–11

■BASIC SWING IN HAND SUPPORT (Fig. PB–12)

SL Beginner.

PT Basic swing in hand support is extremely important and mastery is required prior to learning numerous skills that originate from basic swing. Student must have sufficient arm and shoulder strength to learn this skill. If front hand support position cannot be maintained easily, student will be unable to learn basic swing correctly. From front hand support, swing body forward and backward. As body swings forward, lean slightly backward from shoulders. As body swings backward, lean slightly forward from shoulders. Swing should originate from shoulders, not hips. Swing only as high as swing remains smooth and control can be maintained. Practice will enable a higher swing.

SP Stand to left side. If student appears to be "shaky," place left hand around upper arm and right hand around forearm to keep elbow locked. Two spotters may be used, one at each side. If two spotters are needed, student is probably not ready for this skill. Spotting is not critical if student has sufficient strength and bars are set low. Instructor must use judgment.

CE 1. Failure to keep arms locked and swing from shoulders.

2. Failure to extend from shoulders and keep head erect.

3. Swinging too high when first attempting basic swing.

MO 1. Swing to shoulder stand.

2. Front dismount.

3. Rear dismount.

Figure PB–12

■ FRONT DISMOUNT (Fig. PB–13)

Note: Because the front of the body passes over the bar, this dismount is termed a front dismount even though it is performed on the backswing. Wherever possible, the student's position is determined relative to the apparatus.

SL Beginner.

PT Just prior to peak of backswing, transfer weight to right arm, pushing off left bar with left hand. As front of body passes over right bar, regrip right bar with left hand. Transfer body weight to left hand. Release bar with right hand and lift sideward-upward. Keep lifting head and chest by pushing down with left hand forcing feet down to a stand, with left hip facing bar and left hand still gripping right bar.

SP Stand slightly forward to right. Place left hand on upper right arm. Just after the body passes vertical phase of swing, place right hand on abdomen and help lift body over bar, if needed.

CE 1. Failure to keep legs swinging up and to right side through weight transfer from arm to arm.

2. Failure to keep elbows straight.

3. Failure to keep body and knees completely extended throughout dismount.

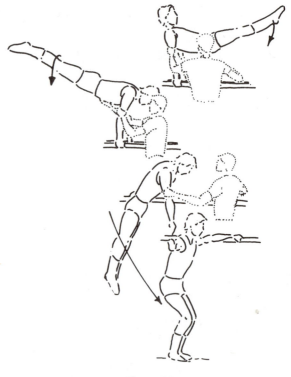

Figure PB–13

■ REAR DISMOUNT WITH 90-DEGREE TURN OUTWARD (Fig. PB–14)

SL Beginner.

PT This dismount is performed on front swing. Hips should be slightly flexed through vertical phase of swing. As body swings forward-upward, transfer body weight onto right arm and push forcefully off with left hand, releasing left bar. Lift left arm upward and to right side. Extend hips and turn 90 degrees outward to right. Continue pivoting body to right around right arm. Make final effort to push bar behind body with right hand prior to releasing bar and landing on mat. Back is to longitudinal axis of bar at completion of dismount.

SP Stand at right side, grasp upper right arm. As body passes vertical phase of swing, reach over bar and place left hand on lower back. As student swings forward-upward, lift and turn hips outward over bar with left hand.

CE 1. Failure to push off with left hand.

2. Failure to keep right arm straight (locked at the elbow) throughout dismount.

3. Failure to turn hips outward while swinging over right bar.

Figure PB—14

■REAR DISMOUNT WITH 180-DEGREE TURN OUTWARD (Fig. PB—15)

SL Beginner.

PT Same as for rear dismount with 90-degree turn, except student must be more aggressive while turning hips outward (to right), pushing off with left hand, and pivoting around right arm. Since right hand and arm are more supinated, push forcefully downward with right hand, hop slightly, turning right hand to right, and immediately regrasp bar. This quick release and regrasp is made at peak of turn to right around right arm and shoulder.

SP Same as for rear dismount with 90-degree turn, with one addition: place more emphasis on supporting student's right arm in case it collapses, causing a possible fall forward toward spotter.

CE 1. Failure to be aggressive through all phases of movement.

2. Failure to keep right arm locked at elbow.

3. Failure to keep body extended throughout turn to landing.

Figure PB—15

■CARTWHEEL DISMOUNT FROM SHOULDER STAND (Fig. PB—16)

SL Beginner.

PT From solid shoulder stand at center of bars, transfer most of body weight to right shoulder allowing body to begin "falling" directly to right over right bar. At the same time, push off left bar with left hand. As body continues to "fall away" to right side, push down and away from right bar with right hand. Body must remain extended at hips with right hand gripping right bar until feet contact mat to a stand.

SP Stand to right and slightly forward of student's back while in shoulder stand position. Place left hand on student's left hip, right hand on right hip. As student "peels off" to right, lift slightly and pull directly sideward. This gives spotter complete control throughout dismount.

CE 1. Failure to assume good shoulder stand position, body extended, tight, with legs together and knees straight.
2. Failure to keep legs together throughout dismount.
3. Allowing hips to bend before landing.
4. Failure to push down and away from bar with right hand.

Figure PB—16

■SINGLE LEG STRADDLE DISMOUNT (Fig. PB—17)

SL Beginner.

PT Assume front hand support at end of bars facing out. Using moderate basic swing, lean forward a bit more than normal as body moves behind head on backswing. At peak of backswing, separate legs with right leg moving over and outside right bar.

At the same time, transfer upper body weight to left arm. Push down on bars with both hands. Release right bar with right hand as right leg is snapped forward over right bar. It is important to snap right leg forward by flexing right hip; student should not rotate hip outward, causing circling movement of right leg. Swing left leg forward in between bars. Make final push off with left hand to lift chest as right leg clears bar. Legs should come together just prior to landing on mat to a stand.

SP Stand directly to left side and grasp left upper arm. As right leg cuts forward, reach over bar placing right hand, palm up, on back of uppermost left thigh. Spotter's left hand may help support left arm, or pull arm slightly forward, depending on student's movements. This enables spotter to maintain control of upper body. The right hand, by lifting momentarily to support the lower body, enables student to complete cut forward of right leg. Whether these actions are necessary depends on how well the skill is executed.

CE 1. Leaning excessively on left arm during weight transfers.

2. Leaning too far forward from shoulders during backswing.

3. Failure to keep one or both arms and legs straight.

4. Waiting too long to cut right leg forward (cut not synchronized with proper segment of backswing).

5. Rotating right hip outward instead of flexing hip to cut leg forward.

6. Failure to push off bars with one or both hands at proper time.

7. Failure to lift chest prior to landing on mat to a stand.

Figure PB–17

■DOUBLE LEG STRADDLE DISMOUNT (Forward) (Fig. PB-18)

SL Intermediate beginner.

PT Before attempting this dismount, student should be able to execute single leg cut dismount to either side. Using moderate basic swing, lean forward a bit more than normal as body moves behind head on backswing. At peak of backswing, separate (straddle) legs, moving them over and outside bars. Flex hips to allow both legs to snap forward. Push down forcefully with both hands and release bars. Lift arms forward-upward, lifting head and chest as legs complete straddle forward. Legs should be together on landing.

SP Stand to one side and in front of student, close enough to grasp upper arms just after vertical phase of swing. Grasp right arm with left hand, left arm with right hand. As student starts to straddle, lift and pull forward. This enables spotter to maintain control of student through critical phase of dismount.

CE 1. Leaning too far forward from shoulders during backswing.

2. Failure to keep arms and legs straight.

3. Failure to straddle legs at peak of backswing.

4. Failure to straddle legs forward forcefully.

5. Straddle not synchronized with backswing.

6. Failure to forcefully push off bars with hands and lift chest.

Figure PB-18

■SINGLE LEG STRADDLE CUT MOUNT (Fig. PB-19)

SL Beginner.

PT Stand at end of bars, facing in. Place hands on bars. With a jump, push down on bars, straightening arms. Immediately transfer weight to right arm and release left hand from left bar. At the same time, move left leg outward to left side of bar and straddle left leg forward over left bar. Swing right leg directly forward between both bars. Join right leg to left leg as straddling movement is completed, and regrasp bar with left hand. Finishing position should be same as completion of moderate front swing.

SP Stand to right side, place right hand on upper right arm. Place left hand, palm up, on back of uppermost right thigh just after right leg swings directly forward and as left leg straddles left bar. With right hand, exert lifting movement to keep right elbow locked and control upper body. With left hand, exert lifting movement to momentarily support hips during critical straddle of left leg over left bar. Some spotters find it easier to spot this skill the same as for the double leg cut mount. Both techniques work equally well.

CE 1. Failure to initially push down on bars with both hands.

2. Failure to keep right arm straight.

3. Failure to swing right leg forward as left leg straddles left bar.

4. Failure to keep legs straight.

5. Leaning back too far from shoulders as mount is completed, causing loss of balance backward.

MO Finish mount to immediate L-seat position.

Figure PB–19

■DOUBLE LEG STRADDLE CUT MOUNT (Fig. PB–20)

SL Intermediate beginner.

PT Before attempting this mount, student should be able to perform single leg straddle mount to either side. Stand at end of bars, facing in. Place hands on bars and, with a jump, push down forcefully, releasing bars with both hands. At the same time, straddle legs outside of both bars and immediately snap legs forward by flexing hips. As straddle is completed, regrasp both bars. Finishing position should be the same as a momentary L-seat in hand support.

SP Stand directly behind student, place hands on hips. As body straddles forward, lift hips to momentarily give support through release and regrasp of bars.

CE 1. Failure to forcefully push down on bars.

2. Failure to aggressively straddle legs forward.

3. Failure to keep legs straight.

4. Allowing shoulders to lean back too far on regrasp, causing loss of balance backward.

MO Regrasp bars in L-seat position and hold.

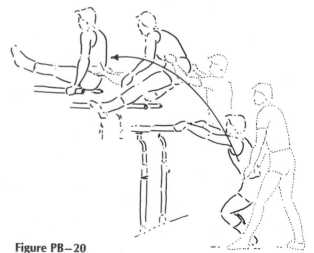

Figure PB–20

Skills with Bars at Regulation Height

■ DROP KIP TO STRADDLE SEAT (Mount) (Fig. PB–21)

SL Intermediate beginner.

PT Stand at end of bars with hands on bars. Feet should be directly under hands. Jump upward pressing down on bars with straight arms and lean backward from shoulders. Immediately flex hips (pike) forcefully to raise legs. The position at this point is similar to the bent hip hang performed on rings. Hold this position as hips swing freely downward and forward. At peak of forward swing, flex hips more tightly. This action enables student to be more explosive with the actual kipping phase. As hips swing down and begin to swing backward, forcefully extend hips, causing legs to move forward and upward at 45-degree angle. At the same moment, press forcefully downward on bars with hands, and open legs to finish in straddle seat position. Entire movement from start to finish should be executed with arms straight.

SP Stand to left side of student and place hands on back and hip. As kipping phase of skill is initiated, lift with right hand to bring upper body above bars. Left hand also imparts a lifting motion to hip area. Just before legs straddle bars, quickly join left to right hand onto student's back. This prevents spotter's left hand from becoming trapped against bar by student's left thigh. Two spotters may be used, the second spotter standing on opposite side.

CE 1. Failure to keep legs and arms straight during entire movement.

2. Extending hips too soon. Hips must be moving back before kipping phase can be executed.

3. Failure to press down on bars forcefully with hands at beginning of skill and at actual moment of kip.

MO 1. Forward shoulder roll to straddle seat.

2. Shoulder stand.

Figure PB–21

■ DROP KIP TO FRONT HAND SUPPORT (Fig. PB–22)

SL Advanced beginner.

PT Same as for drop kip to straddle seat, except that legs stay together and performer finishes kip in hand support position. Drop kip to straddle seat is an excellent lead up to this skill, primarily from a safety standpoint. By finishing in straddle seat position, student avoids any possibility of arms buckling at finish of kip. In this way, student can concentrate on perfecting timing and proper technique involved in executing kip.

SP Same as for drop kip to straddle seat, except left hand is lower on back of left thigh. Left hand also lifts and supports hips until student is in control of hand support position.

MO 1. Swing to shoulder stand.

2. Swing to shoulder roll forward to upper arm support.

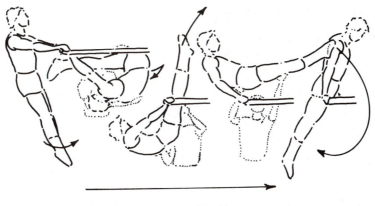

Figure PB−22

■ UPPER ARM KIP TO STRADDLE SEAT (Fig. PB−23)

SL Beginner.

PT Jump to upper arm support in center of bars and initiate basic swing. As body swings forward, flex hips, raising legs directly overhead. It is important to elevate hips at least level with, and preferably above, bars, maintaining tightly piked position. Push down on bars with arms and hands to elevate hips. Once in this position, extend hips forcefully, driving legs forward-upward to 45-degree angle. Just as kipping action occurs, straddle legs. Press down on bars forcefully with hands to raise head and chest above bars. Finish in straddle seat position.

SP Stand to left side. As student swings legs forward flexing hips, place right hand on upper back, left hand in small of back. Be sure to reach in under bars. By lifting with both hands, spotter can position student prior to kip. Lift again as student initiates kip to raise hips and chest to straddle seat position.

CE 1. Failure to elevate hips to bar level or higher prior to kip.

2. Failure to press down on bars with hands while kipping.

3. Failure to extend hips forcefully to initiate kip.

4. Failure to keep legs straight throughout skill.

MO 1. Forward shoulder roll to straddle seat.

2. Shoulder stand.

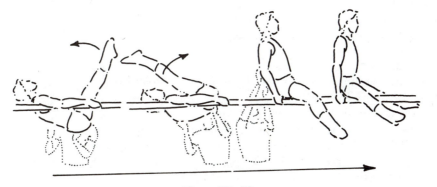

Figure PB−23

■ UPPER ARM KIP TO HAND SUPPORT (Fig. PB–24)

SL Intermediate beginner.

PT Same as for upper arm kip to straddle seat, which, for safety reasons, is a good lead up for this skill. The only exception is that legs stay together. Finish kip in hand support position.

SP Same as for upper arm kip to straddle seat, except place left hand under back of student's thigh, just above knee joint. This enables spotter to give more support to hips as student reaches hand support position. Support to hips at this point will reduce the chance of arms buckling at elbow.

CE Same as 1–4 in upper arm kip to straddle seat.

MO 1. Swing to shoulder stand.

2. Swing to shoulder roll forward to upper arm support.

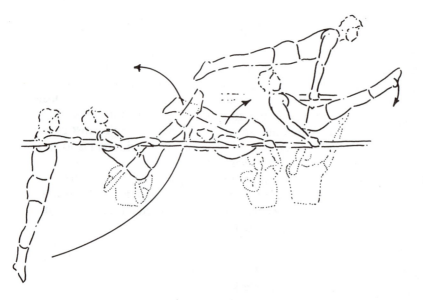

Figure PB–24

■ BASIC SWING IN UPPER ARM SUPPORT (Fig. PB–25)

SL Intermediate beginner.

PT Jump to upper arm support in center of bars. Immediately swing legs forward by first flexing hips slightly. Think of pulling feet as far forward-upward from upper arms (point of support) as possible. When legs and body reach peak of forward swing, relax slightly and allow gravity to initiate downward swing of legs. As legs begin to swing back past vertical phase of swing, drop head forward slightly, push down on bars with arms, and forcefully drive legs backward-upward as high as possible. As body begins downward swing, pull legs forward by slightly flexing hips. Follow through with forward-upward phase of swing. Repeat swing several times.

The beginner will feel some discomfort to upper arms where they contact bars. With practice, a toughening-up process will take place and upper arms will become accustomed to the initial discomfort.

SP Stand to left side and help by placing right hand in small of back and imparting lifting motion to left as student swings forward. During backswing, place left hand on abdomen and impart lifting motion to right.

CE 1. Failure to keep legs straight throughout forward and backward swings.

2. Failure to bear down on bars with arms, allowing shoulders to shrug (uncomfortable position).

3. Failure to swing entire body, not just legs.

4. If student has great difficulty with swing, a lack of sufficient strength is most likely the problem.

MO 1. Back uprise on backswing.

2. Front uprise on forward swing.

Figure PB–25

■ BACK UPRISE FROM UPPER ARM SUPPORT (Fig. PB–26)

SL Intermediate beginner.

PT Jump to upper arm support in center of bars and initiate basic swing. Student should be able to build up enough swing with two to three forward-backward swings. As legs begin to swing backward-upward, bear down on bars with arms and hands and forcefully drive legs backward-upward. As upper arms begin to leave bars, push down more forcefully with hands to finish in straight arm support with legs behind body. Keep hands close to shoulders as backward-upward phase of swing begins.

SP Stand to left side. As legs begin backward-upward swing, reach under bars and place left hand on abdomen. Place right hand on front of lower left thigh and lift through uprise and to hand support. This will also help student "feel" the skill to a correct finishing position.

CE 1. Failure to obtain good swing.

2. Failure to have hands close to shoulders.

3. Failure to keep legs and body extended through uprise.

4. Failure to be dynamic in extending arms to finish in good hand support position.

MO 1. Swing forward in hand support.

2. Swing forward to straddle seat.

3. Swing forward to L-seat.

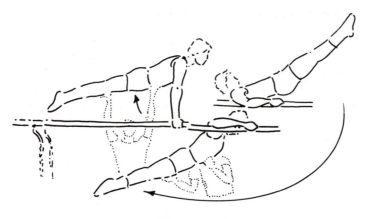

Figure PB–26

■FRONT UPRISE TO STRADDLE SEAT (Fig. PB–27)

SL Intermediate beginner.

PT This is a good lead up for front uprise to hand support. Jump to upper arm support and obtain swing. Grip bar firmly with hands more forward of shoulders than for back uprise. As legs begin forward phase of swing, flex hips slightly, but lead swing with toes. Press downward on bars with hands as legs swing higher. Forcefully and smoothly extend hips while straddling legs and simultaneously extending arms to finish in straddle seat position.

SP Stand to left side. As body begins forward-upward swing, reach under bars and place right hand in small of back. Place left hand lower on buttocks and lift student through uprise to straddle seat.

CE 1. Failure to generate a dynamic forward swing.

2. Failure to press downward with arms and hands on forward swing.

3. Failure to extend hips and arms smoothly to complete uprise forward.

4. Failure to keep legs straight throughout skill.

MO 1. Forward shoulder roll to straddle seat.

2. Shoulder stand.

Figure PB–27

■FRONT UPRISE TO HAND SUPPORT (Fig. PB–28)

SL Intermediate beginner.

PT Same as for front uprise to straddle seat, except legs stay together and uprise is completed to hand support position.

SP Same as for front uprise to straddle seat, except left hand is placed on back of lower left thigh. This enables spotter to give more support to hips, preventing student's arms from possible buckling as uprise is completed.

CE Same as 1–4 of front uprise to straddle seat.

MO 1. Swing to shoulder stand on backswing.

2. Swing to forward shoulder roll to upper arm support.

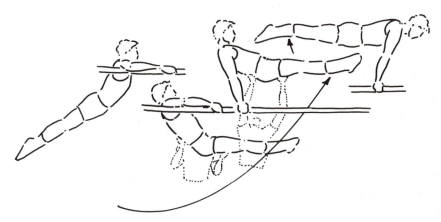

Figure PB–28

■ROLL FORWARD FROM SHOULDER STAND TO UPPER ARM SUPPORT (Fig. PB–29)

SL Intermediate beginner.

PT Assume shoulder stand just behind center of bars. Allow body to overbalance. As gravity causes body and legs to roll forward-downward over shoulders, drop head forward (chin down). Simultaneously, release bars and reach forward quickly regrasping bars firmly in front of upper arms. Press down on bars with arms and hands. Body should remain extended. However, a slight flexion in hips will not hinder performance of roll forward.

SP Stand to left side. As student starts to fall forward, reach in under bars, place right hand, palm up, on lower back. Place left hand, palm up, on back of left thigh. Impart a lifting motion to slow down swing, especially when skill is first attempted.

CE 1. Failure to drop head forward soon enough or not at all.

2. Failure to quickly reach forward, regrasping bars, or missing bars with hands completely.

3. Allowing hips to flex too much.

4. Failure to press down on bars with arms and hands once regrasp forward is made.

MO Back uprise to hand support.

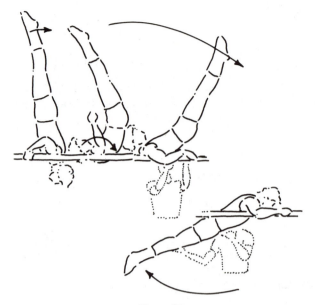

Figure PB—29

Beginning Routine for Parallel Bars (Fig. PB—30)

1. Drop kip to straddle seat.
2. Forward shoulder roll to straddle seat.
3. Shoulder stand.
4. Forward shoulder roll to upper arm support.
5. Back uprise to straddle seat.
6. Straddle travel forward.
7. Double leg straddle dismount.

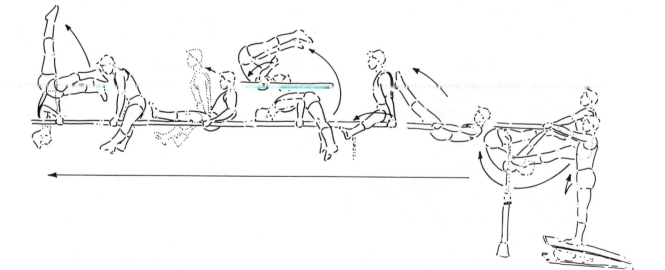

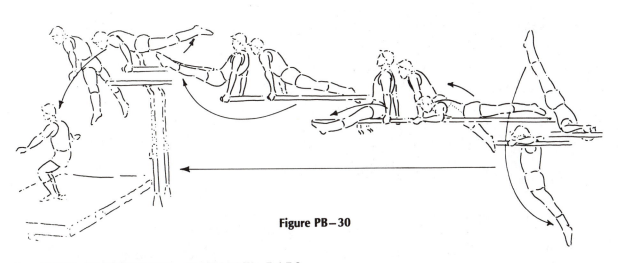

Figure PB—30

▲ TEST QUESTIONS—*PARALLEL BARS*

1. What is the correct distance between the bars?
   a. whatever is most comfortable.
   b. 2 feet.
   c. generally, the distance between each student's elbow and fingertips.
   d. none of the above.

2. When performing a front hand support, the student should
   a. grip the bars tightly.
   b. flip the hips.
   c. extend the elbows and shoulders.
   d. bend the knees.

3. The straddle seat position places most of the body weight on the _____.
   a. hands.
   b. hands and inner thighs.
   c. inner thighs.
   d. hands and thighs.

4. When performing a shoulder stand, how many primary points of balance are employed?
   a. 3
   b. 2
   c. 1
   d. 4

5. When performing a front dismount,
   a. the student dismounts at the forward end of the swing.
   b. the student lands with his or her back facing the bars.
   c. the front of the body passes over the bar.
   d. the student must regrasp the bar.

6. A good basic swing is performed by swinging from
   a. the hips.
   b. the shoulders.
   c. the hands.
   d. the wrists.

7. Which of the following skills is *not* employed to move along the length of the bars?
   a. straddle travel.
   b. basic swing.
   c. hand travel.
   d. shoulder roll.

8. Which of the following physical characteristics is most important in learning parallel bar skills?
   a. upper body strength.
   b. good form.
   c. good hip flexibility.
   d. good shoulder flexibility.

9. In upper arm support, the bars contact the _____.
   a. thighs and hands.
   b. upper arms.
   c. shoulders.
   d. upper arms and hands.

10. The back uprise is performed from _____.
    a. an upper arm support at the forward end of the swing.
    b. a hand support at the backward end of the swing.
    c. an upper arm support at the backward end of the swing.
    d. none of the above.

PARALLEL BARS	Name:

Straddle Seat

Body erect, arms locked _____

Knees straight _____

Held 3 seconds _____

Score _____

Front Hand Support

Arms locked _____

Legs together and straight _____

Held 3 seconds _____

Score

Upper Arm Support

Good body position, legs
   together and straight _____

Elbows pressed toward, hands
   gripping bars _____

Held 3 seconds _____

Score

Bent Hip, Upper Arm Support

Legs together and straight _____

Hips above bars in bent hip
   position _____

Elbows pressed downward,
   hands gripping bars _____

Held 3 seconds _____

Score _____

L-Seat in Hand Support

Arms locked _____

Legs together and straight _____

Upper body, 90 degrees to lower
   body _____

Held 3 seconds _____

Score _____

Hand Travel Forward and Backward

Arms locked, legs straight and
   together _____

Smooth movement forward and
   backward _____

Along length of bars _____

Score _____

Straddle Travel

Arms locked _____

Knees straight throughout _____

Smooth transfer from straddle
   seat to straddle seat _____

Score _____

Swing to Shoulder Stand

Knees and hips straight
   throughout _____

Smooth swing and arm bend to
   vertical position _____

Held 3 seconds _____

Score _____

Forward Shoulder Roll

Legs straight throughout _____

Elbows out during roll _____

Smooth roll with body bent,
   knees straight _____

Finish in good straddle seat _____

Score _____

Basic Swing in Hand Support

Arms locked, legs straight and
   together _____

Smooth swing to horizontal
   position at either end of swing _____

Repeat 3–5 swings _____

Score _____

(Continued)

PARALLEL BARS *(Continued)*

Back Shoulder Roll

Legs straight throughout   ————

Elbows out during roll   ————

Smooth roll with body bent,
   knees straight   ————

Finish in good straddle seat   ————

         Score ————

Shoulder Stand

Knees straight throughout   ————

Smooth press to vertical position   ————

Elbows out, hands gripping bars   ————

Held 3 seconds   ————

         Score ————

Single Leg Straddle Mount

Sufficient jump to cut leg to side   ————

Knee straight on cut   ————

Legs meet at finish of cut   ————

Arms locked   ————

         Score ————

Double Leg Straddle Mount

Sufficient jump to cut legs
   over both bars   ————

Knees straight on cut   ————

Finish in locked arm support   ————

         Score ————

Front Dismount

Good smooth swing   ————

Body at least horizontal prior
   to dismount   ————

Body straight, legs together
   passing to side of bar   ————

Smooth controlled landing   ————

         Score ————

Rear Dismount with 90-Degree Turn Outward

Good smooth swing   ————

Body at least horizontal prior to
   dismount   ————

Body straight, legs together
   passing to side of bar   ————

Smooth controlled landing   ————

         Score ————

Upper Arm Kip to Straddle Seat

Explosive extension from
   bent-hip, upper arm support   ————

Legs straight throughout   ————

Finish in good straddle seat   ————

         Score ————

Upper Arm Kip to Hand Support

Explosive extension from
   bent-hip, upper arm support   ————

Legs straight and together
   throughout   ————

Finish in good hand support
   position   ————

         Score ————

(Continued)

PARALLEL BARS *(Continued)*

Drop Kip to Straddle Seat

Legs and arms straight
   throughout   ————

Good hip compression and
   extension   ————

Smooth rise to straddle seat   ————

          Score   ————

Basic Swing in Upper Arm Support

Press elbows downward   ————

Smooth swing forward-backward
   to horizontal position at both
   ends of swing   ————

Legs together and straight
   throughout   ————

          Score   ————

Drop Kip to Front Hand Support

Legs and arms straight
   throughout   ————

Good hip compression and
   extension   ————

Smooth rise to lock arm support   ————

          Score   ————

Back Uprise from Upper Arm Support

Good smooth swing   ————

Complete uprise with arms
   locked and body extended
   behind hands   ————

Able to swing forward   ————

          Score   ————

Front Uprise to Straddle Seat

Good smooth swing   ————

Complete uprise with arms
   locked and body extended in
   front of hands in straddle
   seat position   ————

          Score   ————

Forward Roll from Shoulder Stand

Good shoulder stand   ————

Legs together, knees straight
   throughout   ————

Good back uprise at peak of
   backswing   ————

Finish in good lock arm support
   position   ————

Able to swing forward   ————

          Score   ————

Front Uprise to Hand Support

Good smooth swing   ————

Complete uprise with arms
   locked and body extended in
   front of hands   ————

Able to swing backwards   ————

          Score   ————

Rear Dismount with 180-Degree Turn Outward

Good smooth swing   ————

Body at least horizontal prior
   to dismount   ————

Body straight, legs together
   passing to side of bar   ————

Smooth controlled landing   ————

          Score   ————

(Continued)

PARALLEL BARS *(Continued)*

Cartwheel Dismount from Shoulder Stand		***Double Leg Straddle Dismount***	
Show good shoulder stand	_____	Good smooth swing	_____
Fall perpendicular to vertical position	_____	Arms locked, legs straight	_____
Land with control	_____	Legs passing crisply outside bars	_____
		Land with control	_____
Score	_____	Score	_____
Single Leg Straddle Dismount		***Final Score***	_____
Good smooth swing	_____	***Final Grade***	_____
Arms locked, legs straight	_____		
Smooth cut to side with straight leg	_____		
Land with control	_____		
Score	_____		

Comments:

Horizontal and Uneven Parallel Bars

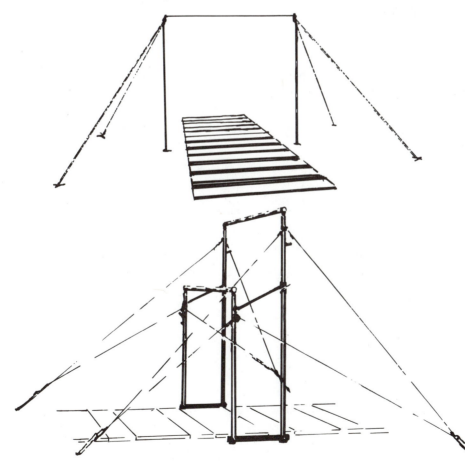

Many skills performed on the uneven parallel and horizontal bars are identical. Two structural differences exist between the two types of equipment, but they do not affect the overall performance technique of the skills involved: (1) the uneven parallel bar diameter is larger than the horizontal bar, and (2) the horizontal bar is made of steel whereas the uneven bar is made of wood or fiberglass.

Since both types of apparatus involve the same performance techniques, this chapter deals with a nucleus of basic skills that are performed on one bar. That bar may be the low bar of the uneven parallel bars or the horizontal bar set lower. A few other skills characteristic of those performed only on the uneven bars are also described.

SAFETY HINTS

1. Prior to each use, make sure the bar supports are secure.
2. Place mats under the bar(s), making sure to cover enough area for mounts and dismounts.
3. Use chalk to insure better grasp and handgrips to help prevent rips.
4. Do not allow students to continue working when their hands feel hot and become red. This indicates that the hands should be given a rest so that they will not rip or tear.
5. Do not allow students on the bar(s) unsupervised.
6. Have a definite skill progression for each class.

Hand Care

Use chalk (carbonate of magnesium) to keep hands from slipping from bar. Students whose hands perspire a great deal will have to use chalk more frequently.

Hand guards can be purchased from gymnastic supply companies or made from 2-inch adhesive tape. They should fit tightly, yet allow freedom of movement. Tape can be put around any finger and then taped around the wrist. If calluses develop, file or shave them carefully. For rips, cut off skin as close to the end of the rip as possible. Wash area, then cover with Vaseline. Keep skin moist to avoid cracking.

Bar Padding

For learning certain skills on the uneven parallel bars, rubber tubing or padding (found in plumbing stores) should be slit and taped tightly around the bar.

Grips

Forward (Fig. HBUB–1)
The forward or overgrip is used for approximately 75 percent of beginning uneven parallel bar and high bar work. Place hands on bars with back of hand facing upward. Thumb may be alongside fingers or around bar when working on uneven bars. Thumb should be around when working on horizontal bar.

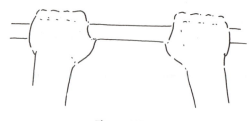

Figure HBUB–1

A grading sheet for horizontal and uneven parallel bar skills appears at the end of this chapter.

Reverse (Fig. HBUB–2)

For reverse or undergrip, place hands on bar with palm facing upward. Thumb may be around bar or alongside fingers on uneven bars but should be around on horizontal bar.

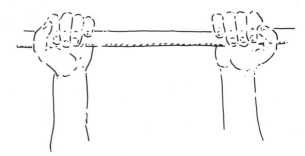

Figure HBUB–2

Mounts

■JUMP TO FRONT SUPPORT (Fig. HBUB–3)

SL Beginner.

PT Stand in front of uneven parallel bar or lowered high bar. Grasp bar with forward grip. Bend knees and spring vertically; extend arms and allow upper thighs to come to rest on low bar. Keep head neutral, legs together and straight, body slightly arched. Keep shoulders forward of bar.

SP Assist students by lifting at waist.

CE 1. Failure to keep elbows straight when support position is achieved.

2. Failure to keep body taut.

3. Allowing shoulders to shrug.

MO 1. Single leg flank to stride support.

2. Front or back hip circle.

3. Squat or straddle stand or dismount.

4. Underswing dismount.

5. Drop kip.

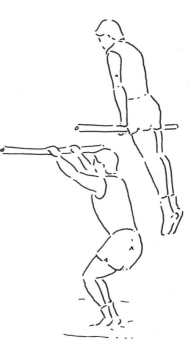

Figure HBUB–3

■HIP PULLOVER TO FRONT SUPPORT ON LOW BAR (Fig. HBUB–4)

SL Beginner.

PT Stand facing bar. Grasp bar with forward grip, elbows bent, and body fairly close to bar. Keep one foot slightly in front of other with weight on back foot. Shift weight to forward foot and simultaneously swing back leg forward and upward to lift hips up and over bar. As hips move under bar, push off with forward foot and allow legs to come together as body is revolving around bar. Keep elbows bent and pull hips to bar. Rotate grip backward to allow wrists to finish over hands to maintain support on hands. Finish in front support by lifting chest and extending arms as pullover is completed.

SP Stand beside student in front of bar. Place near hand on small of back and far hand on back of upper thighs. Keep hips close to bar by lifting hips and legs if necessary.

CE 1. Allowing arms to straighten. When this happens, hips cannot be kept close to bar and student's lower body will drop to mat.

2. Failure to kick or swing vigorously with back leg and push off with forward foot.

3. Failure to rotate hand grip backward.

4. Failure to lift upper body and heels simultaneously to end in front support.

5. Lifting chest too early.

MO Same as for jump to front support.

Figure HBUB–4

■ SINGLE LEG SWING UP TO STRIDE LEG SUPPORT (Fig. HBUB–5)

SL Beginner.

PT Grip bar with forward grip, hands shoulder width apart, and lower upper body below bar. With feet resting on mat, lift right leg, bending knee, and bring leg between and behind both hands. Place back of knee on bar, keep knee bent. Extend left leg forward. By swinging left leg downward-backward and forward-upward several times, student will develop pendulum swing. After two or three swings in this manner, enough swing will be generated for next phase of skill. As left leg swings down and back, forcefully pull down on bar with hands, raising head and chest forward above bar. A final extension of arms moves the body to a stride leg support on bar. Back of right thigh rests on bar.

SP Standing at left side, place left hand just above knee on front of left thigh (straight leg). Place right hand, palm up, on upper back. Spotter may actively help student gain a pendulum swing by pushing left leg downward and backward. Back of right knee must remain bent around bar. On actual ''swing up'' phase, lift with right hand and keep pushing left leg backward to help student raise head and chest above bars.

CE 1. Failure to develop enough swing.

2. Failure to keep arms straight while swinging under bar.

3. Failure to keep left leg straight and swinging backward through ''swing up.''

4. Failure to forcefully pull down on bar with hands during swing up phase.

5. Failure to rotate hands forward to top of bar.

Figure HBUB—5

■ GLIDE KIP (Fig. HBUB—6)

SL Intermediate beginner.

PT Stand in front of bar with hands in forward grip about shoulder width apart. With shoulders relaxed and arms extended, jump upward, lifting hips backward-upward. Lift legs upward so that they are a few inches above mat. Keeping arms and shoulders extended, glide under bar to extended position. As full body extension is achieved, immediately flex hips and lift ankles to bar. As body begins backward swing motion in pike position, force legs up along bar by partially extending hips and forcefully pushing downward with extended arms. As hips reach bar level, legs continue moving outward-downward. The pushing-down action from the extended arms must be followed through until student finishes in front support position with arms and shoulders fully extended and head in neutral position. Just before completing skill, rotate grip slightly forward. After learning skill, student can start approximately 3 feet in front of bar and jump into skill.

SP Two spotters, one on each side of student in front of bar. Reach under bar and place inside hand on lower back and have outside hand ready to place on back of upper thighs as they pass under bar. Keep ankles close to bar in kipping action and then assist in returning to front support position.

CE 1. Failure to thrust hips back and up on jump to bar.

2. Failure to keep arms and shoulders extended on glide.

3. Keeping legs too high on glide.

4. Failure to bring ankles to bar and have back parallel to mat just before kipping action.

5. Failure to keep arms straight and to push down on bar to reach front support position.

MO Same as for front support position.

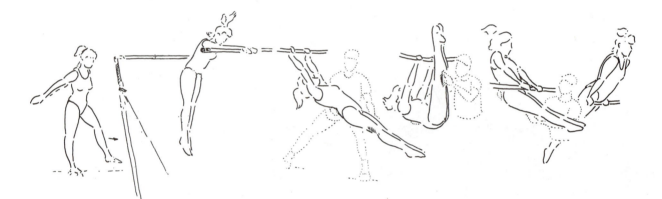

Figure HBUB–6

■ KIP SINGLE LEG SHOOT THROUGH (Fig. HBUB–7)

SL Intermediate beginner.

PT Follow same procedures as for glide kip. When body has reached extended position in glide, force one leg between hands so that it can continue over bar. Keep legs free of bar and finish in wide stride position.

SP Stand on non-shoot-through leg side of student and proceed same as for glide kip.

CE 1. Not forcing leg through arms while hips are forward.

2. Not extending hips as body is ready to pass over bar to final position.

MO 1. Mill circle.

2. Single leg flank dismount.

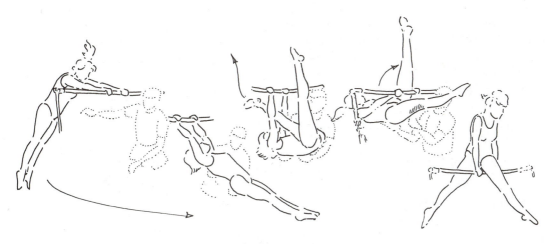

Figure HBUB–7

Single Bar Skills

■SINGLE LEG FLANK TO STRIDE LEG SUPPORT (Fig. HBUB–8)

SL Beginner.

PT From front support position with forward grip, lift left leg upward and sideways over low bar. Remove left hand, allow leg to pass under left hand and over bar, replace hand on bar, and immediately hold stride leg support. Weight is on hands; rest of body is completely free of bar. When lifting left hand off bar, shift weight to right hand. Right arm must remain locked (straight) at all times. The movement, once learned, should be executed briskly.

SP
1. Stand in front of bar, grasp upper arm or elbow of right arm, and keep arm straight until skill is completed.
2. Stand behind bar. Hold ankle that will not be flanking and wrist of hand that will not be leaving bar.

CE
1. Failure to keep shoulders slightly forward of bar until stride position is attained.
2. Failure to keep right arm straight at all times.
3. Failure to lift left leg high enough to clear bar.
4. Failure to keep legs straight.

MO
1. Single leg swing down and up.
2. Single leg flank dismount with quarter turn.
3. Mill circle.

Figure HBUB–8

■CAST (Push Away and Return to Bar) (Fig. HBUB–9)

SL Beginner.

PT From front support position with hands in forward grip, flex hips, bring legs under bar (allow arms to flex slightly), and move shoulders forward of bar. Thrust legs backward-upward, forcing body (except hands) away from bar, and extend arms. Return to bar in fully extended (arched) position.

Hint: Swing legs high enough so that the body parallels the mat.

SP Stand behind bar. Reach under bar with inside hand and place behind elbow (palm against elbow) to force shoulders forward. Place outside hand on upper thigh to lift body away from bar.

CE 1. Allowing arms to bend after hips leave bar.

2. Not keeping head neutral and shoulders forward of bar.

3. Insufficient thrust of legs.

4. Allowing legs to bend.

5. Not returning to bar in extended position.

MO 1. Back hip circle.

2. This movement is also used for the following skills but the body does not return to bar in an extended position before continuing with other skills.
   a. Single leg shoot through to stride support.
   b. Double leg shoot through to rear support.
   c. Squat stand.
   d. Straddle stand.

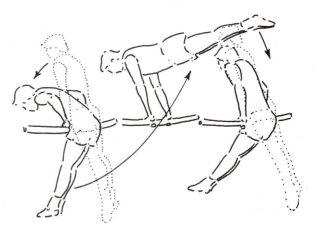

Figure HBUB–9

■SINGLE LEG SHOOT THROUGH TO STRIDE SUPPORT (Fig. HBUB–10)

SL Beginner.

PT From front support position with hands in forward grip, cast away from bar, keeping arms straight and shoulders forward of bar. As body is suspended away from bar, forcefully lift hips and bring one knee to chest; then extend it forward over bar as body is returning to bar. Finish in stride position with entire body weight on hands.

SP Two spotters, one in front of bar, one behind bar. Spotter behind bar stands on nonbending leg side. Grasp leg above knee with inside hand and ankle with outside hand, and keep body suspended by lifting leg until other knee is bent and extended over bar. Spotter in front of bar supports upper arms to make sure shoulders remain forward of bar at all times and to prevent student from collapsing or falling forward.

CE 1. Insufficient cast.

2. Failure to keep shoulders forward of bar.

3. Allowing arms to bend.

4. Failure to bend knee to chest and to extend it over bar in one rapid movement.

5. Allowing knee to be turned out rather than bringing it directly to chest.

MO 1. Mill circle.

2. Single leg flank dismount with quarter turn.

Figure HBUB–10

■BACK HIP CIRCLE (Fig. HBUB–11)

SL Beginner.

PT From front support position with hands in forward grip, cast away from bar and return in straight body position, contacting bar at lower abdominal area. As soon as body contacts bar, flex hips and force legs forward. Bend arms slightly to keep hips close to bar and rotate around bar at hip area. As soon as body has completed a three-quarter circle, rotate hands (grip) around bar and extend entire body to finish in front support position.

SP Stand in front of bar. Reach under bar and place inside hand on back as body returns to bar from the cast, and outside hand on back of upper thigh to rotate and keep hips close to bar. After hips have circled bar, slide outside hand up to arm to maintain front support position.

CE 1. Poor cast.

    2. Failure to keep head in neutral position throughout skill.

    3. Failure to pike as hips contact bar (many beginners pike too soon).

    4. Failure to slightly bend arms and continually pull hips to bar.

    5. Failure to keep legs straight at all times.

    6. Failure to rotate hands (grip) around bar, fully extend arms and shoulders, and open body to finish in front support position.

MO Any skill from front support position.

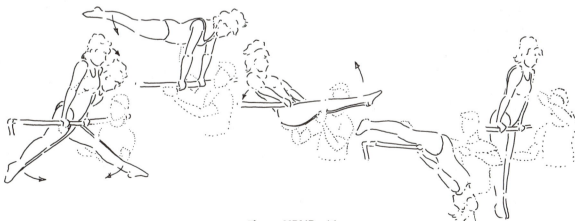

Figure HBUB–11

■MILL CIRCLE (Fig. HBUB–12)

SL Beginner.

PT From stride support (right leg forward) using reverse grip, lift body up from bar and support weight on hands. Keep chest and head up; arch back slightly. Shift weight forward by leading with right foot as if to step forward and extend hips. This movement should force most of body weight over bar and allow body to rotate around bar. For added momentum, lift back leg so that legs are in wide split position. Keep legs apart and body straight throughout skill. As upper body is coming to original position, rotate hands forward around bar, force wrists forward, lift upper body and forward leg to stop momentum, and finish in stride support.

Note: To learn, it sometimes helps to bring legs together while in inverted position; however, weight must be kept on hands, and legs off bar.

SP Stand behind bar, reach under bar with inside hand, and grasp elbow or wrist with palm to keep student's arms straight and to force body around bar by pushing forward and then upward as student comes to original position. Outside hand supports back during last quarter of skill. A second spotter can reach under bar and place inside hand on back of thigh to push leg forward at start of skill.

CE
1. Failure to lift body off bar and support weight with hands before starting forward motion.
2. Failure to step out to allow hips to pass forward of bar and to develop momentum.
3. Not keeping head and chest up throughout skill (chin should drop a bit just before completing skill).
4. Allowing upper body to curl when rotating.
5. Bending arms and legs during skill.
6. Not moving hands around bar with body and not forcing them forward during last quarter of skill.

MO
1. Single leg flank to rear support position.
2. Single leg flank dismount with quarter turn.
3. Single leg flank with half turn to front support.

Figure HBUB–12

■SINGLE KNEE CIRCLE BACKWARD (Fig. HBUB–13)

SL Beginner.

PT From stride leg support with right leg in front, swing left leg forcefully behind body. Push away from bar with hands, allowing head and shoulders to drop back aggressively. At the same time, slide back of right thigh backward along bar. Bar is "hooked" behind right knee. As body continues to rotate around bar backward, keep arms straight. The pivotal points are the hands and the back of the right knee. Pull left leg forward when a three-quarter circle is completed, which at this point increases speed of rotation. At the same time, rotate hands (grip) backward with snapping motion and extend arms to finish in stride leg support position.

SP Stand to left side. Reach under and behind bar, placing right hand (thumb down) around upper left arm. Place left hand on front left thigh just above knee. As student initiates backward rotation, push left leg back with left hand. Pull right arm back and down to give impetus to circling movement around bar. As student finishes a three-quarter circle, switch left hand to left upper arm (thumb up), pushing shoulders up to finish in stride leg support position. Right hand should reach behind bar onto back and be ready to assist student once on top of bar.

CE 1. Failure to swing left leg backward forcefully and push back from bar.

2. Failure to drop head and shoulders back forcefully.

3. Failure to keep arms straight.

4. Failure to rotate grip backward around bar.

5. Bending arms excessively during wrist snap.

Figure HBUB–13

■FRONT HIP CIRCLE (Fig. HBUB–14)

SL Beginner.

PT Assume front support position with hands in forward grip and body resting high on upper thighs; keep head up and move forward and outward, leading with chest, keeping entire body extended. Just before body reaches inverted position, flex hips, bend elbows slightly, and continue rotating around bar. Push down forcefully on bar with hands, and just before body returns to original position, forcefully rotate hands forward, extend arms and shoulders, and finish in front support.

SP Two spotters behind bar, both reaching under bar with inside hand to spot lower back and hip area. As body passes inverted position, place outside hand on back. (Transfer inside hand to legs to control forward movement, if necessary.)

CE 1. Not starting with thighs high enough on bar (insufficient extension of shoulders and arms).

    2. Failure to keep entire body straight at beginning of skill.

    3. Piking too soon or too late.

    4. Failure to keep hips in contact with bar throughout skill.

    5. Failure to extend arms and shoulders upon returning to original position.

MO Any skill from front support position.

Figure HBUB–14

■ DROP DOWN AND UP (Fig. HBUB–15)

SL Beginner.

PT This basic skill should be taught with care, as it requires timing and control in the pike position; it is also the beginning, middle, or end of several other skills. Start in rear seat support with hands in forward grip. Lift body off bar while lifting knees to face. With arms completely straight, drop back and under bar, and remain in tight pike. As soon as backward momentum stops, forward motion will begin. At this point, push down forcefully on bar, remain in tight pike, and move grip forward as body moves back to starting position. Hips extend at this point to finish in rear sitting position.

SP Stand to side of student behind bar. Place inside hand on buttocks and outside hand on back. Go with movement, and assist by pushing on back during latter part of return movement.

CE 1. Bending arms at any time during skill.

    2. Allowing upper body to go forward in the beginning rather than lifting legs to upper body.

3. Trying to return to rear sitting position too soon rather than taking full advantage of swinging action.

4. Failure to maintain pike position throughout skill.

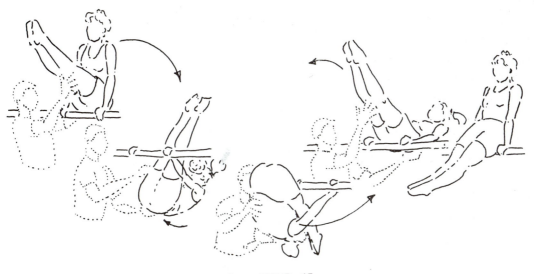

Figure HBUB—15

■DROP KIP FROM SUPPORT POSITION (Fig. HBUB—16)

SL   Intermediate beginner.

PT   From front support position with hands in double overgrip, press down on bar with hands and allow shoulders to fall backward. At the same time, flex hips, pulling feet toward bar. As hips swing down under bar and forward, make an extra effort to pull feet toward bar. Arms must remain straight. As hips begin to swing back under bar, start to extend hips and force legs up and outward at 45-degree angle. At the same time, pull down and toward bar forcefully with straight arms. The pull is exerted from shoulders, not biceps. Rotate wrist forward while pulling down and toward bar. This action raises body back to front support position.

SP   Stand on left side, just in front of bar. Reach under bar with right hand and place on back. Place left hand just behind left knee or a bit lower on leg. Follow student as hips swing down and forward with hands in contact with body. With left hand, keep student's feet close to bar as hips complete forward swing. As hips swing back and up and kipping phase takes place, lift with right hand to bring upper body up to front support. Keep pushing legs into bar with left hand.

CE   1. Failure to keep arms straight (locked elbows) throughout skill.

2. Failure to keep legs straight and feet close to bar especially at completion of forward swing.

3. Kipping too soon. Kipping action takes place just after hips begin to swing backward-upward.

4. Failure to pull forcefully down on bar during kip phase of skill.

5. Failure to rotate wrists forward as skill is completed.

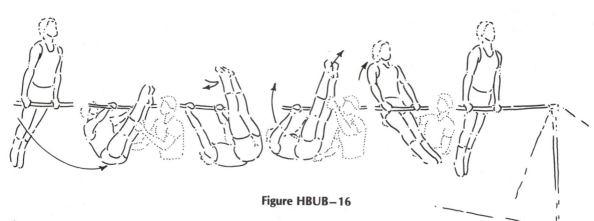

Figure HBUB–16

Dismounts

■SINGLE LEG FLANK WITH QUARTER (90-Degree) TURN (Fig. HBUB–17)

SL Beginner.

PT Assume stride position on bar; right leg in front, right hand in reversed grip, left hand in either forward or reversed grip. Lift (flank) left leg sideways, upward, and over bar. As leg is lifted, support weight with right hand, and take left hand off bar and lift sideways. As left leg passes over bar, extend hips, execute quarter turn, and land on mat with right hand still contacting bar. Turn head to right and land with knees slightly bent to absorb shock and for balance.

ST Stand behind student on supporting-arm side. Place outside hand on elbow of left arm and keep inside hand ready to lift right leg and clear bar.

CE 1. Failure to lift leg high enough to clear bar and to keep legs straight at all times.

2. Failure to keep supporting arm (right in this case) straight at all times.

3. Failure to lift arm as leg passes over bar.

4. Failure to extend hips as leg passes over bar.

5. Failure to keep upper body erect at all times.

6. Failure to maintain contact with bar with supporting hand until feet have reached mat and balance is attained.

VA Single leg flank dismount with three-quarter turn.

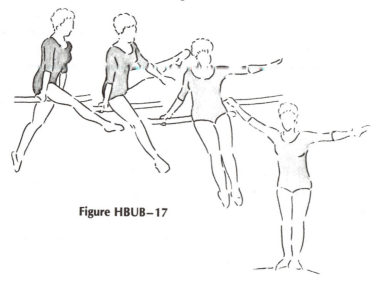

Figure HBUB–17

■ UNDERSWING DISMOUNT (Fig. HBUB–18)

SL Beginner.

PT From front support position on bar with hands in forward grip, keep arms straight, thighs close to bar, and drop back behind bar, lifting legs upward. After hips pass under bar, fully extend body by thrusting hips and legs forward-upward, then outward as hands release bar. Land with knees slightly bent, arms over head, and head between arms.

SP Stand in front of bar beside student. Reach under bar with inside hand and grasp back. As underswing begins, place outside hand on back of upper thighs to lift legs upward. Maintain contact until student has landed.

CE 1. Failure to keep arms straight and head in neutral position as body drops back, then to bend arm slightly as body is extending to push body away from bar.

2. Failure to lift legs upward to keep thighs close to bar until hips pass under bar.

3. Failure to push away from bar (release hands) as body extends upward and outward.

4. Allowing upper body to fall forward on landing (mainly due to allowing hips to flex).

Figure HBUB–18

■ STRADDLE SOLE CIRCLE UNDERSWING DISMOUNT (Fig. HBUB–19)

SL Intermediate beginner (review Fig. HBUB–18).

PT From support position on bar with hands in forward grip, cast away from bar forcefully while leaning forward from shoulders. As body reaches at least horizontal position, flex hips, straddle legs, placing feet on bar just outside of hands. The upper back should be rounded, shoulders extended, head neutral with hips over bar, and arms straight. As hips begin to circle downward-backward, press toes against bar, keeping shoulders extended to help force feet against bar. As hips pass under bar, they should be flexed more tightly, following through with the upswing. As shoulders reach horizontal level of bar, hips and shoulders are extended and feet slide off bar. The arms remain straight. Keep extending hips and shoulders, bringing feet together. The legs now extend outward-downward. The bar is pushed backward from shoulders as hands release bar. Land with knees and hips slightly bent, arms overhead, and head between arms.

SP Stand to left, in front of bar. Reach over bar, place right hand on left shoulder. Spotter can assist cast to straddle stand on bar and momentarily "set" student for circle downward-backward phase of skill. As circle downward-backward begins, move right hand quickly under bar and place on lower back, palm up. Place left hand under back of left thigh. Follow through upswing, lifting with both hands as feet come off bar and body extends. Maintain contact with right hand; left hand moves around and is placed on abdomen to insure proper landing.

CE 1. Cast from bar too weak, causing inability to "set" the straddle stand on bar.

2. Upper back not rounded and shoulders extended throughout skill.

3. Failure to press toes against bar, causing feet to slide off bar too soon.

4. Failure to keep chin down throughout skill.

MO 1. One-half twist to stand facing bar.

2. One-half twist regrasp to mixed grip, swing forward.

Figure HBUB–19

■DROP BACK FLANK CUT DISMOUNT (Fig. HBUB-20)

SL Beginner.

PT From L position on bar with hands in forward grip, lift knees toward head (as if to start back seat circle) and, keeping arms straight, drop back and swing under bar in pike position. As movement upward begins, push downward on bar to force body as far upward as possible. Keeping upper body erect, release right hand, turning 90 degrees to right, and allow legs to flank to left. When body is fully extended, release left hand and land with knees and hips slightly bent.

SP Stand behind student. Grasp hips. Follow movement of skill and maintain contact until balance is achieved on landing.

CE 1. Failure to keep arms straight throughout skill.

2. Failure to keep body (except hands) free of bar throughout skill.

3. Failure to stay in pike position until flank is executed.

4. Failure to push against bar with hands to get as high as possible before flanking.

5. Failure to extend hips as body flanks and to push down on bar with left hand before releasing it to dismount.

Hint: Learn on low bar first.

Figure HBUB—20

■ THREE-QUARTER SOLE CIRCLE DISMOUNT (Legs Straddled) (Fig. HBUB—21)

SL Intermediate beginner.

PT From front support position with hands in forward grip, cast away from bar, flex hips, and straddle legs. Place balls of feet on bar to outside of hands. Round the back, drop chin toward chest, and circle backwards with hips leading downward and under bar. Keep arms and legs straight. Think of extending ankles to keep feet pressed against bar. Following approximate three-quarter circle around bar, lift head and look for end of mat. Release bar and swing forward-upward to lift chest. Push off bar with feet to extend body and land on mat to a stand. Push off bar with knees straight.

SP Stand to either side of student, or use one spotter on each side. If standing at left side, reach under bar and place right hand on upper left thigh. This must be done as soon as feet are placed on bar. As hips start to circle down behind bar, push down with right hand to give impetus to circle. As body starts to circle upward in front of bar (toward spotter), keep lifting hips to help student complete at least a three-quarter circle. As student releases bar, place left hand, palm up, onto chest to lift chest and extend body for a good stand on mat. Quickly place right hand on back to help control landing.

CE 1. Failure to round the back and lower the head toward chest just as feet are placed on bar.

2. Failure to keep legs and arms straight throughout skill.

3. Failure to circle at least three-quarters around bar before releasing bar and pushing off with feet.

4. Failure to extend body as feet push off bar.

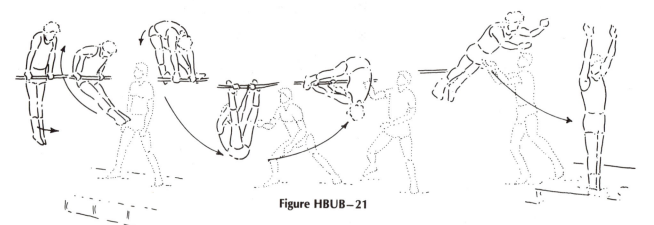

Figure HBUB-21

Uneven Bar Skills

■BEAT SWING SQUAT-OVER MOUNT (From Long Hang on High Bar) (Fig. HBUB-22)

SL Beginner.

PT Jump to long hang on high bar, facing low bar. Use forward grip. Keeping upper body as motionless as possible, force hips backward and lift legs forward and up, then hips forward and legs back. As hips start to move backward, draw knees to chest and extend legs upward. As body moves forward, force hips upward (extend hips) and lower backs of upper thighs to low bar. Extend upper body to finish in rear support.

SP Stand beside student between bars. Place hands on waist to keep upper body motionless. Then pull waist (and hips) back slightly as squat movement is initiated. Lift hips upward if necessary.

CE 1. Improper timing on swing.

2. Failure to lift knees to chest at start of second forward swing of legs.

3. Failure to lower backs of upper thighs onto bar with control.

4. Failure to make beat swing short and forceful.

MO 1. Stem rise to high bar.

2. Pullover to high bar.

3. Kip to high bar.

4. Release high bar, grasp low bar, and perform front or back seat circle.

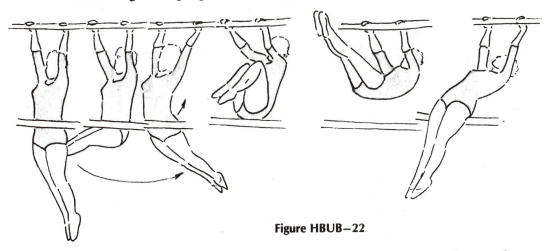

Figure HBUB–22

VA 1. *Beat swing straddle mount* (Fig. HBUB–23). Follow same procedures as for squat mount but lift legs upward and sideward in wide straddle before placing backs of upper thighs on bar; then finish in rear seat support with hands on high bar.

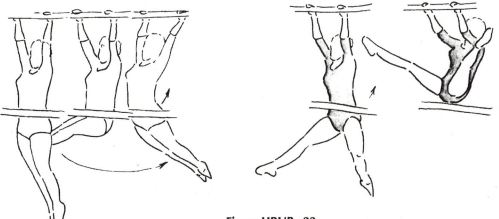

Figure HBUB–23

2. *Beat swing stoop-over mount* (Fig. HBUB–24). Follow same procedures as for squat mount but keep legs straight at all times.

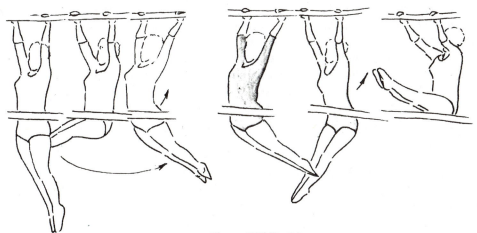

Figure HBUB–24

■BACK HIP CIRCLE MOUNT (Using Vaulting Board) (Fig. HBUB–25)

SL Advanced beginner.

PT After 2-foot takeoff on vaulting board, grasp low bar and allow shoulders to go forward, keeping arms straight. Extend body completely to reach horizontal position. Shoulders are slightly forward of low bar toward high bar. Bring body to bar. When hips contact bar, flex hips and continue with back hip circle.

SP In the beginning, assist at abdomen and upper thigh area by lifting student to horizontal position. Back hip circle portion should be spotted like regular back hip circle (see Fig. HBUB–11).

CE 1. Not allowing shoulders to be over hand position.

2. Not hitting horizontal position with body completely tight.

3. Flexing at hips before contacting bar.

MO Any skill from front support position.

VA Free back hip circle mount.

Figure HBUB–25

■SINGLE LEG SWING, DOWN AND UP (Fig. HBUB–26)

Note: This particular skill is not found in a competitive routine. It is merely a lead up skill for other moves.

SL Beginner.

PT From stride support, right leg in front, hands in forward grip, shift hips backward, bending right leg so knee hooks over bar, and swing back and down under bar. As momentum under bar stops, swing left leg down and backward-upward forcefully, push against bar with hands, and return to stride position. Just as thigh of right leg moves over bar, rotate hands to top of bar and extend arms, right leg, and upper body to finish in stride position.

SP Stand between bars to left of student. As body swings under bar, place outside hand on back to prevent a fall, and as body starts upward motion, reach under bar and place inside hand on upper thigh to assist with pumping action of left leg.

CE 1. Allowing arms to bend and body to curl forward on backswing.

2. Not using left (pumping) leg forcefully.

3. Failure to rotate grip as body returns to stride support position.

4. Failure to extend right leg and upper body as body reaches stride position.

Figure HBUB–26

■MILL CIRCLE CATCH (Fig. HBUB–27)

SL Advanced beginner.

PT Same procedure as for beginning of mill circle. When body is inverted under bar, begin looking for high bar. When body has almost reached original position, grasp high bar, keeping body straight and hips stretching forward.

SP Stand between bars. As soon as student has passed inverted position, place inside hand on lower back and outside hand on upper back, and help to high bar. Maintain contact until catch of high bar is successful.

CE 1. Poor mill circle.

2. Failure to keep eyes open and to look for high bar.

3. Reaching for bar too soon or with one hand at a time.

4. Failure to keep hips moving forward throughout skill.

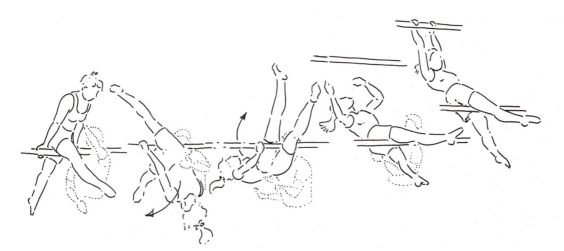

Figure HBUB–27

MO 1. Single or double leg stem rise.

2. Pullover from low to high.

3. Kip from low to high.

■PULLOVER FROM LOW TO HIGH BAR (Fig. HBUB–28)

SL Beginner.

PT From rear sitting position, grasp high bar with forward grip. Place left foot on low bar with left knee forward of foot. Extend right leg over low bar. Lower right leg, then forcefully swing leg up over high bar while simultaneously bending arms to pull, and push with left foot to lift hips to high bar. Bring legs together as hips pass over high bar. Lift head and chest; rotate grip and extend arms to finish in front support on high bar.

SP Stand between bars and assist by pushing hips to high bar. One hand can be placed on shoulder to continue push upward after hips are out of reach. As student reaches support position, grasp ankles to assist with balance.

CE 1. Failure to swing straight leg forcefully to lift hips to bar.

2. Failure to pull with arms and push with foot against low bar.

3. Failure to keep head in neutral position throughout skill.

4. Failure to rotate grip and extend arms, then lift body to front support position.

MO 1. Any skill from front support position.

2. Cast to long hang and any move from that position.

Figure HBUB–28

■DOUBLE LEG STEM RISE (Fig. HBUB–29)

SL Beginner.

PT 1. Grasp high bar with forward grip; place both feet (toes) on low bar. Extend legs, forcing hips to high bar by forcefully pushing downward on high bar. Allow elbows to bend slightly to let shoulders pass over bar. Keep feet on low bar until body is almost to front support position. Rotate grip forward, extend arms and shoulders, and finish in front support.

Note: Timing or coordination of leg extension and arm pull is important on both the single and double leg stem rise. Hips must move backward, then upward as if moving around a large semicircle.

2. Start in L position (toes on low bar). Keep legs straight at all times. Pull up slightly with arms while pushing against low bar. Lower body to original L; then forcefully pull with hands and push against bar with feet until in front support position.

SP   Stand under high bar. Place outside hand on hip, inside hand on back of upper thigh. Assist in backward, then upward movement.

CE   1. Failure to extend legs backward as body is being pulled to bar by arms.

2. Not allowing shoulders to pass over bar.

3. Allowing feet to leave low bar before body is ready to extend to front support position.

4. Failure to slightly bend elbows to allow shoulders to move forward of the bar.

5. Failure to rotate grip, extend arms, and lift head and chest to end in front support.

MO   1. Any skill from front support position on low bar.

2. Underswing to stride support.

3. Cast to long hang.

4. Underswing dismount over low bar.

5. Handstand, quarter-turn dismount.

6. Handstand; squat, straddle, or stoop dismount.

7. Double leg shoot through to stand on low bar.

8. Cast to straddle stand or free straddle support.

Figure HBUB–29

■ KIP FROM LOW TO HIGH BAR (Short Kip) (Fig. HBUB–30)

SL   Intermediate beginner.

PT   From rear support on low bar, grasp high bar with forward grip. Keep eyes focused on high bar or on object in back of high bar until kipping action is almost completed; then look over high bar. Bring ankles to high bar; then forcefully move legs upward as hips are extended and simultaneously push down on high bar with hands to bring hips to high bar. As legs are moving up bar, then outward, hips are extending. Rotate grip forward, extend arms and shoulders, and end in front support.

SP Place inside hand on back of upper thigh, outside hand on shoulder or upper back, and assist in entire movement to front support.

CE 1. Allowing head to be forward.

2. Sluggish movement throughout skill.

3. Kipping downward rather than upward, then outward (failure to force legs up bar).

4. Allowing arms to bend.

5. Failure to rotate grip, extend arms and shoulders, and end in front support.

MO Same as for stem rise.

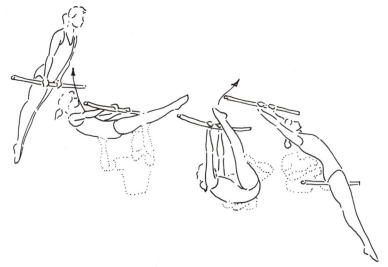

Figure HBUB—30

■ UNDERSWING TO STRIDE SUPPORT (Fig. HBUB—31)

SL Beginner.

PT From front support position on high bar with hands in forward grip, allow upper body to drop backward (arms remaining straight), keeping thighs as close to bar as possible. As body moves under bar, lift left leg, and lower right leg so that it is extended behind low bar and left leg is extended in front of low bar. Extend hips forward, and lower body to stride position on low bar with control.

SP Stand under high bar and support hips with outside hand and back of upper thigh of left leg with inside hand.

CE 1. Failure to keep arms straight as body drops behind high bar.

2. Failure to keep thighs close to bar on underswing.

3. Failure to control underswing as body passes under high bar.

4. Failure to extend hips as forward leg passes over low bar.

5. Failure to lower body to stride support with control.

MO 1. Maintain grip on high bar:
a. Pullover low to high bar.

b. Single or double leg stem rise after bringing back leg to bar.

c. Bring back leg over bar to rear sitting (hanging) support and kip to high bar.

2. Change hands to low bar:
a. Mill circle.

b. Mill circle catch.

c. Single leg flank dismount with quarter turn.

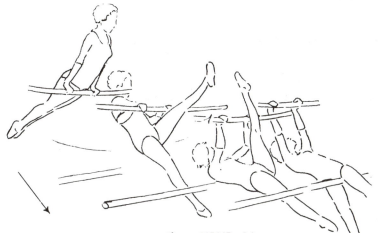

Figure HBUB-31

■FORWARD ROLL TO REAR SEAT SUPPORT ON LOW BAR (Fig. HBUB-32)

SL Beginner.

PT From front support position on high bar with hands in forward grip, lower body forward (pike), rotate grip forward, and slowly lower body to rest on back of upper thighs on low bar. Hands remain in forward grip throughout skill.

SP Stand between bars. Put outside hand on back as pike is achieved and inside hand on back of upper thigh to lower legs to low bar.

CE 1. Bending legs.

2. Failure to rotate grip.

3. Failure to maintain forward grip throughout skill.

4. Failure to control movement to rear sitting support on low bar, resulting in a bouncing action.

MO 1. Maintain grip on high bar:

a. Pullover low to high bar.

b. Single or double leg stem rise.

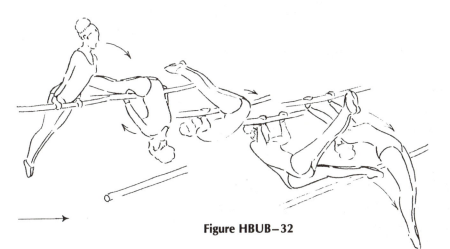

Figure HBUB-32

High Horizontal Bar Skills

■ CAST FROM HIGH BAR TO HIP CIRCLE ON LOW BAR (Cast Wrap) (Fig. HBUB−33)

Lead up: First learn hip circle from long hang, then cast to long hang to hip circle on low bar.

Figure HBUB−33

1. *Hip circle from long hang* (Fig. HBUB−34):

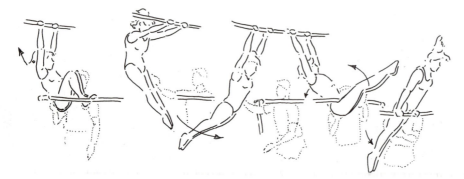

Figure HBUB−34

SL   Advanced beginner.

PT   Hang on high bar. Spotter between bars initiates swing. As contact is made on low bar in long hang position, forcefully pike (bringing knees toward head). When and only when this tight pike position is attained should the performer release high bar to regrasp low bar and continue with hip circle. It may be advisable to have a certain number of swings and pikes before releasing high bar, such as release on third contact with low bar. As movement continues around low bar, bend arms slightly to allow hips to be pulled to low bar (as in hip circle from cast). As movement is almost completed, rotate grip, extend arms and shoulders, head up, and finish in front support.

SP One spotter between bars initiates swing by pushing hips toward low bar. As pike position is achieved, other spotter in front of low bar places hands on backs of upper thighs to force body around bar. As student reaches front support position, inside spotter can grasp legs and upper arm to maintain front support position.

CE 1. Allowing hips to pike (flex) before contacting bar.

2. Not forcing legs toward head after contacting low bar.

3. Releasing high bar too soon or too late.

4. Failure to maintain contact of hips on low bar during hip circle.

5. Failure to rotate grip rearward, extend upper body, and finish in front support position.

2. *Cast to long hang* (Fig. HBUB–35):

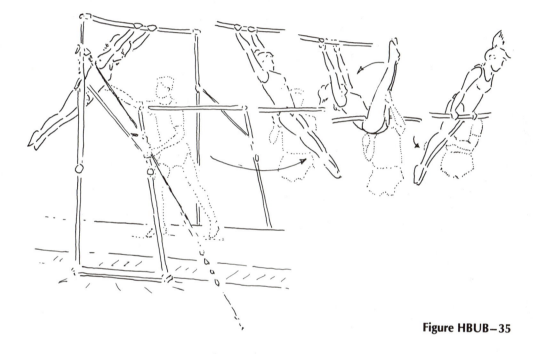

Figure HBUB–35

SL Advanced beginner.

PT From front support position on high bar with hands in forward grip, bring legs forward under bar; force legs backward-upward and extend arms to push body away from bar with control. Keep body fully extended and swing under high bar toward low bar.

Note: Leg action does not have to be very forceful if arms are extended properly. Remember to extend arms so entire body weight will not be supported by hands and shoulders in a jarring or jerky movement to long hang position.

SP Stand behind high bar and grasp legs and lower body throughout swing. Second spotter can stand under high bar to assist student from losing grip. To stop momentum of swing, place hands on abdominal area.

CE 1. Jerky cast allows arms to bend, knees to bend, or legs to separate.

2. Failure to keep body tight throughout long hang.

Note: At this point, if student feels confident with each part of skill, the two may be combined. One spotter spots cast to long hang and other spots hip circle.

CE Of combined skills:

    1. Jerky or insufficient cast.

    2. Failure to keep body tight until hips have contacted low bar.

    3. Failure to flex hips when they contact low bar.

    4. Releasing high bar too soon or too late.

    5. Failure to rotate grip, extend arms, raise upper body, and end in front support.

MO 1. Any skill from front support position.

    2. Pop glide kip.

    3. Hecht dismount.

■LONG HANG KIP FROM REAR SEAT ON UNEVEN BAR (Fig. HBUB–36)

SL Advanced beginner.

PT From a sitting position facing high bar, grasp high bar with forward grip. Lower heels to develop momentum for leg lift and hip thrust off the bar to a long hang swing forward. At peak of forward swing, immediately flex hips, pulling ankles to bar. Extend hips and force legs up and out at 45-degree angle while simultaneously pulling downward on the high bar. Rotate hands forward as body extends and shoulders move forward of the bar, ending in a front support position.

SP Stand between bars. Place one hand on back and other on back of upper thighs. As body leaves bar, push hips forward with hand on back. At peak of forward swing, help lift legs to bar with hand on back of thighs. As the kipping action begins, hold legs close to bar and lift upper body by pushing on the lower back until a front support position is attained.

CE 1. Failure to initiate momentum by not driving the heels backward simultaneously with coming off the bar.

    2. Failure to keep the arms straight throughout the skill.

    3. Failure to move ankles to the bar while the back is parallel to the floor.

    4. Failure to pull forcefully downward on the bar during the kip phase of the skill.

    5. Failure to quickly rotate wrists forward as skill is completed.

MO Any skill from the front support position.

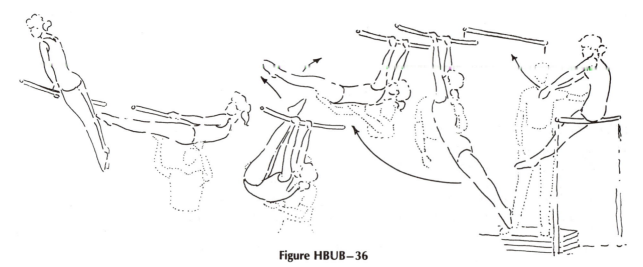

Figure HBUB–36

■ BASIC SWING IN HANG (Fig. HBUB–37)

SL Intermediate beginner.

PT Stand behind bar, jump to forward grip, and immediately flex hips to initiate pendulum swing forward. At peak of forward-upward swing, extend hips and shoulders smoothly, which raises the center of gravity higher. Maintain the extended position as body swings backward to vertical hang position. Flex hips slightly while passing through vertical hang. As body swings backward-upward, extend hips to lead backward swing with heels. Shoulders should be relaxed, head neutral. At peak of backswing, tighten body, flex hips slightly, and simultaneously loosen grip; rotate grip forward, regrasping bar with a forward grip. Body now swings downward-forward. Swing should be repeated several times to perfect the technique. Care should be taken not to swing too high, causing possible loss of grip on the backswing.

SP Stand facing student's left side, close enough; however, leave room for the swing. Place right hand on small of back and push to help forward swing. On backswing, place left hand on abdomen and push to help backswing. Be especially alert to the possibility of student's hands slipping off bar on backswing.

CE 1. Failure to keep head in neutral position throughout swing.

2. Failure to keep knees straight and legs together at all times.

3. Swinging too high.

4. Failure to rotate hands forward at peak of backward swing.

MO Kip at forward end of swing. Single leg shoot through end of swing.

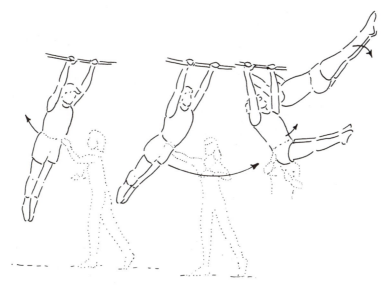

Figure HBUB–37

■ LONG HANG KIP (Fig. HBUB–38)

SL Advanced beginner.

PT The same technique used in executing the basic swing is necessary to prepare for the kip. At the peak of forward-upward swing, flex hips sharply, pulling ankles to bar. This position must be executed prior to hips beginning downward-backward swing. As hips start to swing under bar, extend hips and force legs up outward at 45-degree angle. At same time, pull down forcefully with straight arms toward bar. The pull is exerted from the shoulders and upper back, not the biceps. Snap wrists forward as shoulders reach bar level and continue pushing down and pulling forward with arms extended until front support position is attained. Note that the preparatory pendulum swing should not be great. The kip is more readily completed from a moderate swing.

SP Stand to left side of student on stacked mats or similar safety device. Spotter's head should be close to level of bar. Place right hand on lower back as body swings forward past bar. As hips flex and ankles are pulled to bar, place left hand behind left knee. As kipping action takes place, help keep student's feet close to bar with left hand. As hips swing downward-backward, impart lifting, pushing action at lower back with right hand through to front support position.

CE 1. Failure to keep arms straight throughout skill.

2. Failure to forcefully flex hips and pull ankles to bar prior to downward-backward swing of hips.

3. Kipping too soon. Kipping action takes place just as hips begin to swing downward-backward.

4. Failure to forcefully pull down on bar, keeping arms straight during kipping phase of skill.

5. Failure to rotate wrists forward as skill is completed.

6. Failure to continue pushing down and pulling forward until front support position is attained.

7. Initiating too much swing prior to flexion of hips toward forward end of swing.

MO Any skill from front support position.

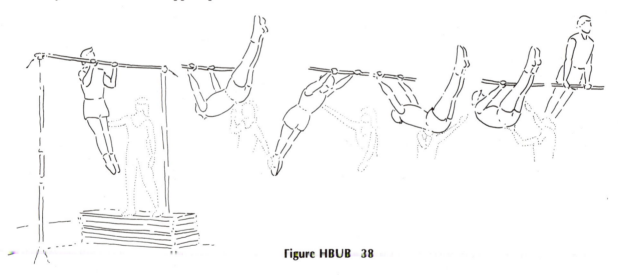

Figure HBUB 38

Beginning Routine for Uneven Parallel Bars (Fig. HBUB—39a)

1. From stand under high bar, grasp low bar, front hip pullover to front support.
2. Back hip circle.
3. Single leg flank over bar to stride leg support.
4. Reach back, grasp high bar, pull over to front support.
5. Underswing to stride leg support.
6. Mill circle forward.
7. Flank quarter turn, single leg swing dismount.

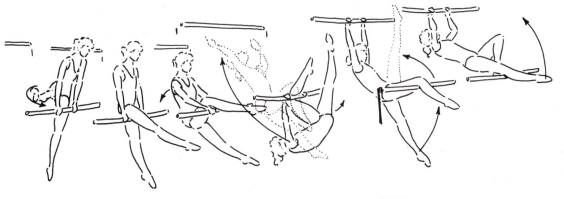

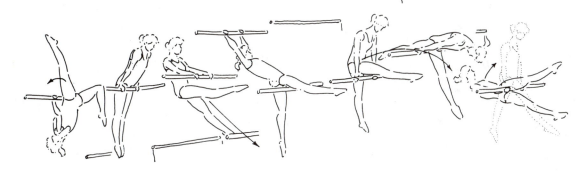

Figure HBUB–39a

Beginning Routine for Uneven Parallel Bars (Fig. HBUB–39b)

1. Jump to long hang on high bar.
2. Beat swing straddle over low bar to rear support.
3. Pullover to high bar.
4. Cast, back hip circle.
5. Underswing to stride leg support.
6. Cut leg back to front support.
7. Straddle sole circle underswing dismount.

Figure HBUB–39b

Beginning Routine for Horizontal Bar (Fig. HBUB–40)

1. Jump to long hang.
2. Front hip pullover.
3. Cast, back hip circle.
4. Underswing to long hang to back swing.
5. Swing forward, single leg shoot through to stride leg support.
6. Flank with quarter turn to front support.
7. Underswing to long hang, dismount at peak of back swing.

Figure HBUB–40

▲ TEST QUESTIONS—HORIZONTAL BAR AND UNEVEN PARALLEL BARS

1. The pullover mount presents several problems to beginners. Which of the following problems is most likely to happen and cause negative results?
   a. hands in reverse grip.
   b. extending arms.
   c. letting one leg follow the other.
   d. tilting the head forward.

2. On the double leg stem rise, students get stuck at the top bar and cannot get to the front support position because they
   a. fail to keep the arms straight.
   b. bend the knees.
   c. push and pull simultaneously with arms and feet.
   d. fail to bend elbows and allow shoulders past the bar.

3. When performing the mill circle, students have difficulty completing the last portion of the skill because of which of the following?
   a. flexing hips during circle.
   b. rotating hands around bar with body.
   c. dropping head backward.
   d. grip is too tight on bar.

4. What grip is used for the mill circle and knee circle forward?
   a. mixed.
   b. reverse.
   c. forward.
   d. does not make a difference.

5. What is the proper spotting technique for the front hip circle (facing away from high bar)?
   a. in front of bars—back and hips.
   b. in front of bars—wrist and back.
   c. between bars—hip and back.
   d. between bars—back and wrist.

6. Why do students often bounce around the bar on the back hip circle?
   a. they fail to come to the bar before piking.
   b. they tuck around the bar.
   c. inadequate cast.
   d. they use a forward grip.

7. What are the hand positions for spotting any underswing dismount?
   a. wrist and back.
   b. waist and back.
   c. back and neck area.
   d. back and upper thigh.

8. When performing the glide kip, when must the ankles come to the bar?
   a. immediately after jump.
   b. on backswing, when hips are under bar.
   c. before body extends in front pike.
   d. just prior to finishing front glide.

9. Why should handgrips be worn?
   a. to help prevent rips.
   b. instead of using chalk.
   c. to ensure a better grip.
   d. all of the above.

10. For a beginner learning an underswing dismount, which of the following is the *most* common error?
    a. a cast backward prior to underswing.
    b. failure to lift legs upward and keep thighs close to bar until hips pass under bar.
    c. keep head neutral.
    d. keep arms straight throughout skill.

HORIZONTAL AND UNEVEN PARALLEL BARS	Name:

Jump to Front Support

Hands in forward grip _____

Jump upward explosive _____

Arms straight, thighs resting on bar _____

Held 3 seconds _____

Score _____

Glide Kip

Hips thrust back upward _____

Legs together and straight in pike glide _____

Full body extension achieved prior to ankles coming to bar _____

Hips extend (kip) forcefully as arms push on bar _____

Front support position attained _____

Score _____

Hip Pullover

Elbows bent throughout skill, then straightened in support _____

Kick-push coordinated with arm pull to get hips to bar _____

Rotation smooth _____

Finish in front support _____

Score _____

Kip Single Leg Shoot through

Initial hip thrust back upward _____

Total body extension in glide _____

Lead leg through arms while body extended _____

Hip thrust and arm push simultaneous _____

Front support position attained _____

Score _____

Single Leg Swing to Stride

Arms straight in underswing _____

Extended leg adequately uses "pumping" action _____

Shoulders move over bar on upswing _____

Arms bend, then straighten in stride _____

Score _____

Single Leg Flank to Stride

Weight shifted to support side as other leg lifted _____

Hand removed as leg crosses bar _____

Shoulder kept slightly in front of bar _____

Score _____

Cast (Push Away)

Slight give in arms and hips as legs move forward _____

Total body extension on backward movement _____

Shoulders forward of bar throughout skill _____

Score _____

Single Knee Circle Backward

Arms straight as body drops backward onto bent knee _____

Extended leg swings back forcefully _____

Hands rotated on upward portion _____

Finish in stride support _____

Score _____

(Continued)

HORIZONTAL AND UNEVEN PARALLEL BARS *(Continued)*

Single Leg Shoot Through

Slight give in arms and hips as
legs move forward _____

Total body extension on
backward movement _____

Knee tucked and leg extended
over bar _____

Head and shoulders forward and
up throughout _____

Score _____

Front Hip Circle

Body extended resting on thighs _____

Aggressive forward move of
chest _____

Hands rotate, *slight* elbow bend
to allow shoulders over bar _____

Finish in front support _____

Score _____

Back Hip Circle

Cast sufficient _____

Return to bar with body
extended prior to piking _____

Rotation smooth at hips _____

Hands rotated/shoulders and
arms extended _____

Finish in support position _____

Score _____

Drop Down and Up

Body lifted off bar in pike
position, hips over bar _____

Arms straight and body in tight
pike on drop under bar _____

Remained in pike on return
movement _____

Extended hips as they passed
over bar _____

Score _____

Mill Circle

Body extended in stride and
supported _____

Weight shift aggressive and
forward of bar _____

Legs in stride throughout _____

Body extended throughout _____

Grip rotates smoothly _____

Score _____

Drop Kip from Support

Arms straight throughout _____

Drop backward into pike with
control _____

Kipping action forceful _____

Returned to front support _____

Score _____

Single Leg Flank Dismount

Weight shift as leg extends
outward and across bar _____

Quarter turn made as hips
clear bar _____

Landing with control and slight
hip and knee flexion _____

Score _____

Single Leg Swing Down and Up

Arms straight on drop backward _____

Bent knee hooking bar freely _____

Extended leg working as
pumping action _____

Upper body extended and stride
supported achieved _____

Score _____

(Continued)

HORIZONTAL AND UNEVEN PARALLEL BARS *(Continued)*

Drop Back Flank Cut Dismount

Drop back and swing under bar
   in good pike   _____

Arms straight throughout   _____

Legs extended to side and arm
   released as hips near bar   _____

Landing with control, head and
   chest up   _____

         Score _____

Mill Circle Catch

Body extended in stride position
   throughout   _____

Hands reach simultaneously for
   high bar   _____

Hips extend forward at time of
   catch   _____

         Score _____

Beat Swing Squat-Over Mount

Body extended in long hang,
   heels back   _____

Beat forward and backward
   aggressive   _____

Legs tucked and extended over
   bar to support on back of
   thighs   _____

         Score _____

Pullover—Low to High

Hips extended over above low
   bar with one leg straight and
   one bent   _____

Kick-push action of legs
   simultaneous with arm bend
   and pull   _____

Hips lifted above high bar   _____

Chest lifted and arms extended
   to front support   _____

         Score _____

Back Hip Circle Mount

Takeoff from board sufficient   _____

Arms straight and body extended
   back upward   _____

Shoulder movement slightly
   forward as thighs contact bar   _____

Circle around bar smooth   _____

End in front support   _____

         Score _____

Double Leg Stem Rise

Legs extended through toe push
   against bar   _____

Coordination of arm pull and leg
   extension adequate   _____

Grip rotated as shoulders pass
   over bar   _____

Ends in front support with
   control   _____

         Score _____

Kip from Low to High Bar

Ankles brought to bar   _____

Kip action explosive   _____

Ending in front support   _____

Arms basically straight
   throughout   _____

         Score _____

Forward Roll to Rear Seat

Rotated grip during forward
   upper body movement   _____

Arms bent and supporting weight
   in roll   _____

Land in rear support position
   with control   _____

         Score _____

HORIZONTAL AND UNEVEN PARALLEL BARS *(Continued)*

Underswing to Stride Support

Upper body drops back with
control and arms straight _____

Leg extended as hip thrust is
made over low bar _____

Body placed on low bar with
control _____

Score _____

Cast Wrap

Body cast to extended position
with control _____

Body extended until contact with
low bar _____

Hips flex around low bar and
arms release simultaneously to
catch low bar _____

Skill ends in controlled front
support position _____

Score _____

Final Score _____

Final Grade _____

Comments:

Chapter 11

Individual Activities, Dual Activities, and Pyramids

Although individual and dual activities and pyramid building are not part of competitive gymnastics, they should be an integral part of the physical education program. The activities can supplement the gymnastics unit.

Because of the nature of these activities, all students can participate by performing an individual skill or by being part of a pyramid. The activities and pyramid building also provide an opportunity for creative design in symmetry and asymmetry.

The following positions can be used separately or in combination to form pyramids for any number of students. They are described to one side for clarity; however, they may be varied by moving an arm or leg to a different position.

A spotter can stand close to students practicing dual activities to help them attain proper position when needed and to prevent collapse, loss of balance, or over-rotation.

INDIVIDUAL ACTIVITIES

Note: Even though these positions are basic, they should be performed with some kind of rhythm or counting system.

■ HANDS AND KNEES (Fig. IA–1)

PT Bend right leg and lower body to kneeling position as left leg bends and joins the right leg. Lean forward gently and place hands on floor under shoulders.

252

Figure IA-1

■STRADDLE STAND (Fig. IA-2)

PT From standing position, lift right leg sideward, shift weight to right, and place right leg on mat while simultaneously lifting arms to side horizontal position.

Figure IA-2

■PRONE PUSH-UP (Fig. IA-3)

PT From squat position, lean forward, placing hands under shoulders. Extend legs rearward, one at a time. Do not allow body to sag or be piked.

Figure IA-3

■SUPINE PUSH-UP (Fig. IA–4)

PT From sitting position, reach backward approximately 15–20 inches. Place hands on mat and extend hips upward until body is totally stretched.

Figure IA–4

■SUPPORTED PIKE (Fig. IA–5)

PT From standing position, reach forward and place hands on floor approximately 20–30 inches in front of feet. Keep legs straight and head between arms.

Figure IA–5

■STANDING PIKE (Fig. IA–6)

PT From standing position, bend forward at hips maintaining straight back. Hands may be placed on knees for support.

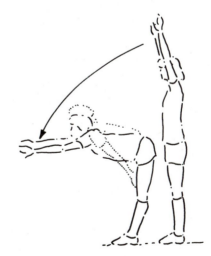

Figure IA–6

■ STRADDLE SEAT (Fig. IA–7)

PT From sitting position, move legs outward simultaneously to straddle position while moving arms to vertical position.

Figure IA–7

■ CRAB (Fig. IA–8)

PT From sitting position, bend knees and bring heels close to hips. Place hands rearward approximately 15 inches and force hips upward.

Figure IA–8

■ SPLITS (Fig. IA–9)

PT From standing position, step forward with right foot. Turn left foot to left and slide both feet in their respective directions until legs and hips contact floor. Keep shoulders and hips forward (square) at all times. Arms move to side, forward, backward, vertical, or any combination.

Figure IA–9

■ V-SEAT (Figs. IA–10 and IA–11)

PT From sitting position, lean back slightly while lifting legs toward upper body.

VA From sitting position, bend knees to chest. Place hands slightly to rear on mat while vertically extending legs.

Figure IA–10

Figure IA–11

■ LUNGE (Fig. IA–12)

PT From standing position, vertically lift arms while stepping forward on right foot. Land in lunge position with right knee bent and back leg straight.

Figure IA–12

■BACKBEND (Bridge) (Figs. IA–13 and IA–14)

PT From supine position, bend knees to place heels close to hips and place hands, palms down, under shoulders. Push hips upward while extending arms and legs simultaneously; keep head between arms.

VA From stand, lift arms vertically while stretching total body upward. As upper body moves backward, allow hips to move over toes as knees bend slightly. Place hands on floor approximately 18–25 inches from feet.

Figure IA–13

Figure IA–14

■TRIPOD (Fig. IA–15) (See p. 52 for detailed description)

PT From squat position, place hands on mat at least shoulder width apart. Place head (at hairline) on mat to make triangle. Place one knee at a time on elbows.

Figure IA–15

■HEADSTAND (Fig. IA–16) (See p. 53 for detailed description)

PT Form triangle with head and hands. Go into tripod, then lift legs to vertical position.

Figure IA–16

■FOREARM BALANCE (Fig. IA–17)

PT From kneeling position, lean forward and place forearms on mat just outside shoulders. Extend right leg backward. Push off with bent left leg as right leg kicks vertically. Do not allow body to sag.

Figure IA–17

■HANDSTAND (Fig. IA–18) (See pp. 58–60 for detailed description)

PT Lift arms overhead as you step to lunge position. Step onto bent front leg and push while simultaneously kicking with back leg. Keep arms straight and shoulders over hands, allow legs to reach vertical position.

Figure IA–18

DUAL ACTIVITIES

■INVERTED TRIANGLE (Fig. DA–1)

PT Stand facing partner. Lock wrists. Keeping entire body rigid, lean backward until arms are straight.

VA Stand with backs together.

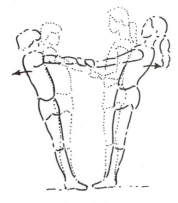

Figure DA–1

■ LUNGE TRIANGLE (Fig. DA–2)

PT Stand approximately 4 feet apart facing each other. Step forward into a lunge (partner A on left, partner B on right). Lift arms vertically to form peak of triangle.

Figure DA–2

■ SIDE LUNGE (Fig. DA–3)

PT Stand beside partner. Place feet side by side and grasp wrists. Partner A steps to right on right and partner B steps to left on left. Allow bodies to stretch to wide lunge position.

Figure DA–3

■ HANDSTAND SUPPORT (Figs. DA–4, DA–5, and DA–6)

PT Stand 2 feet in front of partner. Place hands on floor while extending right leg backward. Gently lift left leg backward so partner may place it over left shoulder. Repeat with right leg. Keep arms straight at all times.

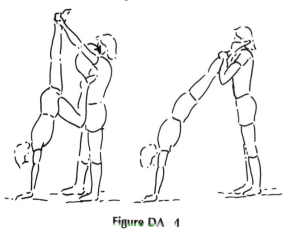

Figure DA–4

VA 1. Stand to side of partner. Kick to handstand placing hands approximately 15 inches from partner's feet. Standing partner can grasp legs above knee or at ankle area for temporary support. Handstand performer lowers legs one at a time to standing position.

Figure DA–5

2. Partner A sits in straddle seat position with hands ready to control handstand at hip and waist area. Partner B stands 3 feet in front of partner A and kicks to handstand placing hands on partner A's thighs or ankles or on floor between straddled legs.

Figure DA–6

■HEADSTAND SUPPORT (Figs. DA–7a and DA–7b)

PT Use same variations as for handstand position.

1. (Fig. DA–7a)
2. (Fig. DA–7b)

(a)

(b)

Figure DA–7

■ DOUBLE CRAB (Fig. DA–8)

PT   Partner A assumes crab position with partner B standing by A's left shoulder. Partner B reaches over and places left hand on A's left shoulder, then left foot on left knee. Partner B shifts body weight to left hand and foot while lifting right hand on right shoulder and right foot on right knee. Keep hips up at all times.

Figure DA–8

■ PRONE SUPPORT ON PARTNER'S HANDS AND KNEES (Fig. DA–9)

PT   Partner A is on back with knees bent, feet flat on floor, arms ready to support legs of partner B. Partner B straddles partner A at shoulders, leans forward, places hands on A's knees, and keeps them straight as right, then left, leg is lifted to be supported by A. Partner A must keep legs rigid to prevent collapse and arms straight to keep B in horizontal position.

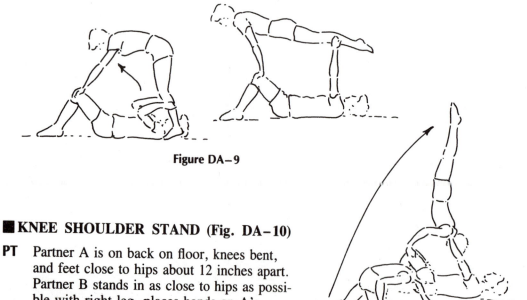

Figure DA–9

■ KNEE SHOULDER STAND (Fig. DA–10)

PT   Partner A is on back on floor, knees bent, and feet close to hips about 12 inches apart. Partner B stands in as close to hips as possible with right leg, places hands on A's knees, leans forward straightening arms, rests shoulders in A's hands, then kicks up to handstand. Partner A must keep knees rigid and arms straight to prevent collapse.

Figure DA–10

■45-DEGREE HANDSTAND SUPPORTED BY STRADDLE SEAT (Fig. DA-11)

PT Partner A is in straddle seat position with partner B standing to left side. As B leans forward to place hands on mat or legs of A, partner A reaches in to grasp waist and hip area for support. Partner B continues kick-push action to get to handstand position, then comes down one leg at a time.

Figure DA-11

■AIRPLANE (Fig. DA-12)

PT Partner A stands in front of partner B. Partner B stands with legs apart, bends both legs, and grasps A at waist. Partner A grasps wrists of B as right, then left, foot is placed on B's thigh. Partner B leans back slightly to control balance. As A straightens legs, B slides hands from waist to upper thighs. Partner A moves arm sideways.

Figure DA-12

■ANGLE BALANCE (Fig. DA-13)

PT Partner A is on back on mat with knees slightly bent. Partner B moves forward enough so that A can place feet on B's hips and thigh area (toes slightly pointing out). Grasp hands as A lifts B to horizontal position. When balance is gained, release hands.

Figure DA-13

■CHEST STAND (Fig. DA–14)

PT Partner A is in hand knee position. Partner B rests chest on A's back and places arms under A's chest. With one leg squat and other extended, kick to vertical position. Lower one leg at a time. Partner A must keep rigid position to prevent collapse.

Figure DA–14

PYRAMIDS (Figs. P–1 to P–15)

Pyramids can be most any size and shape desired—small, medium, large, symmetrical, asymmetrical, circular, square, high, low. Some of the basic pyramid positions are shown below and on the following pages.

Figure P–1

Figure P–2

Figure P–3

Figure P–4

Figure P—5

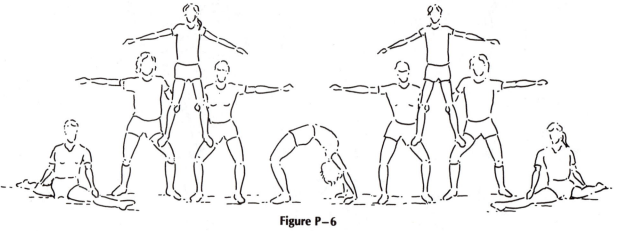

Figure P—6

Figure P—7

Figure P—8

Figure P–9

Figure P–10

Figure P–11

Figure P–12

Figure P–13

Figure P–14

Figure P–15

Chapter 12

Modern Rhythmic Gymnastics

Rhythmic gymnastics is one of the oldest forms of mass exercise, originating in Europe. When Europeans came to the United States, they maintained these activities as a form of exercise at cultural gatherings. Practice of these activities diminished for a time; however, revitalized interest in gymnastics also brought a rejuvenation of today's modern rhythmics. The exercises are done in a rhythmic manner with apparatus that can be held and maneuvered by hand. This apparatus includes balls, ropes, hoops, ribbons, clubs, and sometimes flags or scarves.

Modern rhythmics is an excellent activity for large groups. Skills can be best taught in a staggered line formation or a large circle. Students need ample room between each other for full range of movement of apparatus.

After a basic skill is taught, it should be performed to music. This develops a sense of rhythm in students, especially when music with a steady beat is used.

Three types of apparatus activities are included in this chapter: balls, ropes, and hoops. These three activities tend to be the popular with mass groups and the apparatus is relatively inexpensive and easy to store.

BALLS

Whether you are sitting, kneeling, standing, or running, hand contact with the ball is the same. The fingers are spread to push the ball evenly, never allowing the palms to touch. Push the ball as long as possible. The lower you are to the floor, the less force you use on the ball, in that it does not rebound as high as it does when you are standing. Learn to bounce equally well with both right and left hands. Keep arms and shoulders relaxed.

Note: Letters in parentheses indicate positions in which the exercises should be done (refer to the figures showing the various positions).

■ BOUNCING WHILE SEATED
❑ Positions (Fig. BALL–1)

Exercises

  1. Bounce with right hand in front of legs (positions a, b). (Fig. BALL–2)

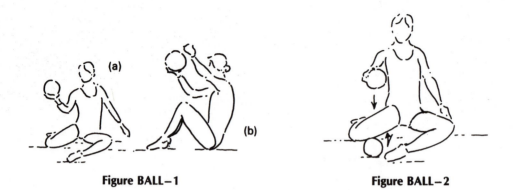

        Figure BALL–1   **Figure BALL–2**

  2. Bounce to right side of body (positions a, b), repeat to left. (Fig. BALL–3.)
  3. Bounce in semicircle (positions a, b). (Fig. BALL–4.)

        Figure BALL–3   **Figure BALL–4**

■ BOUNCING WHILE KNEELING
☐ Positions (Fig. BALL–5)

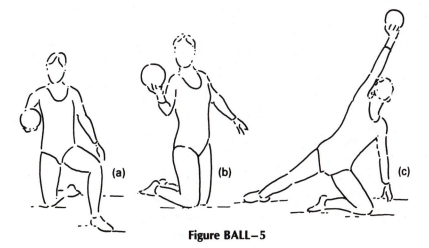

Figure BALL–5

Exercises

1. Left knee up, bounce with right hand (position a). (Fig. BALL–6.)

Figure BALL–6

2. Right knee up, bounce with left hand (position a). (Fig. BALL–7.)

Figure BALL–7

3. Bounce around body (positions a, b). (Fig. BALL–8.)

Figure BALL–8

4. Do knee spin bounce in circle (position a). (To perform knee spin, place right knee where left knee is and pick up left knee.) (Fig. BALL–9.)

Figure BALL–9

5. Bounce in semicircle toward hand on floor (position c). (Fig. BALL–10.)

Figure BALL–10

■BOUNCING WHILE STANDING

❑Positions (Fig. BALL–11)

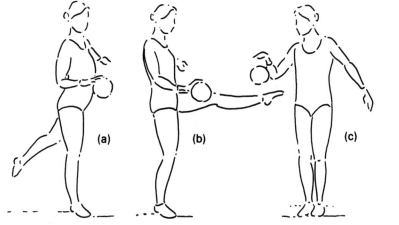

Figure BALL–11

Exercises

1. Bounce to right side of body with right hand (positions a, b, c). (Fig. BALL–12.)

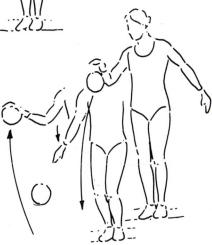

Figure BALL–12

2. Bounce from right to left and back with right (positions a, b, c). Repeat from left. (Fig. BALL–13.)

Figure BALL–13

3. Bounce from right hand; change and bounce
   left to right (positions a, b, c). (Fig. BALL–14.)

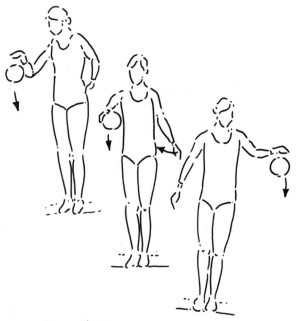

Figure BALL–14

4. Bounce around body (positions a, c). (Fig.
   BALL–15.)

Figure BALL–15

■ BOUNCING WHILE MOVING
□ Positions (Fig. BALL–16)

(a) Walking

(b) Jumping

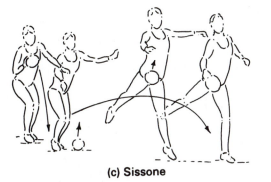

(c) Sissone

(e) Running

(d) Step hop

(f) Grapevine

(g) Chassé

Figure BALL–16

Exercises

1. In place, bounce ball to front and to right of body (positions a, b, e). Repeat to left. (Fig. BALL–17.)

Figure BALL–17

2. Moving forward slowly, bounce ball in front to right of body with right hand (positions a, b, c, d, e, g). Use other hand. (Fig. BALL–18.)

3. Move backward slowly, bouncing ball to front and right of body (positions a, b, c, d). Use other hand. (Fig. BALL–19.)

Figure BALL–18

Figure BALL–19

4. Grapevine to right and left (position f). (Fig. BALL–20.)

Figure BALL–20

BOUNCE WITH LEG LIFTS
Positions (Fig. BALL–21)

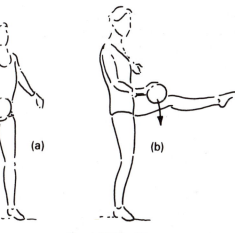

(a)   (b)

Figure BALL–21

Exercises

1. Bounce to right as left leg lifts (positions a, b). Repeat to left. (Fig. BALL–22.)

Figure BALL–22

2. Bounce under left and catch with left (positions a, b). Bounce under right. (Fig. BALL–23.)

Figure BALL–23

■THROWING AND CATCHING

❏Throwing (Tossing) (Fig. BALL–24)

PT With knees, hips, and elbows slightly bent, hold ball in one or both hands resting on palms with fingertips lightly cupped around ball. Before tossing or throwing ball, lower hand slightly, then return and continue upward, allowing ball to roll out of palms past fingertips and into air as entire body extends. Arms should follow through by extending.

Figure BALL–24

❏Catching (Fig. BALL–25)

PT With extended arms reach toward ball. Make contact first with fingertips and allow ball to roll into palms while simultaneously flexing (giving) elbows, knees, and hips.

Figure BALL–25

VA 1. With ball in right hand, throw and catch in right. Throw from right to catch in left. (Fig. BALL–26.)

Figure BALL–26

2. Stand in straddle position. Bend forward with ball in both hands. Toss ball between legs over back and stand to catch in front. (Fig. BALL–27.)

Figure BALL–27

3. Hop, skip, or chassé while throwing and catching. Remember, when you are moving forward, ball must be given forward-upward impetus so that it will travel forward with body. (Fig. BALL–28.)

Figure BALL–28

4. **Throw ball directly over head from right to left and reverse action. (Fig. BALL–29.)**

Figure BALL–29

5. **Hold ball in right hand to side of body. Rotate wrist forward, bend elbow, continue turning ball under forearm. As hand has made 360-degree move, toss ball upward, rotate hand back to normal position, and catch ball. "Give" with upper body as ball is being turned under arm. (Fig. BALL–30.) Ball could also be tossed overhead and caught by other hand. (Fig. BALL–31.)**

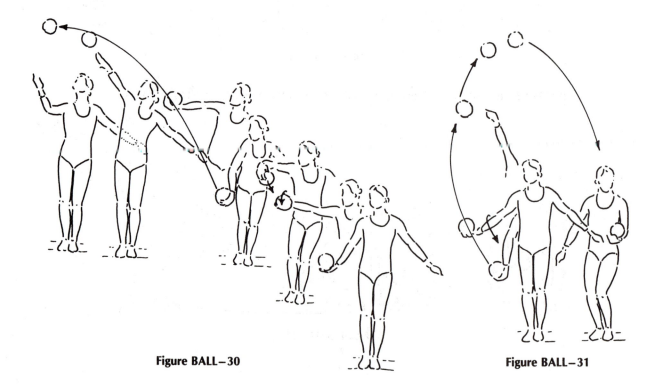

Figure BALL–30   **Figure BALL–31**

■ ROLLING (FIG. BALL–32)

PT Releasing ball on the floor is the same technique used for throwing. Roll ball off palm, then fingertips, as arm extends in direction of intended throw.

Figure BALL–32

VA 1. Starting with ball in right hand, swing arm backward, then forward, as body bends. Release ball slowly and move forward (chassé, skip, cartwheel, etc.) to get in front of ball so it may be caught in right hand in squat position behind body. (Fig. BALL–33.)

Figure BALL–33

2. Roll ball from one side of body to catch in the other hand. (Fig. BALL–34.)

Figure BALL–34

Beginning Routine for Balls (Fig. BALL—35)

1. Chassé left while bouncing with right. Chassé right while bouncing with right (a).
2. Step hop on left, bounce with left, and catch with right. Extend right leg back to lunge position, right hand with ball forward, left hand to side. Make half turn to right, bring feet together, with both hands on ball in front of body (b).
3. Swing backward, then forward with right. Bounce ball in front twice with both hands, then catch with left (c).
4. Swing backward, then forward with left. Bounce in front twice with both hands, then catch with right (d).
5. Make one-quarter turn right and bring feet together. Swing backward and forward and change to left. Repeat on left and change to right (e).
6. Make two circles under arm with right hand and catch each time. Swing forward and backward; change to left. Swing backward and forward; make two circles under arm twice with left hand and catch each time (f).
7. Make one-quarter turn left, roll ball, run, and sit to catch (g).

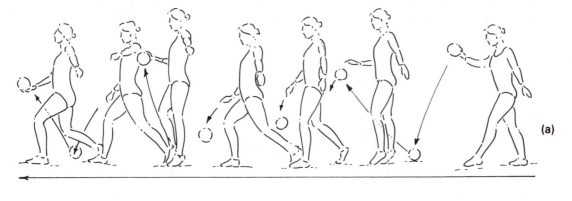

(a)

(b)

Figure BALL—35

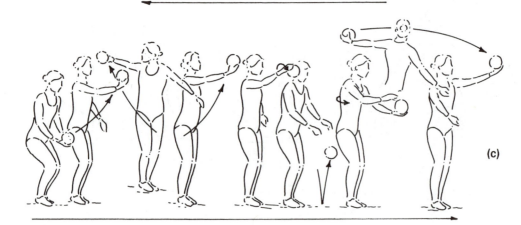

(c)

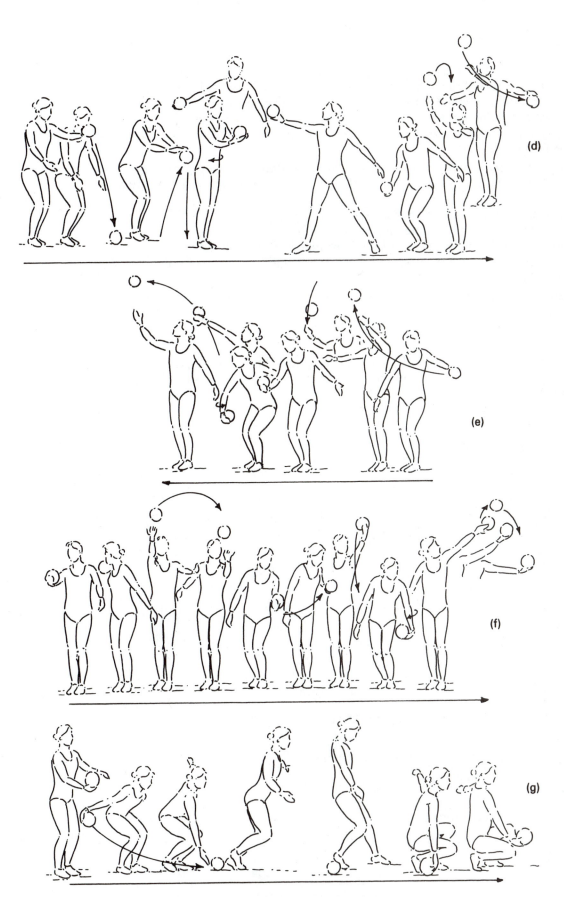

(d)

(e)

(f)

(g)

Figure BALL–35 *(continued)*

ROPES

Jumping rope, especially to music, with poise and grace and allowing the rope to contact the floor silently takes hours of practice. As the body leaves the floor on each jump, toes leave last and point toward floor while suspended in the air. Upon landing on one foot or two, toes touch first never allowing weight to rest on heels.

The rope is turned by wrist action with the arms extended from the body in approximately a 90-degree angle.

Since jumping rope is a strenuous activity, individuals must develop great stamina to perform a routine with precision. Beginners should jump in short intervals with frequent rests.

Rope routines are usually a combination of jumping, swinging, dancing with the rope, and throwing and catching the rope while turning or leaping.

Even though an official rope is used for competition, nylon or hemp is less expensive when cut into several sizes for classes. Measure the length of the rope by doubling the distance from the shoulder to the floor.

■ROPE JUMPING SKILLS

❑Double Jump (Fig. ROPE–1)

PT   Start with rope behind body with middle hanging just above ankles. As rope passes under and continues backward-upward portion of swing, execute a small bounce or jump with both feet.

Figure ROPE–1

VA   1. Make a quarter turn after each double jump.
    2. Move forward on each large jump.
    3. Turn rope backwards.
    4. Turn rope twice before landing.

❏Double Hop, Alternating Feet (Fig. ROPE-2)

PT As rope comes under feet, hop to right on right and as rope continues backward-upward, step on left and back to right. As rope comes forward again, be ready to step to left on left followed by a quick right and left.

VA Turn in a circle while hopping.

Figure ROPE-2

❏Figure 8 Crossover (Figs. ROPE-3 and ROPE-4)

PT Use double jump. Cross arms in a half figure 8 motion as rope passes head position. After jump is made, rope continues backward-upward, and when it is ready to pass overhead again, lift arms upward to continue figure 8 motion. Hands never

Figure ROPE-3

pause during figure 8 motion. If rhythm is not smooth and continuous, rope will become entangled with feet.

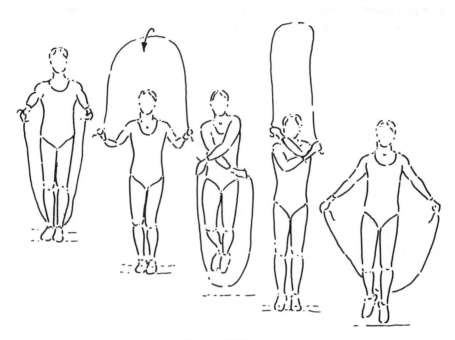

Figure ROPE–4

■ ROPE SWINGING SKILLS

❏ Rope Swinging—Vertical Circles (Figs. ROPE–5 to ROPE–7)

PT Double rope. Hold in right hand. Keeping elbow close to side of body, bend arm and swing rope forward in circular pattern in the vertical plane.

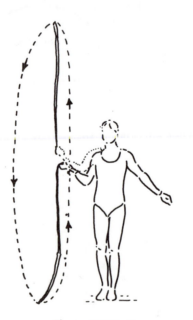

Figure ROPE–5

VA   1. Swing rope backward in circular pattern. Extend arm and make large circle with arm and rope both forward and backward. Repeat on left side.

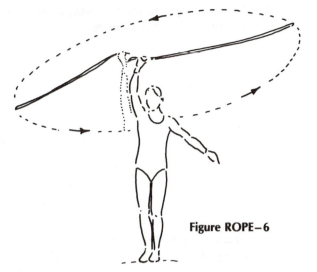

Figure ROPE–6

2. Make figure 8 motion in front of body with rope doubled and held in right hand. Repeat using left hand.

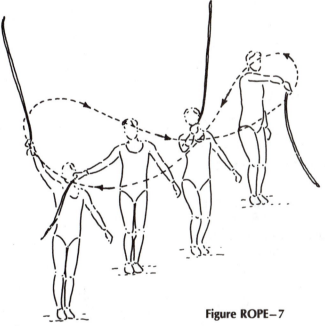

Figure ROPE–7

☐ Rope Swinging—Horizontal Circles (Figs. ROPE–8 to ROPE–10)

PT   With rope doubled and held in one hand, make small circle to side of body. This type of circling requires total wrist control.

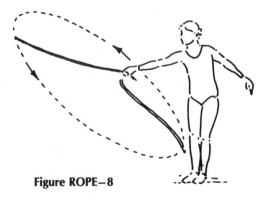

Figure ROPE–8

VA 1. Make large circle on floor and jump over rope as it passes under feet.

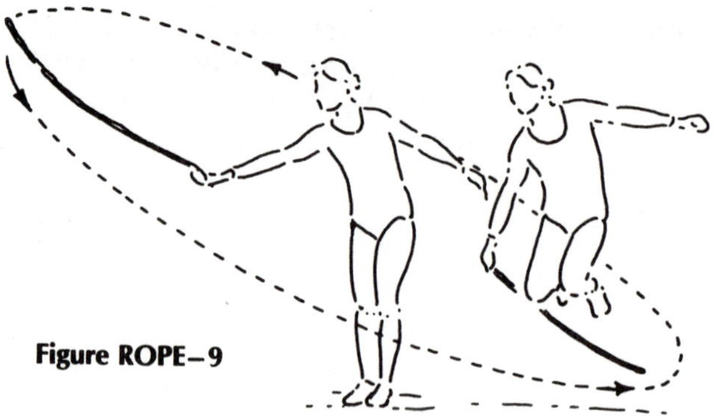

Figure ROPE–9

2. Extend arm vertically to make small and large circles in horizontal plane overhead.

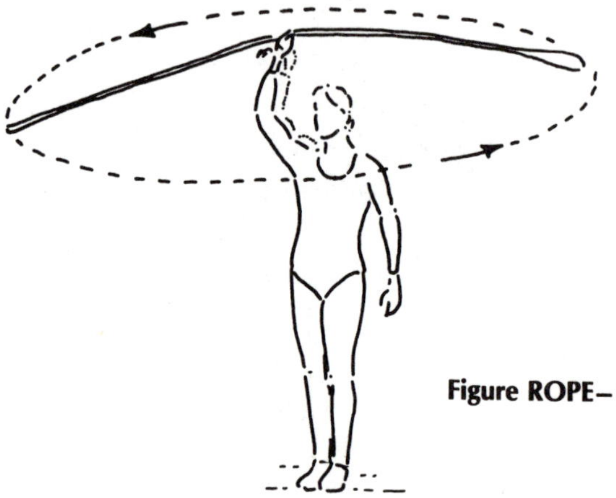

Figure ROPE–10

❑ Rope Swinging—Open Movements (Figs. ROPE–11 to ROPE–13)

PT Hold rope to side of body with hands approximately 14 inches apart. Bend and extend knees rhythmically at the beginning of forward and backward swing.

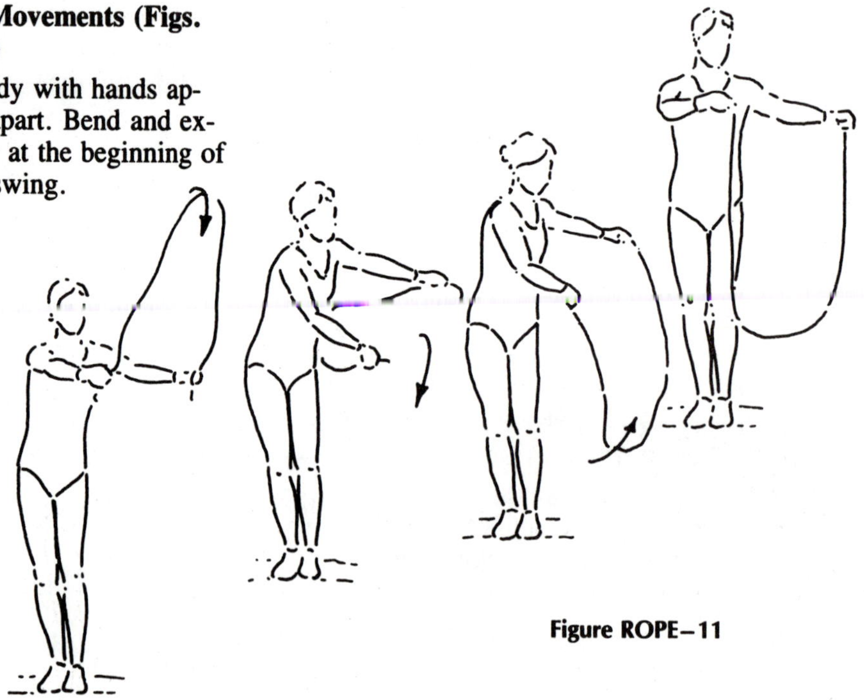

Figure ROPE–11

VA 1. Swing rope forward on right, cross to other side of body backward to left. Swing forward left, then back to right backward position.

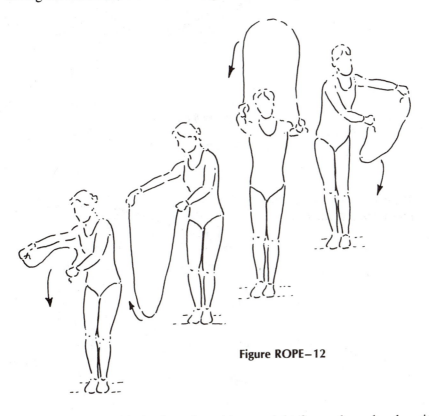

Figure ROPE–12

2. Swing from right side backward position to right forward overhead position. Make circle backward to right forward overhead position and continue across body to left side backward position.

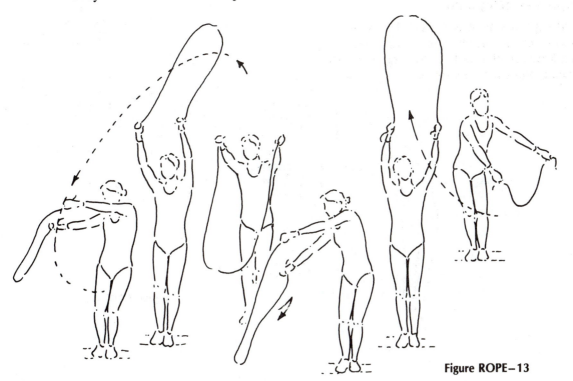

Figure ROPE–13

❏ Rope Folded in Fourths (Fig. ROPE–14)

PT Fold rope into four equal parts. Stretch rope tight with both hands. Hold rope in front or at side of body or overhead while performing a chassé, tour jeté, sissone, skip, chaîné, piqué, or other locomotor movements and turns. Make sure shoulders are relaxed at all times.

Figure ROPE–14

VA Create various body waves, keeping rope taut at all times.

Beginning Rope Routines (Fig. ROPE–15a–e)

Counts

a
1. Vertical circle right hand forward.
2. Vertical circle right hand forward.
3. Cross over figure 8 to left.
4. Cross over figure 8 to right.

1. Cross over figure 8 to left, change rope to left.
2. Circle vertical left side.
3. Cross over figure 8.
4. Cross over figure 8, change to right hand.

b
1. Chassé step hop right. Circling through vertical.
2. Chassé step hop right. Circling through vertical.
3. Chassé step hop left. Circling through vertical.
4. Chassé step hop left. Circling through vertical.

c
1. Circle overhead with both hands.
2. Circle overhead with both hands.
3. Open rope continue to circle.
4. Move to starting position for jumping.

d

1. Double jump.
2. Double jump.
3. Double jump.
4. Double jump.

1. Double hop.
2. Double hop.
3. Double hop.
4. Double hop.

1. Double jump.
2. Double jump.
3. Open swing to left side backward, then forward.
4. Open swing to left side backward, then forward.

e

1. Put both ends of rope in right hand.
2. Circle overhead horizontally.
3. Circle on floor and jump over rope.
4. Circle overhead and catch other end with left hand, feet in lunge position.

(a)

Figure ROPE–15

(b)

(c)

(d)

Figure ROPE–15 *(continued)*

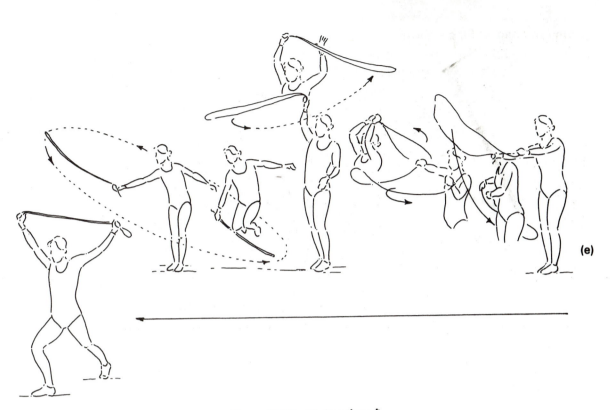

Figure ROPE–15 *(continued)*

HOOPS

The hoop is a versatile apparatus that can be rolled on the body or floor, rotated around the body or body parts, danced in and around, jumped through, over, or in and out of, and tossed to oneself or a partner.

To hold the hoop, wrap fingers around with thumb on inside of hoop. With this grip, the thumb and first finger control the hoop while the other fingers are relaxed.

■SWING

PT   Swing movements are executed with straight arm from the shoulder allowing a little suppleness in elbow. As with other apparatus, knees generally bend and extend slightly with the swing to allow for smooth motion and a greater range of movement.

☐Forward Backward, Sagittal Plane

PT   When hoop is swung in a forward-backward direction, movement resembles pendulum in a clock. As hoop reaches desired height, there is a slight pause before returning in opposite direction. On downward swing, bend knees; on upward swing, extend knees. Also fully extend ankles to be on toes. Allow upper torso to turn slightly on backswing; eyes follow movement of hoop.

Counting—Do movement to four counts: back-and-front-and; front-and-back-and; or one-and-two-and-three-and-four.

❑Swing in Sagittal Plane, Switch Hands (Fig. H–1)

PT Start with backswing and continue forward. When hoop is directly forward, change to other hand and continue rhythm in backswing on that side. Counting—Same as for swinging to side.

Figure H–1

❑Toss in Sagittal Plane (Fig. H–2)

PT Start with backswing. As hoop reaches 45-degree angle upward from horizontal, extend fingers to release hoop upward. As hoop reaches its peak, have outstretched hand ready to grasp and continue with downward and backward swing without loss of rhythm. Free hand can be held horizontally to side of body. Start with low toss and gradually increase height.

Figure H–2

□ Toss in Sagittal Plane, Switch Hands (Fig. H–3)

PT Start with backswing. On forward swing just before releasing to change hands, toss slightly. Catch with other hand and continue rhythm through backswing. As confidence is gained, make toss higher.

Figure H–3

□ Roll in Sagittal Plane (Fig. H–4)

PT Start with forward, then backward swing. On return forward swing, place hoop on floor, push it forward slightly. Take three small running steps alongside hoop, grasp it, and pause. Pick up hoop and repeat.

Rhythm—Up and back and 1-2-3 pause, or 1 and 2 and 1-2-3 pause.

Figure H–4

☐ Roll and Turn (Fig. H–5)

PT Same as roll above, only make half turn on second and third steps to grasp hoop with opposite hand and return to starting position when repeating movement. Rhythm—Same as for roll in sagittal plane.

Figure H–5

☐ Figure 8 (Fig. H–6)

PT Hold hoop in front of body with right hand toward floor, and bring arm and hoop to left side of body. Continue lifting hoop back upward as palm of hand rotates upward; extend arm and hoop above head level. Cross body in front of face and start downward swing with palm facing outward. On back upward swing, rotate hand so palm is forward again.

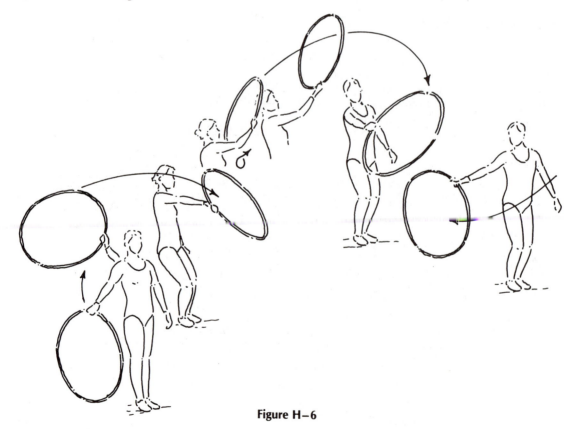

Figure H–6

❑Swing in Frontal Plane (Fig. H–7)

PT Hold hoop in front of body with right hand and feet together or in second position. Step to right on right extending left toe (lunge position) on floor while lifting hoop upward to right. As hoop moves downward in front of body, bring legs together (plié), then continue to lift hoop to left as you step left (lunge).
Rhythm—1 and 2 and, or side and side and, or up-down-up and (4 beats).

Figure H–7

❑Circle Hoop in Frontal Plane (Fig. H–8)

PT Hold hands in middle of each side of hoop with arms in front of body, elbows bent, and hands about chest height. Starting to right, make circle. As circle is completed, continue hoop to right and extend arms as far as possible. As peak of stretch is almost reached, step to right on right allowing further extension. Repeat motion to left. As circle is completed, step with feet together and prepare step to left with left.
Rhythm—1 and 2 and 1 and 2 and.

Figure H–8

❑Rotate Hoop Around Wrist in Frontal Plane (Fig. H–9)

PT Stretch right arm forward with palm down. With slight circular action, keep arm straight and hoop will rotate without too much effort. This can be done with knees straight or maintaining a rhythm of bending and extending.

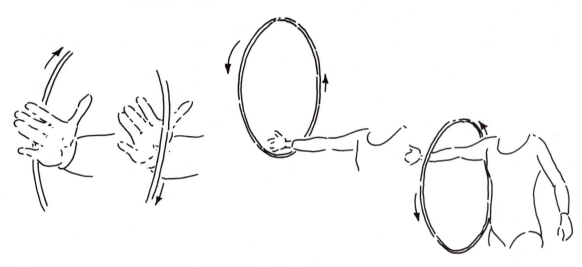

Figure H–9

VA 1. Rotate around finger and thumb. Using same technique, place hoop on back of hand, extend thumb, and allow hoop to rotate around fingers.

2. Rotate on wrist in sagittal plane. Same as above but to side.

❑Rotate Hoop Around Neck (Fig. H–10)

PT Place hoop so that it rests on shoulders with back of hoop close to neck. With slight push of hoop with hands to right (or left), start moving upper torso forward and backward to maintain movement.

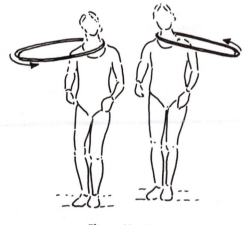

Figure H–10

■JUMPING THROUGH HOOP (Figs. H–11 and H–12)

PT With both hands near top, hold loop in front of body resting hoop on floor. Tilt hoop forward, then swing it backward so as to jump into or through it. Hoop may continue back upward and overhead like a jump rope (Fig. H–11) or be moved forward and backward. (Fig. H–12.)

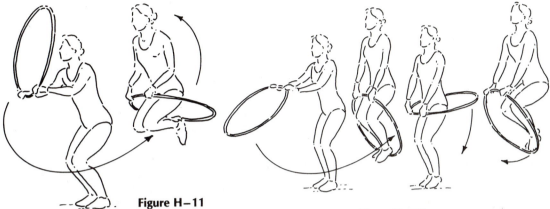

Figure H–11

Figure H–12

■ JUMPING IN AND OUT OF THE HOOP (Figs. H–13 to H–15)

PT Place hoop on floor in front of body. Using rhythms below, jump in and out of hoop.

Rhythm 1—Both feet in and out: jump, bounce, jump, bounce.
Rhythm 2—One foot in at a time: 1, 2, 3, 4 or right in, left in, right out, left out.
Rhythm 3—Step, quick step: step, close step: disco beat 1, 2, 3 or right in, left in touch lightly, right; then left out, touch lightly with right, left.

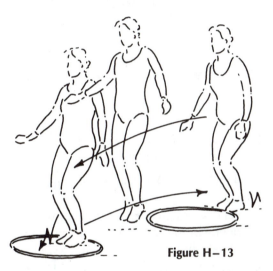

Figure H–13

Figure H–14

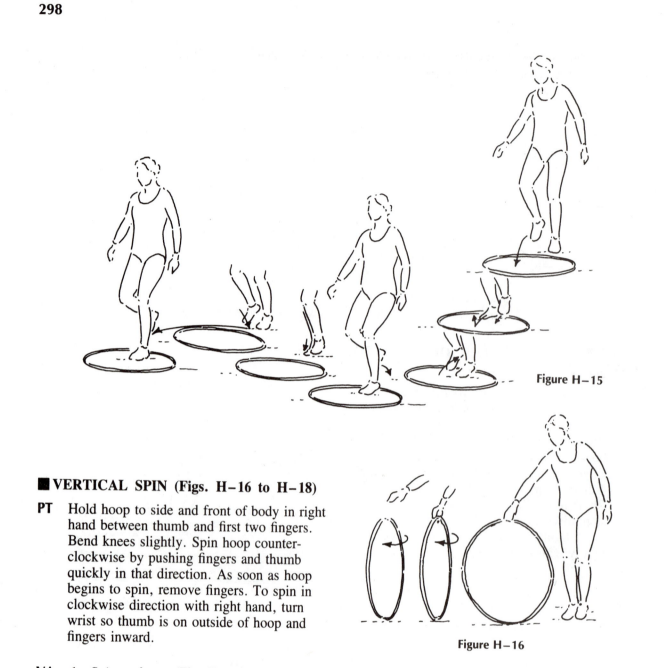

Figure H–15

■ VERTICAL SPIN (Figs. H–16 to H–18)

PT Hold hoop to side and front of body in right hand between thumb and first two fingers. Bend knees slightly. Spin hoop counter-clockwise by pushing fingers and thumb quickly in that direction. As soon as hoop begins to spin, remove fingers. To spin in clockwise direction with right hand, turn wrist so thumb is on outside of hoop and fingers inward.

Figure H–16

VA 1. *Spin and turn* (Fig. H–17). After initiating spin, make 360-degree turn before regrasping hoop.

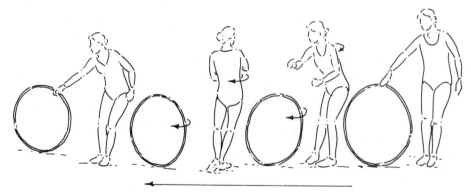

Figure H–17

2. *Swing forward and back before spin* (Fig. H–18). On return of backswing, place hoop just in front and to side of body and spin as it makes contact with floor.

Figure H–18

■ SPIN WITH FINGERS IN FRONTAL PLANE (Figs. H–19 and H–20)

PT   Hold hoop at chest level with both hands. Extend arms and with thumb and first two fingers spin hoop.

VA   *Spin hoop overhead* (Fig. H–20). Using same technique as above, reach upward, slightly arching body and raising up on toes while spinning hoop.

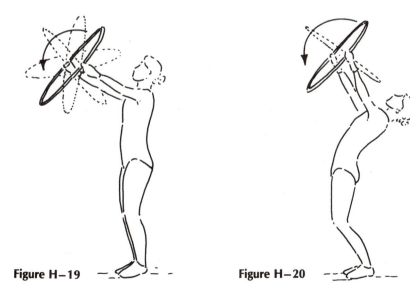

Figure H–19   **Figure H–20**

■DANCE AND LOCOMOTOR SKILLS WITH HOOP (Figs. H–21 and H–22)

PT Using basic locomotor skills such as skip, gallop (chassé), leap, run, slide, and walk, students can choreograph creative combinations. The basic swing forward and backward in the sagittal plane lends itself well to blending with hops, skips, and jumps.

Instead of running to catch a rolled hoop, students can leap, pas de chat, or do other moves to the hoop to reach it before it falls. A locomotor skill can also be combined with a static position when capturing the hoop after a roll. Students can do jazz moves, body waves, and various turns while holding the hoop in front of the body with both hands.

VA 1. *Circle in front, then turn in arabesque* (Fig. H–21).

Figure H–21

2. *Roll, run, sit, and catch; pose* (Fig. H–22).

Figure H–22

■STATIC POSITIONS WITH HOOP

PT Many static positions used on beam and in floor exercise can also be used with the hoop. The most important thing to keep in mind is that these positions must be moved into and out of with utmost grace. The hoop can be held tight for the beginner moving into and out of these static positions and may be spun or rotated by more advanced students.

Selected Bibliography

GENERAL

American Alliance for Health, Physical Education, Recreation and Dance. *Gymnastics Guide: 1982–1984*. Reston, VA: AAHPERD, 1982.

Bayles, Mary Ann, and Gail G. Evans. *Administration of Gymnastics Meets: A Handbook for Teachers and Coaches*. Reston, VA: AAHPERD, 1978.

Boone, William, T. *Better Gymnastics: How to Spot the Performer*. Reston, VA: Anderson World, 1979.

Carroll, M. E., and Manners. *Gymnastics Seven-Eleven: A Session-by-Session Approach to Key Stage 2*. Bristol, PA: Taylor & Francis, 1992.

Conner, Bart, and Paul Ziert. *Bart Conner: Winning the Gold*. New York: Warner, 1982.

Cornelius, William L. *Beginning and Intermediate Gymnastics*. Jostens, 1983.

Danskin, Elizabeth. *Women's Gymnastics*. Hancock House, 1983.

Duden, Jane. *Men's & Women's Gymnastics*. New York: Macmillan Children's Book Group, 1992.

Fodero, Joseph M., and Ernest E. Furblur. *Creating Gymnastic Pyramids & Balances*. Champaign, IL: Leisure Press, 1989.

George, Gerald S., ed. *USGF Safety Manual*. Indianapolis, IN: United States Gymnastics Federation, 1985.

Gluck, Michael. *Mechanics for Gymnastics: Coaching Tools for Skill Analysis*. Springfield, IL: Charles C. Thomas, 1982.

Goodbody, John. *The Illustrated History of Gymnastics*. New York: Beaufort, 1983.

Gule, Denise A. *Dance Choreography for Competitive Gymnastics*. Champaign, IL: Leisure Press, 1990.

Hartley-O'Brien, Sandra J. *Coaching the Female Gymnast*. Springfield, IL: Charles C. Thomas, 1983.

Kaneko, Akitomo. *Olympic Gymnastics*. New York: Sterling, 1980.

Maddux, Gordon, and Arthur Shay. *Forty Common Errors in Women's Gymnastics and How to Correct Them*. Chicago: Contemporary Books, 1979.

Noble, Dancy K. *Gymnastics for Kids Ages 3–7*. Champaign, IL: Leisure Press, 1983.

Pica, Rae. *Dance Training for Gymnastics*. Champaign, IL: Leisure Press, 1988.

Sands, Bill. *Coaching Women's Gymnastics*. Champaign, IL: Human Kinetics, 1984.

———, and Michael Conklin. *Everybody's Gymnastics Book*. New York: Scribner's, 1984.

Sands, William A. *Modern Women's Gymnastics.* New York: Sterling, 1983.

Schmidt, Darlene. *A Scientific Approach to Women's Gymnastics.* Horizons, 1980.

Silverstein, Herma. *Mary Lou Retton & the New Gymnasts.* New York: Watts & Franklin, 1985.

Smith, Garry L. *Parallel Bars: An Instructor's Complete Developmental Program for Students of All Ages.* Byron, CA: Front Row Experience, 1990.

————, and Frank Alexander. *Fun Stunts & Tumbling Stunts: An Instructor's Complete Developmental Program for Students of All Ages.* Byron, CA: Front Row Experience, 1989.

Smith, Tony. *Gymnastics: A Mechanical Understanding.* London: Hodder & Stoughton, 1982.

Thomas, Kurt. *Kurt Thomas on Gymnastics.* New York: Simon & Schuster, 1980.

Turoff, Fred. *Artistic Gymnastics: A Comprehensive Guide to Performing & Teaching Skills for Beginners and Advanced Beginners.* Madison, WI: Brown & Benchmark, 1991.

United States Gymnastics Federation Staff. *Make the Team: Gymnastics for Girls.* New York: Little, Brown, 1991.

Wettstone, Eugene, ed. *Gymnastics Safety Manual: The Official Manual of the United States Gymnastics Safety Association,* 2d ed. University Park, PA: Penn State University Press, 1979.

YMCA Gymnastics. Champaign, IL: Human Kinetics, 1991.

CLASSICS

Cooper, Phyllis. *Feminine Gymnastics,* 3d ed. Minneapolis: Burgess, 1980.

Frederick, A. Bruce. *Gymnastics for Men.* Dubuque, IA: William C. Brown, 1969.

Gault, Jim. *World of Women Gymnasts.* Millbrae, CA: Celestial Arts, 1976.

George, Gerald S. *Biomechanics for Women's Gymnastics.* n.p., 1980.

Murray, Mimi. *Women's Gymnastics: Coach, Participant, Spectator.* Boston: Allyn & Bacon, 1979.

Ryser, Otto E., and James R. Brown. *A Manual for Tumbling and Apparatus Stunts,* 7th ed. Dubuque, IA: William C. Brown, 1980.

Tonry, Don. *Sports Illustrated Women's Gymnastics: The Vaulting, Balance Beam, and Uneven Parallel Bars Events.* New York: Thomas Y. Crowell, 1980.

RHYTHMIC GYMNASTICS

Balazs, Eva. *Gymnastique Modern.* 3 vols. Waldwick, NJ: Hoctor, 1968.

Greathouse, Helena. *Competitive Rhythmic Gymnastics.* Waldwick, NJ: Hoctor, 1979.

Provaznik, Marie, and Norma Zabka. *Gymnastics Activities with Hand Apparatus.* Minneapolis: Burgess, 1965.

Schmid, Andrea. *Modern Rhythmic Gymnastics.* Palo Alto, CA: Mayfield, 1975.

PERIODICALS

International Gymnast. Sundby Publications, 225 Brooks, Oceanside, CA 92054.

ORGANIZATIONS

National Association for Girls and Women in Sport (NAGWS). 1900 Association Drive, Reston, VA 22091.

National Collegiate Athletic Association (NCAA). Box 1906, Shawnee, KS 66222.

United States Gymnastics Federation (USGF). 201 S. Capitol Avenue, Indianapolis, IN 46225.

Index

About the Authors

Dr. Phyllis S. Cooper is a full professor at Trenton State College. She received her B.S. from the University of Maryland, M.Ed. from Temple University, and Ed.D. from Nova University. Dr. Cooper has coached and taught gymnastics for twenty years, including junior high school, college, and national and international teams. She held a national judges rating for twenty years, and her doctoral research was in the area of stress management for sport performance enhancement.

Milan Trnka, assistant professor in the Department of Health Sciences at West Chester University, received his A.B. from Syracuse University and M.S. from the University of Illinois. Professor Trnka has coached gymnastics for twenty-five years at all levels, was a competitor and coach for the Sokol USA team as well as for Syracuse University, and has judged competitions for ten years.

ISBN 0-02-324701-0